A FAREWELL TO THE YAHWIST?

Society of Biblical Literature

Symposium Series

Christopher R. Matthews,
Editor

Number 34

A FAREWELL TO THE YAHWIST?

The Composition of the Pentateuch
in Recent European Interpretation

A FAREWELL TO THE YAHWIST?

The Composition of the Pentateuch in Recent European Interpretation

Edited by

Thomas B. Dozeman and Konrad Schmid

Society of Biblical Literature
Atlanta

A FAREWELL TO THE YAHWIST?

Library of Congress Cataloging-in-Publication Data

A farewell to the Yahwist? : the composition of the Pentateuch in recent European interpretation / edited by Thomas B. Dozeman and Konrad Schmid.
     p. cm. — (Society of biblical literature symposium series ; no. 34)
   Includes bibliographical references and indexes.
   ISBN-13: 978-1-58983-163-6 (paper binding : alk. paper)
   ISBN-10: 1-58983-163-2 (paper binding : alk. paper)
    1. J document (Biblical criticism) 2. Bible. O.T. Genesis—Criticism, interpretation, etc. 3. Bible. O.T. Exodus—Criticism, interpretation, etc. I. Dozeman, Thomas B. II. Schmid, Konrad, 1965– III. Series: Symposium series (Society of Biblical Literature) ; no. 34.
   BS1181.4.F37 2006
   222'.106—dc22   2006003095

14 13 12 11 10 09 08 07 06   5 4 3 2 1
Printed in the United States of America on acid-free, recycled paper
conforming to ANSI/NISO Z39.48-1992 (R1997) and ISO 9706:1994
standards for paper permanence.

Contents

ABBREVIATIONS

AASF	Annales Academiae scientiarum fennicae
AB	Anchor Bible
ABD	*Anchor Bible Dictionary.* Edited by D. N. Freedman. 6 vols. New York: Doubleday, 1992.
AOAT	Alter Orient und Altes Testament
ATANT	Abhandlungen zur Theologie des Alten und Neuen Testaments
ATD	Das Alte Testament Deutsch
BBB	Bonner biblische Beiträge
BET	Beiträge zur biblischen Exegese und Theologie
BETL	Bibliotheca ephemeridum theologicarum lovaniensium
BHH	*Biblisch-historisches Handwörterbuch: Landeskunde, Geschichte, Religion, Kultur.* Edited by B. Reicke and L. Rost. 4 vols. Göttingen: Vandenhoeck & Ruprecht, 1962–66.
Bib	*Biblica*
BK	*Bibel und Kirche*
BN	*Biblische Notizen*
BTS	*Bible et terre sainte*
BWANT	Beiträge zur Wissenschaft vom Alten und Neuen Testament
BZAW	Beihefte zur Zeitschrift für die alttestamentliche Wissenschaft
CANE	*Civilizations of the Ancient Near East.* Edited by J. Sasson. 4 vols. New York: Scribner, 1995.
CBET	Contributions to Biblical Exegesis and Theology
CBQ	*Catholic Biblical Quarterly*
ConBOT	Coniectanea biblica: Old Testament Series
DBAT	*Dielheimer Blätter zum Alten Testament und seiner Rezeption in der Alten Kirche*
DBAT.B	Dielheimer Blätter zum Alten Testament und seiner Rezeption in der Alten Kirche. Beiheft
ETR	*Etudes théologiques et religieuses*
EvT	*Evangelische Theologie*
FAT	Forschungen zum Alten Testament
FOTL	Forms of the Old Testament Literature
FRLANT	Forschungen zur Religion und Literatur des Alten und Neuen Testaments

HAT	Handbuch zum Alten Testament
HKAT	Handkommentar zum Alten Testament
HSM	Harvard Semitic Monographs
JAOS	*Journal of the American Oriental Society*
JBL	*Journal of Biblical Literature*
JBS	Jerusalem Biblical Studies
JBT	Jahrbuch für biblische Theologie
JNSL	*Journal of Northwest Semitic Languages*
JR	*Journal of Religion*
JSOT	*Journal for the Study of the Old Testament*
JSOTSup	Journal for the Study of the Old Testament Supplement Series
KHC	Kurzer Hand-Kommentar zum Alten Testament
LD	Lectio divina
MdB	*Le Monde de la Bible*
NIB	*The New Interpreter's Bible*
OBO	Orbis biblicus et orientalis
OTL	Old Testament Library
QD	Quaestiones disputatae
RB	*Revue biblique*
RHPR	*Revue d'histoire et de philosophie religieuses*
RTP	*Revue de théologie et de philosophie*
SBAB	Stuttgarter biblische Aufsatzbände
SBLMS	Society of Biblical Literature Monograph Series
SBS	Stuttgarter Bibelstudien
SBTS	Sources for Biblical and Theological Study
SHAW	Sitzungsberichte der Heidelberger Akademie der Wissenschaften
TB	Theologische Bücherei: Neudrucke und Berichte aus dem 20. Jahrhundert
ThWAT	*Theologisches Wörterbuch zum Alten Testament*. Edited by G. J. Botterweck and H. Ringgren. Stuttgart: Kohlhammer, 1970–.
TRE	*Theologische Realenzyklopädie*. Edited by G. Krause and G. Müller. Berlin: de Gruyter, 1977–.
TRu	*Theologische Rundschau*
TZ	*Theologische Zeitschrift*
VF	*Verkündigung und Forschung*
VT	*Vetus Testamentum*
VTSup	Supplements to Vetus Testamentum
WMANT	Wissenschaftliche Monographien zum Alten und Neuen Testament
ZAW	*Zeitschrift für alttestamentliche Wissenschaft*
ZTK	*Zeitschrift für Theologie und Kirche*

INTRODUCTION

Thomas B. Dozeman and Konrad Schmid

The Pentateuch Seminar of the Society of Biblical Literature provides the context and the point of origin for our study *A Farewell to the Yahwist?* The Pentateuch Seminar was formed in the early 1980s by a small group of leading researchers in North America, including John Van Seters, Rolf Knierim, George Coats, Simon De Vries, and John Gammie. These scholars were drawn together by a growing uneasiness over the lack of direction in pentateuchal studies in the wake of the influential synthesis of Martin Noth and Gerhard von Rad, which had provided creative direction for the field in the early and middle periods of the century. The aim of the Pentateuch Seminar was to assess the present state of the field, to explore new theories of composition, and to reevaluate the organization and the meaning of pentateuchal literature.

The Pentateuch Seminar quickly attracted many of the leading Jewish and Christian researchers in the world. Hans Heinrich Schmid presented his work on the linguistic and theological affinity of the Yahwistic texts in the Tetrateuch to Deuteronomic and Deuteronomistic literature. Thomas L. Thompson explored the growth of pentateuchal tradition as the linking of material through literary chains. Jacob Milgrom contributed new insights in the composition of the Priestly tradition, which was undergoing a renaissance in Jewish scholarship. Rolf Knierim refined his interest in more conceptually oriented methodology. George Coats continued to explore the relationship of the Pentateuch to the Deuteronomistic History, focusing in particular on the book of Joshua. John Van Seters was advancing his research on comparative historiography. Finally, Rolf Rendtorff joined the conversation with his theory of "complexes of tradition" in the literary development of the Pentateuch, a theory of composition that reevaluated the role of the Yahwist author in the work of his teacher, Gerhard von Rad.

The Pentateuch Seminar was a moment of enormous creativity, as the participants explored new directions in the study of the Pentateuch. As often happens at moments of such innovation, it was not always easy to relate the new and emerging methodologies or to see the implications of the distinct theories of composition for the broader interpretation of the Pentateuch. The work of the Pentateuch Seminar continued to crystallize in the decades of the 1980s and 1990s to the point where the research of its members now provides the methodological framework for many who work in pentateuchal studies in the twenty-first century. *A Farewell to the Yahwist?* would not be possible without the groundbreaking work of the members of the Pentateuch Seminar.

The present volume carries on Rolf Rendtorff's theory of "complexes of tradition" in the growth of the Pentateuch. In *Das überlieferungsgeschichtliche Problem des Pentateuch*, Rendtorff raised questions about the combination of tradition history and source criticism in the research of Martin Noth and Gerhard von Rad.[1] Both von Rad and Noth recognized the existence of smaller, independent units of tradition in the formation of the Pentateuch, especially in light of the form-critical work of Hermann Gunkel and Hugo Gressmann. But von Rad and Noth refashioned form criticism, with its tendency to identify the smallest units of tradition, into tradition history by identifying larger complexes of tradition, including the ancestors, exodus, Sinai, wilderness wandering, and the acquiring of the land. Their focus, however, remained on the early stages of tradition. They judged the combination of the distinct complexes of tradition to have taken place already in the oral formation of the historical credo. Thus, what interested von Rad and Noth most was "the unity of the material as such rather than its literary unity";[2] consequently, the literary development of the separate themes never became an object of study.

Rendtorff argued that the one-sided focus on early complexes of tradition left a gap in methodology between the smaller units of tradition and the final literary development of the Pentateuch. Von Rad and Noth filled the gap by assuming the existence of sources in the literary formation of the Pentateuch, but this presented a methodological problem for Rendtorff, who concluded that the literary formation of the Pentateuch had not yet received enough analysis to support the theory of continuous and unified literary sources, especially in light of the insights from tradition history concerning the independent status of the complexes of tradition. What was required, according to Rendtorff, was a new

---

1. Rolf Rendtorff, *Das überlieferungsgeschichtliche Problem des Pentateuch* (BZAW 147; Berlin: de Gruyter, 1977). For a partial English translation, see *The Problem of the Process of Transmission in the Pentateuch* (trans. J. J. Scullion; JSOTSup 89; Sheffield: Academic Press, 1990).

2. Gerhard von Rad, "The Form-Critical Problem of the Hexateuch," in *The Problem of the Hexateuch* (London: Oliver & Boyd, 1966), 16. Martin Noth (*A History of Pentateuch Traditions* [trans. B. A. Anderson; Chico, Calif.: Scholars Press, 1981], 31 n. 115) shares von Rad's disinterest in the literary development of the Pentateuch. He writes that the Sinai literature had already reached such a "complicated compilation within the Pentateuchal tradition that today an intelligible analysis can no longer be successfully undertaken."

study of the literary reworking of the independent complexes of tradition and their arrangement in the present form of the Pentateuch, which von Rad had attributed to the Yahwist author writing in the early monarchical period and Noth to a *Grundschrift* composed even earlier.

Rendtorff sought to fill the gap in methodology between oral tradition and literary development through a study of the ancestral stories in Genesis, which were organized around the theme of the divine promise. His study had two goals. The first was to investigate the literary development of the individual elements of the theme of promise, including land, descendants, blessing, guidance, and divine self-introduction. Rendtorff was especially interested in recovering the process of transmission by which the individual elements of the theme of promise were combined to create the present form of the text. The methodology would provide a partial test of whether the composition of the ancestral complex of tradition supported source criticism or required a new model. The second goal was to examine the distribution of the theme of the promise to the ancestors in other tradition complexes in the Pentateuch, including the exodus, the wilderness wandering, and the revelation at Sinai in Exodus–Numbers. The distribution would provide insight into the organic relationship of the distinct tradition complexes.

Rendtorff's study of the tradition complex of the ancestors provided the basis for his rejection of source criticism as the methodology that best explained the literary process of transmission. First, he concluded that the theme of the promise to the ancestors underwent a multilayered process of composition in which the combination of the elements of the promise (e.g., posterity, land, blessing) served to relate the separate traditions of the individual ancestors into a larger literary complex. The literary process favored a theory of supplementation or "planned theological editing" rather than source criticism. Second, Rendtorff also noted that the theme of the promise to the ancestors, so central to the reworking of Genesis, was nearly absent in Exodus–Numbers. He concluded that the Moses story was reworked from an entirely different point of view than the ancestral stories and that the few cross-references to the promise to the ancestors in Exodus–Numbers were late literary developments to relate the two tradition complexes, which had developed separately and thus did not belong together in any organic way. This conclusion also argued against the theory of source criticism, with its presupposition of an early Yahwistic source that included literature from Genesis through Numbers or Joshua. Rendtorff was clear in his rejection of a Yahwistic author writing in the monarchical period, but he was less clear on the identity of the author(s) who created the Pentateuch by linking the separate tradition complexes, avoiding a decision about whether a Deuteronomistic or a Priestly layer first brought together the different themes of the Pentateuch.

An important step beyond the initiative taken by Rendtorff was provided by the studies on the composition of the Pentateuch by Erhard Blum.[3] After a thorough literary analysis, he formulated a proposal on the process of its compositon that focused on two main subsequent, but nearly contemporaneous, compositional layers: a Deuteronomistic one (KD) and a Priestly one (KP). Before them, the traditions in Genesis, on the one hand, and in Exodus through Numbers/Deuteronomy, on the other, *literarily* grew independently from each other. They were, however, *conceptionally* linked; that is, the narrative continuation of Genesis into Exodus was already part of a given intellectual matrix for the literarily still-unconnected traditions. In a recent contribution Blum has stressed further the literary gap between Genesis and Exodus and has limited the literary extension of KD from Exodus to Numbers/Deuteronomy.[4] Therefore, KP formulated the first literary connection between Genesis and Exodus.

Comparable in this regard, Albert de Pury and Thomas Römer argued already in the late 1980s and the early 1990s for the pre-Priestly independence of the stories in Genesis, on the one hand, and in Exodus, on the other.[5] The main line of their thesis is that the first literary outline of the Pentateuch was not that of the Yahwist of the monarchical period or even the pre-Priestly, exilic Yahwist (as stated, for example, by John Van Seters) but that of the Priestly author in the postexilic period. A counterpart to this thesis is that the non-Priestly literature presupposing the same master narrative of salvation history was the composition of a post-Priestly redactor who was dependent on the Priestly material. Before the Priestly author, the ancestral story and the exodus story most likely existed side by side, presenting two different and competing views and concepts of Israel's origins and identity: the ancestral story developed a geographically autochthonous concept of Israel and a theologically inclusive notion of God, while the exodus story presented the allochthonous origin of Israel in Egypt and advocated an exclusive understanding of God.

---

3. See Erhard Blum, *Die Komposition der Vätergeschichte* (WMANT 57; Neukirchen-Vluyn: Neukirchener, 1984); idem, *Studien zur Komposition des Pentateuch* (BZAW 189; Berlin: de Gruyter, 1990).

4. Erhard Blum, "Die literarische Verbindung von Erzvätern und Exodus: Ein Gespräch mit neueren Endredaktions-hypothesen," in *Abschied vom Jahwisten: Die Komposition des Hexateuch in der jüngsten Diskussion* (ed. J. C. Gertz et al.; BZAW 315; Berlin: de Gruyter, 2002), 119–56. See also his contribution in this volume.

5. See, e.g., Albert de Pury, "Le cycle de Jacob comme légende autonome des origines d'Israël," in *Congress Volume: Leuven, 1989* (ed. J. A. Emerton; VTSup 43; Leiden: Brill, 1991), 78–96; idem, "Osée 12 et ses implications pour le débat actuel sur le Pentateuque," in *Le Pentateuque: Débats et recherches* (ed. P. Haudebert; LD 151; Paris: Cerf, 1992), 175–207; Thomas Römer, *Israels Väter: Untersuchungen zur Väterthematik im Deuteronomium und in der deuteronomistischen Tradition* (OBO 99; Fribourg: Universitätsverlag; Göttingen: Vandenhoeck & Ruprecht, 1990).

A Farewell to the Yahwist? discusses from various perspectives the thesis of the literary interrelationship between Genesis and Exodus, namely, whether the Priestly author was the first to combine the tradition of the ancestors with the story of Moses and the exodus, creating the master narrative of salvation history as a progression from the divine promise of land, posterity, and blessing to the ancestors to the exodus from Egypt and the journey to the promised land. This book has a forerunner in the German volume *Abschied vom Jahwisten*, which was published in 2002 and collected papers of some of the major exponents of this theory.[6] The present volume also contains voices critical to the general literary separation of the pre-Priestly material in Genesis and Exodus, so its title ends, contrary to its German predecessor, with a question mark. One of the goals of this volume is to facilitate communication between European and North American scholars and to provide a critical discussion of recent directions of pentateuchal studies in Europe.

The essays in *A Farewell to the Yahwist?* are organized loosely into three parts. In the opening section Thomas Römer (University of Lausanne, Switzerland) reviews the history of research surrounding the identification of the Yahwist in "The Elusive Yahwist: A Short History of Research." He catalogues the many modifications that have taken place in the definition of J throughout the scholarly constructs in the nineteenth and twentieth centuries, taking the reader through to the recent work of Rolf Rendtorff. Konrad Schmid (University of Zürich, Switzerland) presents the thesis of the volume in "The So-Called Yahwist and the Literary Gap between Genesis and Exodus." He examines the lack of narrative unity between Genesis and Exodus, the redactional links between the two books, and the literary connection between the patriarchs and the exodus in Priestly literature. His essay concludes with a summary of the implications of attributing the original linking of Genesis and Exodus to Priestly literature for the study of the history of religion and for theology.

The middle portion of the volume includes a series of more narrowly focused exegetical studies on the transition between Genesis and Exodus in Gen 50, Exod 1, and the call of Moses in Exod 3–4. Albert de Pury (University of Geneva, Switzerland) provides the point of departure by summarizing his research on the separation of the Jacob story and the story of Moses until the writing of the Priestly history under the influence of the reign of Cyrus in "The Jacob Story and the Beginning of the Formation of the Pentateuch." De Pury explores the independent status of the Jacob story in the northern kingdom, the tension between the Jacob legend and the prophetic emphasis on Moses in Hos

---

6. Jan Christian Gertz, Konrad Schmid, and Markus Witte, eds., *Abschied vom Jahwisten: Die Komposition des Hexateuch in der jüngsten Diskussion* (BZAW 315; Berlin: de Gruyter, 2002).

12, and the combination of the two origin traditions in the Priestly history. Jan Christian Gertz (University of Heidelberg, Germany) provides a close reading of the literary transition in Gen 50–Exod 1 from the patriarchs and Joseph to Moses in "The Transition between the Books of Genesis and Exodus." Gertz argues that the transition between Gen 50 and Exod 1 is the decisive thematic connection within the pentateuchal narrative and that it was first established by the Priestly author. Once it originated, all succeeding redactors were required to embrace this connection as the historically accurate and theologically intended sequence. Thus, for Gertz, "The string holding the pearls of the non-Priestly pentateuchal narratives was furnished by P!" Erhard Blum (University of Tübingen, Germany) broadens the study of the literary connection between Genesis and Exodus in "The Literary Connection between the Books of Genesis and Exodus and the End of the Book of Joshua." Blum interprets the literary transition between Gen 50–Exod 1 and the call of Moses in Exod 3–4 in conjunction with a series of related texts stretching from the purchase of Shechem (Gen 35) to the burial of the bones of Joseph (Josh 24). The compositional and editorial fabric of the motif of Joseph's bones creates a profile of related texts including Gen 50:24–26; Exod 1:6, 8; Judg 2:6–8; and Josh 24:28–31, which represent a redactional stratum by the same author, who sought to fashion a "Hexateuch" (or, more precisely, the "book of the Torah of God" [Josh 24:26]). The compositional stratum is dependent on both pre-Priestly tradition and the Priestly material in the Pentateuch, which identifies the author as post-Priestly. The dependence of this author on the Priestly composition of Exod 1:1–5 in composing Gen 50:24–26 and Exod 1:6, 8 suggests that the Priestly author was the first to bring together the major traditions of the Pentateuch, including the primeval history, the narratives of the patriarchs, and the exodus narrative. In "The Commission of Moses and the Book of Genesis," Thomas B. Dozeman (United Theological Seminary, Dayton, Ohio) compares the commission of Moses in Exod 3–4 to the Priestly version in Exod 6–7 to evaluate whether the composition is pre-Priestly or post-Priestly. A comparison of the form of the commission in conjunction with a study of its central motifs suggests that the commission of Moses in Exod 3–4 is a pre-Priestly composition and that the Priestly version in Exod 6–7 is dependent upon it. The form-critical and literary study leads to the conclusion that the pre-Priestly author of Exod 3–4, rather than the Priestly author, was the first to relate the books of Genesis and Exodus into the master narrative of the Pentateuch.

The volume concludes with three responses to the thesis that the Priestly author was the first to create the master narrative of the Pentateuch. Christoph Levin (University of Munich, Germany) underscores areas of agreement with the thesis of the volume, including the late combination of the books of Genesis and Exodus, the nature of the non-Priestly texts as not forming a coherent work from the beginning, and the formation of the narrative of the Tetrateuch in the postexilic period. But he disagrees that the relationship between Genesis and Exodus is the central problem in the formation of the Pentateuch, while he also identifies a pre-Priestly Yahwistic (J) editor as the redactor who first fashioned the continuous narrative of the Tetrateuch. John Van Seters (Waterloo, Canada) agrees with the criticism of the early dating of the Yahwist to the monarchical period but is critical of the emphasis on redaction and complex editorial processes to account for the formation of the Pentateuch. Van Seters argues, instead, for von Rad's original understanding of the Yahwist as an author and historian. He seeks to demonstrate through a study of Gen 50 and Exod 1 that the pre-Priestly, exilic Yahwist was the author who combined the ancestral material in Genesis with the story of Moses in Exodus–Numbers, creating in the process a historiography of the origin of ancient Israel. David M. Carr (Union Theological Seminary, New York) provides a broad overview of the arguments in the volume. He clarifies that the debate over the identification of a pre-Priestly Pentateuch has nothing to do with the J source of classical source criticism. This holds true even for those who continue to use the term *Yahwist,* as in the case of Christoph Levin and John Van Seters. His response also surveys the different methodological models employed for joining the traditions of the ancestors and the exodus in both Priestly and non-Priestly literature. In addition, Carr provides a more detailed literary study of Gen 50 and Exod 1, distinguishing between Priestly and pre-Priestly tradition. His response closes by examining the identification of post-Priestly material in the Pentateuch.

A Farewell to the Yahwist? is the outgrowth of a special session of the Pentateuch Section held during the Society of Biblical Literature 2004 Annual Meeting in San Antonio. The session, which was conceived and organized by Thomas B. Dozeman, Thomas Römer, and Konrad Schmid, included the papers by Thomas Römer, Konrad Schmid, Jan Christian Gertz, Thomas B. Dozeman, Christoph Levin, and David M. Carr. Because Albert de Pury's and Erhard Blum's contributions were not part of that session, the responses in this volume do not refer to them. The editors thank Christopher R. Matthews for accepting this work for publication in the Society of Biblical Literature's Symposium Series and for providing advice in the editorial process.

THE ELUSIVE YAHWIST: A SHORT HISTORY OF RESEARCH

Thomas Christian Römer

1. INTRODUCTION

The current scholarly debate on the Torah is characterized by a quite paradoxical situation. On the one hand, a growing number of authors, especially in Europe, have given up the classical Documentary Hypothesis as a relevant model for explaining the composition of the Pentateuch, including the theory of a distinct Yahwistic source or author (J). Even scholars still holding to this model, such as Horst Seebass, for instance, must concede: "Among all source critical-theories about the Pentateuch, J is the most unstable one."[1] On the other hand, recent textbooks or publications for a larger audience still present the Documentary Hypothesis as a firmly established result of source criticism and historical exegesis, and the so-called "J" source, in particular, continues to play a preeminent role in the presentation and discussion of the theory.[2]

Typically such textbooks and introductions will present J as the oldest document of the Pentateuch, written under the reign of Solomon, and containing already the narrative structure of the Pentateuch (or Hexateuch), starting with the creation of humanity and ending with the conquest of the promised land. In this model J is thus defined as the first historian or the first theologian in the Hebrew Bible.[3] Although this conception is presented as the traditional view on J, a critical survey of scholarship on J reveals that it actually corresponds only to a rather late development of the theory under the influence of G. von Rad. For this reason the first part of this paper will be devoted to a brief state

---

1. "Unter den quellenkritischen Hypothesen des Pentateuch ist die des J die unstabilste" (Horst Seebass, "Jahwist," *TRE* 16[1987]: 441–51).

2. See, for instance, Antony F. Campbell and Mark A. O'Brien, *Sources of the Pentateuch: Texts, Introductions, Annotations* (Minneapolis: Fortress, 1993); Richard Elliott Friedman, *The Bible with Sources Revealed* (San Francisco: HarperSanFrancisco, 2003).

3. Peter F. Ellis, *The Yahwist, The Bible's First Theologian: With the Jerusalem Bible Text of the Yahwist Saga* (Chicago: Fides, 1968).

of the question of J. The aim of the paper is not to offer an exhaustive history of pentateuchal research[4] but to focus on the major modifications occurring in the definition of J in the nineteenth and twentieth centuries. After this short overview the second part of the paper will be devoted to a closer analysis of the different conceptions connected with the Yahwist,[5] which will demonstrate the elusive character of this scholarly construct.

2. The Life, or Lives, of the Yahwist: From Birth to Death—or to Resurrection?

2.1. The Birth of the Yahwist

The Yahwist was fathered in the eighteenth century through the work of Henning Bernhard Witter (1711) and Jean Astruc (1753). Both authors, working on the book of Genesis and trying to explain the different divine names, came to the conclusion that the Pentateuch was compiled from different documents.[6] Astruc distinguished several documents, especially a document "A" speaking of God as "Elohim" and a document "B" using the divine name "Jehova." In his 1780 *Introduction to the Old Testament,* Eichhorn distinguished, apparently independently from Astruc, two sources for the book of Genesis: an

---

4. Many of those have been written recently, see, for instance, Félix García López, *El Penta-teuco: Introducción a la lectura de los cinco primeros libros de la Biblia* (Estella: Verbo Divino, 2003); Cees Houtman, *Der Pentateuch: Die Geschichte seiner Erforschung nebst einer Auswertung* (Kampen: Kok Pharos, 1994); Otto Kaiser, "The Pentateuch and the Deuteronomistic History," in *Text in Context: Essays by Members of the Society for Old Testament Studies* (ed. A. D. H. Mayes; Oxford: Oxford University Press, 2000), 289–322; Ernest Nicholson, *The Pentateuch in the Twentieth Century: The Legacy of Julius Wellhausen* (Oxford: Clarendon, 1998); Thomas Römer, "La formation du Pentateuque: Histoire de la recherche," and Christophe Nihan and Thomas Römer, "Le débat actuel sur la formation du Pentateuque," in *Introduction à l'Ancien Testament* (ed. T. Römer et al.; MdB 49; Genève: Labor et Fides, 2004), 67–84, 85–113; Jean-Louis Ska, *Introduction à la lecture du Pentateuque: Clés pour l'interprétation des cinq premiers livres de la Bible* (Brussels: Lessius, 2000); John Van Seters, *The Pentateuch: A Social Science Commentary* (Sheffield: Sheffield Academic Press, 1999); Erich Zenger, "Theorien über die Entstehung des Pentateuch im Wandel der Forschung," in *Einleitung in das Alte Testament* (ed. E. Zenger; 5th ed.; Studienbücher Theologie 1/1; Stuttgart: Kohlhammer, 2004), 74–123.

5. For presentations of J, see, besides the article of Seebass mentioned above, Albert de Pury, "Yahwist ("J") Source," *ABD* 6 (1992): 1012–20; Jean-Louis Ska, "The Yahwist, a Hero with a Thousand Faces: A Chapter in the History of Modern Exegesis," in *Abschied vom Jahwisten: Die Komposition des Hexateuch in der jüngsten Diskussion* (ed. J. C. Gertz et al.; BZAW 315; Berlin: de Gruyter, 2002), 1–23; and Peter Weimar, "Jahwist," *Neues Bibel Lexikon* 1 (2001): 268–71.

6. Henning B. Witter, *Jura Israelitarum in Palestiniam terram* (Hildesheim, 1711); Jean Astruc, *Conjectures sur la Genèse (1753): Introduction et notes de Pierre Gibert* (Paris: Noêsis, 1999).

"Elohim document" and a "Jehova document." Both are, according to Eichhorn, limited to the book of Genesis. The rest of the Pentateuch consists of various documents from the time of Moses. In his fourth edition (1823), Eichhorn gave up the notion of Mosaic authorship for the Pentateuch and attributed the gathering and the grouping of the main documents of Genesis and of the other books to a compiler.[7] Since he limited the Jehova and Elohist documents to the book of Genesis and postulated the existence of other documents for the following books, Eichhorn's conception of the formation of the Pentateuch came very close to a fragmentary theory, such as it was defended by Alexander Geddes in 1792.[8]

The next step in the creation of the Yahwist can be found in the work of Karl David Ilgen on the sources of the Pentateuch, of which only the first part dealing with the book of Genesis actually appeared.[9] Ilgen locates the sources of the Pentateuch in the temple archives of Jerusalem. He distinguishes seventeen different sources and attributes these sources to three "compilers" or "writers" whom he labels according to their use of the divine name: the first and the second Elohist, and the Jehovist (Ilgen does not speak of a "Yahwist," since the usual pronunciation of the Tetragrammaton in his time was "Jehova"). As Eichhorn before him, Ilgen was aware that the use of the divine name was not sufficient to attribute the texts to one of these three writers. He thus added further criteria such as repetitions and differences in ideology, style, and vocabulary.[10]

After de Wette's isolation of Deuteronomy as an independent source, which could be dated in the seventh century B.C.E., the work of H. Hupfeld constitutes a major advance toward the establishment of the "new Documentary Hypothesis." In his 1853 book, which deals again with Genesis, Hupfeld confirms Ilgen's idea of two Elohists (an earlier E, which would become later the Priestly source, and a second, later E) as well as a "Yahwist" (which he labels "Jhwh-ist"). The Yahwist is for Hupfeld the youngest document of the three. The first Elohist is the *Urschrift,* which the redactor of the Pentateuch takes as

---

7. Johann Gottfried Eichhorn, *Einleitung in das Alte Testament I–III (1780–83)* (4th ed.; Göttingen: Rosenbusch, 1823). In English one may consult *Introduction to the Study of the Old Testament: A Fragment Translated by G. T. Gollop* (from the 3rd German edition; n.p.: privately published, 1803).

8. Alexander Geddes, *The Holy Bible: Or the Books Accounted Sacred by Jews and Christians; Otherwise Called the Books of the Old and New Covenants I* (London: Davis, 1792).

9. Karl David Ilgen, *Die Urkunden des jerusalemischen Tempelarchivs in ihrer Urgestalt, als Beytrag zur Berichtigung der Geschichte der Religion und Politik* (Halle: Hemmerde & Schwetschke, 1798).

10. On Ilgen, see Bodo Seidel, *Karl David Ilgen und die Pentateuchforschung im Umkreis der sogenannten Älteren Urkundenhypothese: Studien zur Geschichte der exegetischen Hermeneutik in der späten Aufklärung* (BZAW 213; Berlin: de Gruyter, 1993).

the basis and within which he incorporates as completely as possible the later Elohist as well as the Yahwist.

2.2. The Yahwist as Oldest Source of the Documentary Hypothesis

The transformation of the Yahwist into the oldest source of the Pentateuch occurred when the so-called first Elohist was gradually acknowledged to be not the earliest source but the latest in light of the research of Eduard Reuss and Karl Heinrich Graf.[11] This new paradigm was essentially taken over by Abraham Kuenen and Julius Wellhausen. Interestingly, Kuenen's Yahwist is again defined on the basis of observations made by the Dutch scholar on the book of Genesis: "We also find in *Genesis* ... another set of narratives or pericopes, which are connected together, and which often run parallel to E in matter, though departing from it in details and language. This group must be derived from a single work which we call Yahwistic document."[12] As is well known, Kuenen and Wellhausen were very close and influenced each other considerably. In his *Composition of the Hexateuch* as well as in his *Prolegomena to the History of Israel*,[13] Wellhausen laid the foundations of the Documentary Hypothesis for at least the next century. However, and this point is often overlooked, Wellhausen himself had a limited interest in the Yahwist. He was most skeptical about the possibility of sorting out this source by means of literary-critical analysis. On the contrary, one frequently finds in his work (especially in the *Composition of the Hexateuch*) the statement that J and E are so closely interwoven that it is not only impossible but even unnecessary to separate both documents.[14] He thus prefers to speak of a "Jehovist," a term that classically designates now the combination of the Yahwistic and Elohistic documents. Yet for Wellhausen even this "Jehovist" is *not* a coherent work, in contrast to Q (that is, our P source); rather, it passed through different hands before coming to its present form. One

---

11. For more details, see Robert J. Thompson, *Moses and the Law in a Century of Criticism since Graf* (VTSup 19; Leiden: Brill, 1970).

12. Abraham Kuenen, *Historisch-critisch onderzoek naar het ontstaan en de verzameling van de boeken des Ouden Verbonds I* (Leiden: Engels, 1861); English translation: *A Historical-Critical Inquiry into the Origin and Composition of the Hexateuch* (trans. H. P. Wicksteed; London: Macmillan, 1886), 140. According to Ska ("The Yahwist," 9), Kuenen was the first to create the term "Jahwist."

13. Julius Wellhausen, *Die Composition des Hexateuchs und der historischen Bücher des Alten Testaments (1899)* (Berlin: de Gruyter, 1963); Julius Wellhausen, *Prolegomena zur Geschichte Israels* (sixth ed.; 1927; repr., Berlin: de Gruyter, 2001); English translation: *Prolegomena to the History of Israel* (trans. J. S. Black and A. Menzies; 1885; Scholars Press Reprints and Translations Series; repr., Atlanta: Scholars Press, 1994).

14. Wellhausen, *Composition des Hexateuchs*, 35.

should therefore distinguish at least three different editions of J (J^1, J^2, J^3) and three different editions of E (E^1, E^2, E^3).[15] Interestingly, the problematic results arising from his analysis of J were used against Wellhausen by those among his contemporaries, such as August Dillmann, who were critical of the new Documentary Hypothesis. Wellhausen did not attempt to provide a precise dating for the composition of J. He limited himself instead to locating the Jehovist in the Assyrian period and affirmed: "One cannot give precise information for a period earlier than the century before 850–750.... It was only at this time that literature flourished."[16] In fact, since Wellhausen was primarily interested in reconstructing the evolution of the Israelite religion from a natural, familiar, and local form of the cult to a regulated, hierarchical, and priestly controlled form of worship (with the Deuteronomistic reform as intermediate state), the Jehovist represented for him the first real document on the original state of Israelite religion. The attempt to distinguish systematically between J and E was, in his eyes, both methodologically unsure and, to a certain extent, even historically pointless. Finally, it should also be noted that for Wellhausen, as for scholars before him since Witter, Astruc, and Ilgen, Genesis played a major role in describing the "Jehovistic history book." Wellhausen concluded: "The story of the patriarchs ... characterizes this document the best."[17]

As Wellhausen before him, Kuenen often treated J and E together. He also differentiated further between two major blocks in the Hexateuch, "the Deuteronomistic-prophetic sacred history (D + JE)" and "the historico-Priestly work (P)," both of which existed independently until the time of Ezra and Nehemiah.[18] As a matter of fact, many scholars at the end of the nineteenth century were not interested in distinguishing precisely between J and E. This is also the case, for instance, with Willy Staerk, who was one of the first to emphasize a major tension within the Jehovistic work. He pointed out two different conceptions of Israel's possession of Canaan: a "naive and popular one" (in his own terms), which is found in the patriarchal narratives; and a second one, more developed and based on a concept of salvation history ("eine reflektierte und heilsgeschichtliche Konzeption"), which can be found in the exodus tradition.[19] Staerk was actually much more interested in this opposition than in the profile of the Jehovist.

---

15. Ibid., 7 and 207.

16. Julius Wellhausen, *Grundrisse zum Alten Testament* (ed. R. Smend; Munich: Kaiser, 1965), 40.

17. "Die Patriarchengeschichte ... charakterisirt [*sic*] diese Schrift am besten" (Wellhausen, *Prolegomena*, 7, German edition).

18. Kuenen, *Historical-Critical Inquiry,* 313.

19. Willy Staerk, *Studien zur Religions- und Sprachgeschichte des alten Testaments* (2 vols.; Berlin: Reimer, 1899), 1:50–51.

Nevertheless some attempts were also made to describe the "personality" of the Yahwist, as for instance in the work of Bernhard Luther,[20] who praised the Yahwist as a literary genius and a strong personality.[21] Luther's Yahwist comes very close to the ideals of liberal Protestantism, since he is opposed to everything cultic and shares the ethical concerns of the preexilic prophets. Heinrich Holzinger and Samuel Rolles Driver also tried to establish lexicons of the Yahwist on the basis of his vocabulary and his style.[22] However, these approaches, which presuppose the unity and the literary homogeneity of J, were quite at odds with the results attained by other scholars, such as Charles Bruston, Karl Budde, and Rudolf Smend senior.[23] The latter scholars followed in general Wellhausen concerning the lack of homogeneity of J, and they tried to identify more precisely discrete editions of the Yahwistic document, even to the point of postulating the existence of two more documents behind J.[24] The attempt to identify pre-J documents remained popular during the first half of the twentieth century (Otto Eissfeldt; Georg Fohrer; Robert H. Pfeiffer).[25]

2.3. THE YAHWIST AND THE *FORMGESCHICHTE*

The diachronic differentiation of the Yahwistic source was also adopted by Hermann Gunkel in his commentary on Genesis,[26] where he distinguished two

---

20. Bernhard Luther, "Die Persönlichkeit des Jahwisten," in Eduard Meyer, *Die Israeliten und ihre Nachbarstämme: Alttestamentliche Untersuchungen* (Halle, 1906; repr., Darmstadt: Wissenschaftliche Buchgesellschaft, 1967), 106–73.

21. Ibid., 169.

22. Heinrich Holzinger, *Einleitung in den Hexateuch: Mit Tabellen über die Quellenscheidung* (Freiburg: Mohr, 1893); Samuel R. Driver, *An Introduction to the Literature of the Old Testament* (9th ed.; 1913; repr., Edinburgh: T&T Clark, 1960).

23. Charles Bruston, "Les deux Jéhovistes," *RTP* 18 (1885): 5–34, 429–528, 602–37; Karl Budde, *Die biblische Urgeschichte (Gen 1–12,5)* (Giessen: Ricker, 1883); Rudolf Smend Sr., *Die Erzählung des Hexateuch auf ihre Quellen untersucht* (Berlin: Reimer, 1912).

24. See also Cuthbert A. Simpson, *The Early Traditions of Israel: A Critical Analysis of the Pre-Deuteronomic Narrative of the Hexateuch* (Oxford: Blackwell, 1948).

25. Otto Eissfeldt, *Hexateuch-Synopse: Die Erzählung der fünf Bücher Moses und des Buches Josua mit dem Anfange des Richterbuches* (Leipzig: Hinrichs, 1922; repr., Darmstadt: Wissenschaftliche Buchgesellschaft, 1962 [1987]); see in English: *The Old Testament: An Introduction* (New York: Harper & Row, 1965): he distinguishes the Yahwistic source in J and L ("lay source"); Georg Fohrer, *Einleitung in das Alte Testament* (11th ed.; Heidelberg: Quelle & Meyer, 1969): he speaks of N (nomadic source) instead of L; Robert H. Pfeiffer, *Introduction to the Old Testament* (2nd ed.; New York: Harper & Brothers, 1948) separated the Yahwistic source of the patriarchal narratives into J and S ("Southern Source"). For more details, see Nicholson, *Pentateuch in the Twentieth Century,* 43–45. Today Jacques Vermeylen defends the existence of a "proto-J" who wrote during the reign of David; see his "Les premières étapes littéraires de la formation du Pentateuque," in *Le Pentateuque en question* (ed. A. de Pury and T. Römer; 3rd ed.; MdB 19; Genève: Labor et Fides, 2002), 149–97.

Yahwists for the primeval history (J^e [a Yahwist using the divine name *elohim*] and J^j [a Yahwist using the Tetragrammaton], as well as no less than three other Yahwists for the patriarchal narratives (two parallel sources J^a and J^b, and a Yahwistic redactor J^r). This meticulous distribution of J into numerous Yahwistic fragments conflicts with Gunkel's statement that it is impossible to define more precisely the relation of these different Yahwists: "It is relatively insignificant what the individual hands contributed to the whole because they are very indistinct and can never be identified with certainty."[27] It is well known that Gunkel was actually not interested in source criticism and the reconstitution of written documents. His main concern was the investigation of oral tradition, which, he believed, generated all the narratives of the book of Genesis. In contrast to the composition of P, which Gunkel considered to be the work of an author, the different Yahwists (as well as the Elohistic school) were just collectors, very much like the Grimm brothers of his time, whose work was apparently well known to Gunkel.[28] The Yahwistic collectors neither organized nor altered the stories that they transmitted and that, besides, had already been gathered into cycles (*Sagenkränze*). As Gunkel states, these Yahwistic collectors "were not masters but rather servants of their subjects."[29]

2.4. The Yahwist as Author and Theologian

Gunkel's notion of several collectors has retained little influence in the contemporary study of the Yahwist. The current conception of the Yahwist is for the most part the invention of Gerhard von Rad. What is more, the Yahwist of von Rad would probably never have been conceived without the strong influence of Karl Barth's dialectical theology. In his 1938 essay on the form-critical problem of the Hexateuch,[30] von Rad resurrected the Yahwist as an author, a theologian, and the architect of the Hexateuch. He conceded that J "was certainly a collector, and as such had an interest in preserving the ancient

---

26. Hermann Gunkel, *Genesis übersetzt und erklärt* (3rd ed.; HKAT 3/1; Göttingen: Vandenhoeck & Ruprecht, 1910); English translation: *Genesis* (trans. M. E. Biddle; Macon, Ga.: Mercer University Press, 1997).

27. Gunkel, *Genesis*, lxxiii, English edition.

28. Gunkel was probably unaware of the fact that a great number of their tales did not stem from storytellers they were listening to; they took them over from already-existing literary collections; see, for instance, Ernst Axel Knauf, *Die Umwelt des Alten Testaments* (Neuer Stuttgarter Kommentar: Altes Testament 29: Stuttgart: Katholisches Bibelwerk, 1994), 226.

29. Gunkel, *Genesis*, lxiv, English edition.

30. Gerhard von Rad, "Das formgeschichtliche Problem des Hexateuch," in idem, *Gesammelte Studien zum Alten Testament* (ed. R. Smend; 4th ed.; TB 8; Munich: Kaiser, 1971), 9–86. English translation: "The Form-Critical Problem of the Hexateuch," in idem, *The Problem of the*

religious motives of his material."[31] Yet von Rad blames Gunkel for his "complete failure to take into account the co-ordinating power of the writer's [= J] overall theological purpose."[32] Against Gunkel, and probably against the history of religion school in general, von Rad wrote: "The Yahwist speaks to his contemporaries out of concern for the real and living faith, not as more or less detached story-tellers."[33] Von Rad is also the first to find a very precise location for the Yahwist by associating him with the time of Solomon, which he characterizes as a period of "enlightenment." As a writer of the Solomonic court, J offers a theological legitimation of the new state created by David and consolidated by Solomon. But J is not only Israel's first (and probably greatest ever) theologian; he is also the creator of the Hexateuch. As such he takes over the old Israelite creed, which is attested in Deut 26:5–9, Josh 24:2–13, and elsewhere. The creed included the motifs of the descent to Egypt, the liberation from Egyptian oppression, and the settlement in the land. On the basis of this credo, J composed the Pentateuch by inserting the Sinai tradition between the exodus and the settlement and by prefacing his work with the addition of the primeval history. The creation of the Hexateuch by J occurred through a further development, which von Rad considers "perhaps the most important factor of all," that is, the "integration of the patriarchal history as a whole with the idea of settlement."[34] By this combination of two independent traditions, the Yahwist altered the purpose of the divine promises to the patriarchs, which were originally related to the establishment of the patriarchs in Canaan without a connection to the exodus-settlement tradition. Von Rad's recognition of the original difference between the patriarchal narratives and the settlement tradition was based on the work of Kurt Galling, who emphasized the ideological differences between the two traditions and attributed their literary combination to L (the so-called "lay" source) and J.[35]

Von Rad's conception of the Yahwist profoundly influenced M. Noth, whose source-critical identification of J was to become canonical.[36] Yet Noth

---

Hexateuch and Other Essays (trans. E. W. Trueman Dicken; Edinburgh: Oliver & Boyd, 1966; repr., London: SCM, 1984), 1–78.

31. Von Rad, "Problem," 69, English edition.

32. Ibid., 51.

33. Ibid., 69.

34. Ibid., 60.

35. Kurt Galling, *Die Erwählungstraditionen Israels* (BZAW 48; Giessen: Töpelmann, 1928), see esp. 56–63.

36. Martin Noth, *Überlieferungsgeschichte des Pentateuch* (Stuttgart: Kohlhammer, 1948); English translation: *A History of Pentateuchal Traditions* (trans. B. W. Anderson; Eaglewood Cliffs, N.J.: Prentice Hall, 1972; repr., Atlanta: Scholars Press, 1981).

also differed from von Rad on several major issues.[37] First, Noth gave up the idea of a Hexateuch: since he considered the books of Deuteronomy and Joshua as belonging to the Deuteronomistic History, he claimed that the hand of the Yahwist was not to be found in Joshua. Therefore Noth had to postulate that the end of the Yahwist was lost when the Deuteronomistic History was linked with the pentateuchal sources.[38] Second Noth claimed that the Yahwist as well as the other sources of the Pentateuch "cannot be regarded as 'authors.' "[39] According to Noth, J did not invent the literary connection between the major themes of the Pentateuch (guidance out of Egypt, guidance into the arable land, promise to the patriarchs, guidance in the wilderness, revelation at Sinai). This connection preexisted in a common *Grundlage* (basis), whether oral or written, which was shared by both J and E. The only creative act of J was the addition of the primeval history to the themes already present in this *Grundlage*. Nevertheless, at the end of his book Noth himself contradicted this introductory statement by concluding that all the pentateuchal sources should be traced to the work of authors instead of being ascribed to schools.[40] In fact, Noth himself appears to have hesitated as to how the nature of the J source should be precisely defined.[41] He was also aware that the patriarchal tradition was only poorly connected with the following themes of the Pentateuch. In this context, Noth even observed that this connection appears only explicitly in "the traditio-historically late passage Gen 15."[42] In addition, Noth also suspected the Joseph story to be a late insertion between the patriarchal narratives and the exodus story.[43] But since the themes of the Pentateuch (excepted the primeval history) had already been combined before the Yahwist, according to Noth, the different theological profiles of

---

37. See, for instance, Campbell and O'Brien, *Sources of the Pentateuch*, 7–10. Contrarily to Noth, von Rad was not much interested in the concrete problems of source criticism.

38. Noth, *History of Pentateuchal Traditions*, 16 and 72.

39. Ibid., 2.

40. Ibid., 228.

41. As John Van Seters argues in a forthcoming book, of which he kindly communicated me some chapters, Noth astonishingly described the Yahwist as being very different from the Deuteronomist.

42. Noth, *History of Pentateuchal Traditions*, 200. Like von Rad, Noth quotes positively Galling: "the theme of the patriarchal history, as Kurt Galling has already seen quite correctly, was only secondarily placed before the following themes" (46). See also the comments of Nicholson, *Pentateuch in the Twentieth Century*, 84–85, and Konrad Schmid, *Erzväter und Exodus: Untersuchungen zur doppelten Begründung der Ursprünge Israels innerhalb der Geschichtsbücher des Alten Testaments* (WMANT 81; Neukirchen-Vluyn: Neukirchener, 1999), 8–10.

43. *History of Pentateuchal Traditions*, 202. Noth considers the Joseph story "a traditio-historically late construction."

the patriarchal and the exodus traditions were automatically relegated to the oral prehistory of the Torah.

In North America Noth's conception of J was further developed in the work of Frank Moore Cross with his own conception of the ancient "epic sources" that supposedly underlie the Hebrew Bible. Cross agreed with Noth that J is based on older traditions, some of which were already written. But for Cross the older material could be characterized more precisely as epic traditions, which the Yahwist transformed into prose accounts. The story of the conflict at the sea provides an example. The poem in Exod 15 is part of the epic tradition, according to Cross, which still reflects the Canaanite mythic pattern of the divine battle against the sea. The Yahwist transforms this epic into a prose narrative through the composition of Exod 14.

The conception of the Yahwist that has appeared in textbooks since the 1950s is mostly a combination of the views of von Rad and Noth, which, in North America, has been further combined with Cross's notion of an old demythologized epic tradition. Thus, to give only a few examples, Robert Pfeiffer praised the "superb literary form" of the Yahwist and ascribed to him the "injection of the future conquest of Canaan into the patriarchal stories by means of divine promises and significant itineraries."[44] Peter F. Ellis described J as "the theological opus of an ancient genius … the earliest monumental theologian in history."[45] And in a 2003 *Commentary on the Bible* David Noel Freedman still "adheres to the common, if somewhat conservative, view that J dates from the United Monarchy … and finds the complete fulfillment of the promise to the fathers not in the original settlement under Joshua but in the conquests and kingdom of David."[46]

2.5. The Death of the Yahwist

The challenge to the conception of the Yahwist as an author writing in the tenth century B.C.E., and more broadly to the whole Documentary Hypothesis in general, rapidly gained ground by the end of the 1970s. Of course, there were some important forerunners, such as the Danish scholar Bentzen, who claimed already in his 1949 introduction: "There is a widespread distrust in the Documentary Hypothesis." The reason according to Bentzen was the "strong

---

44. Pfeiffer, *Introduction to the Old Testament*, 156. Ellis also highlighted J as author and theologian (*Yahwist*, 23–24).

45. Ellis, *Yahwist*, viii.

46. David Noel Freedman, "The Pentateuch," in *Eerdmans Commentary on the Bible* (ed. J. D. G. Dunn and J. W. Rogerson; Grand Rapids: Eerdmans, 2003), 25–31, 27.

tendency to separate Gen. from Ex.–Num. as originally different complexes of tradition."[47] Quite similarly, Winnett argued in a 1965 article that the book of Genesis is the work of a "late J," who wrote in the early Persian period and composed the book of Genesis by using older documents (an "early J" for Abraham and Jacob and an "E" document for the story of Joseph). According to Winnett, it was P who, still later in the postexilic period, supplemented the work of the "late J" and prefixed it to the "Mosaic tradition." P also separated the book of Deuteronomy from the Deuteronomistic History and reworked it as the conclusion for the entire Pentateuch.[48]

The hiatus between the patriarchs and the exodus story was also a main argument of Rolf Rendtorff, who claimed in his 1976 monograph that Old Testament scholars never had a clear idea about the Yahwist, which led him to the conclusion that the whole Documentary Hypothesis should definitely be abandoned.[49] Rendtorff took over Noth's idea of independent pentateuchal themes but argued that these themes and traditions had been put together at a much later stage by redactors who wer influenced by Deuteronomistic language and theology. As Staerk before him, Rendtorff insists on the fact that the Moses story does *not* presuppose the theme of the promise of the land made to the patriarchs. Analyzing the story of Moses' call, Rendtorff comments: "The land is introduced here as an unknown land.... there is not a word which mentions that the patriarchs have already lived a long time in this land and that God has promised it to them and their descendants as a permanent possession. Following the terminology of the land in Genesis, those addressed here would be the 'seed' for whom the promise holds good. But they are not spoken to as such."[50] Rendtorff's ideas were taken over by E. Blum, who replaced the Yahwist and the Documentary Hypothesis by a theory of two main "compositions" (D and P), which created two different accounts of Israel's origins during and after the Babylonian exile, by incorporating into their work older, originally independent stories and collections of laws.[51]

---

47. Aage Bentzen, *The Books of the Old Testament* (vol. 2 of *Introduction to the Old Testament*; (Copenhagen: Gads, 1949), 60.

48. Frederick V. Winnett, "Re-examining the Foundations," *JBL* 84 (1965): 1–19.

49. Rolf Rendtorff, *Das überlieferungsgeschichtliche Problem des Pentateuch* (BZAW 147; Berlin: de Gruyter, 1976); English translation: *The Problem of the Process of Transmission in the Pentateuch* (trans. J. J. Scullion; JSOTSup 89; Sheffield: JSOT Press, 1990). See also Rolf Rendtorff, "The 'Yahwist' as Theologian? The Dilemma of Pentateuchal Criticism," *JSOT 3* (1977): 2–10.

50. Rendtorff, *Problem of the Process*, 128.

51. Erhard Blum, *Die Komposition der Vätergeschichte* (WMANT 57; Neukirchen-Vluyn: Neukirchener, 1984); idem, *Studien zur Komposition des Pentateuch* (BZAW 189; Berlin: de Gruyter, 1990).

2.6. The Rebirth of the Yahwist

For other scholars, who were equally convinced that the classical documentary theory had to be abandoned, the "old Yahwist" had indeed to die, but only to enable a new Yahwist to rise rejuvenated from his ashes. Martin Rose followed the observations developed by H. H. Schmid in his book on the "so-called Yahwist," where he had pointed out the Deuteronomistic influence on the vocabulary and ideology of the texts that Noth had attributed to J.[52] Rose transformed J into a Deuteronomist of the second or third generation and considered his work in Genesis to Numbers as a prologue and—simultaneously—a "theological amendment" to the Deuteronomistic History.[53] Quite similarly John Van Seters considered the Yahwist to be a later expansion of the Deuteronomist's work.[54] But, in contrast to Rose, Van Seters' Yahwist is above all an antiquarian historian who freely composes his work, rather than integrating older documents that one could reconstruct, except in the case of the Jacob and Joseph stories.[55] Following Winnett, Van Seters argues that J is a contemporary of Second Isaiah and shares his universal perspective. Like von Rad, Van Seters attributes the integration of the patriarchal tradition and the exodus to J,[56] but for Van Seters this development took place only at the end of the exilic period. In the Deuteronomistic History the combination of the two traditions is still lacking.[57]

Christoph Levin[58] also locates J in the exilic period, later than the book of Deuteronomy but nevertheless earlier than the Deuteronomistic History. J

---

52. Hans Heinrich Schmid, *Der sogenannte Jahwist: Beobachtungen und Fragen zur Pentateuchforschung* (Zürich: Theologischer Verlag, 1976).

53. Martin Rose, *Deuteronomist und Jahwist: Untersuchungen zu den Berührungspunkten beider Literaturwerke* (ATANT 67; Zürich: Theologischer Verlag, 1981); for the same approach, see in English Frederick H. Cryer, "On the Relationship between the Yahwistic and the Deuteronomistic Histories," *BN* 29 (1985): 58–74.

54. John Van Seters, *Prologue to History: The Yahwist as Historian in Genesis* (Zürich: Theologischer Verlag, 1992); idem, *The Life of Moses: The Yahwist as Historian in Exodus-Numbers* (Louisville: Westminster John Knox, 1994). For the primeval history, Van Seters suggests that J is directly dependent on the Babylonian version of the flood, which is conserved in the Epic of Gilgamesh (see also his *Pentateuch*, 119–20).

55. According to Dozeman: "the Yahwist of Van Seters has nothing to do with the Yahwist of the documentary hypothesis": Thomas B. Dozeman, "Geography and Ideology in the Wilderness Journey from Kadesh through the Transjordan," in Gertz et al., *Abschied vom Jahwisten*, 173–89, 188.

56. See Van Seters, *Pentateuch*, 153–54.

57. John Van Seters, "Confessional Reformulation in the Exilic Period," *VT* 22 (1972): 448–59.

58. Christoph Levin, *Der Jahwist* (FRLANT 157; Göttingen: Vandenhoeck & Ruprecht, 1993).

represents the perspective of a more popular form of religion, as well as the concerns of the Diaspora. For this reason Levin argues that J defends the diversity of the cultic places where Yhwh may be worshiped, as opposed to the authors of Deuteronomy, who wish to limit the location of the cultic site. According to Levin, J is foremost a collector and a redactor; he is the first to combine his older sources into a narrative, which covers (more or less) the extent of the Pentateuch.[59] Levin actually combines a fragmentary theory with a supplementary theory in his description of the work of the Yahwist, since more than half of the non-Priestly texts of the Pentateuch are supplements, which numerous redactors added to the combined Yahwistic and Priestly narrative. Finally, alongside the work of scholars such as Rose, Van Seters, and Levin, other authors continue to advocate the traditional view of J as a work of the monarchical period (thus, in addition to Freedman, also Nicholson and Seebass).

This overview already reveals that the current state of the debate about the Yahwist is rather confused. Several scholars have buried him; others, on the contrary, remain loyal to the "old" Yahwist of von Rad and Noth, while still others have attempted to rejuvenate him. To make things even more complicated: a closer look at the advocates of the Yahwist reveals that not everyone defends the same conception of J; quite the contrary.

3. The Various Identities of the Yahwist

3.1. Redactional Process, School, or Author?

The present survey has already demonstrated that there has never been any real consensus about the meaning of the symbol J. For Wellhausen, J was not homogeneous but had developed through various stages. Wellhausen also argued that in many cases J and E could not be distinguished clearly from each other, an observation that prompted him to use the term "Jehowist," under which he subsumed virtually almost all pre-Deuteronomic and pre-Priestly texts of the Hexateuch. Ernest Nicholson currently defends a quite similar idea about J when he argues: "Not all that can be attributed to J ... was written at one sitting, so to speak."[60] In a sense, Gunkel extended and made even more radical

---

59. In a recent article Levin still argues, as in his book, that the end of J may be lost; see Christoph Levin, "Das israelitische Nationalepos: Der Jahwist," in *Große Texte alter Kulturen: Literarische Reise von Gizeh nach Rom* (ed. M. Hose; Darmstadt: Wissenschaftliche Buchgesellschaft, 2004), 63–86, 74. In a recent reconstruction of J, which Prof. Levin kindly sent to me, he identifies, however, the end of J in Num 25:1 and Deut 34:5, 6*.

60. Nicholson, *Pentateuch in the Twentieth Century*, 195. See quite similarly Otto Kaiser, *Die erzählenden Werke* (vol. 1 of *Grundriß der Einleitung in die kanonischen und deuterokanonischen*

Wellhausen's view, since he understood J as a school of collectors who were interested in transmitting faithfully the oral traditions of the Hebrew Bible. Noth is rather hesitant to describe the profile of J, an observation already significant in itself. Nevertheless, he comes very close to Gunkel in his idea of a common basis (*Grundlage*) underlying J and E. Noth concluded that at the time when J wrote his documents the different themes of the Pentateuch (excepted the primeval history) had already been combined, and J merely took over this earlier synthesis of traditions.

This idea of a Yahwistic school (or of different Yahwists) stands in complete opposition to the conception of J as a personality (B. Luther), a notion that blossomed in the work of von Rad. With von Rad the Yahwist has become not only an author but also above all a theologian.[61] For Van Seters, J is also an author, but he lives five centuries later and is more a historian than a theologian. For Levin, J is a redactor; his Yahwist shares the exilic location with Van Seters's Yahwist, but Van Seters would never agree with the idea of J as a redactor.[62] And in addition there continues to be a bewildering diversity in the historical location of J: today one may find proposals for virtually each century between the tenth and the sixth centuries B.C.E.[63]

3.2. THE PROBLEM OF THE YAHWIST'S EXTENT AND PROFILE

The same diversity of views exists with respect to the extent and the profile of the Yahwist. For an extended period of time there was consensus that the Documentary Hypothesis did not apply to a Pentateuch but to a *Hexateuch*. The attempts to locate the end of J in Judges or even in Samuel and Kings never found much support.[64] However, since the J source emphasized the importance of the patriarchal narratives and the divine promises of the land, it was assumed that the J source would end with the fulfillment of these promises in the book of

---

Schriften des Alten Testaments; Gütersloh: Mohn, 1992), 63, who considers "J" as a long redactional process starting in the ninth and ending in the fifth century B.C.E.

61. See also Hans Walter Wolff, "Das Kerygma des Jahwisten," *EvT* 24 (1964): 70–98.

62. John Van Seters, "The Redactor in Biblical Studies: A Nineteenth Century Anachronism," *JNSL* 29 (2003): 1–19.

63. Tenth century: von Rad ("Solomonic enlightenment"); ninth century: Wellhausen; eighth century: Seebass; seventh century: H. H. Schmid; Philip J. Budd, *Numbers* (WBC 5; Waco, Tex.: 1984), xxiv–xxv; sixth century: Van Seters, Levin.

64. Karl Budde, *Die Bücher Richter und Samuel, ihre Quellen und ihr Aufbau* (Giessen: Ricker, 1890); Immanuel Benzinger, *Jahvist und Elohist in den Königsbüchern* (BZAW 21; Berlin: Kohlhammer, 1921); Gustav Hölscher, *Geschichtsschreibung in Israel: Untersuchungen zum Jahvisten und Elohisten* (Skrifter utgivna av Kungl. Humanistiska Vetenskapssamfundet i Lund 50; Lund: Gleerup, 1952).

Joshua. This is why von Rad was displeased with Noth's invention of the Deuteronomistic History, since this theory deprived the Yahwist of its end. Noth was indeed forced to claim that this end had been lost, and it is still this position that is advanced today by Levin. Another possibility for the advocates of an exilic or postexilic Yahwist is to consider his work as a prologue to the Deuteronomistic History (Rose, Van Seters). Does this mean, therefore, that J tried to establish a narrative that begins with Genesis and ends with Kings? And, if this is the case, who then was responsible for the concept and/or publication of the Pentateuch as a discrete document or collection of documents?[65]

There is also no consensus regarding the definition of J's style. Since Hans Heinrich Schmid underscored the close literary relationship between the Yahwist and the Deuteronomistic style and theology, some scholars have proposed that J must be closely related to the Deuteronomistic school (Rose, Cryer). Others, on the contrary, claim that the Yahwist has nothing to do with the language and concerns of this school (Levin, Seebass). Thus for Van Seters, even though J may use some Deuteronomistic vocabulary and expressions, which he took over from the Deuteronomistic History, his theology should definitely not be described as "Deuteronomistic."[66] Recently Levin has sought to produce a list of J's favorite expressions,[67] yet one finds in this list words such as אח, טוב, מאד, ראה, and so on. Levin argues that these very common terms appear in typical Yahwistic combinations, but one may ask if his demonstration is really more convincing than the ideas of his forerunners.

3.3. THE PROBLEM OF THE "MESSAGE" OF J

Finally, there is also considerable disagreement regarding the problem of the theology or the "message" proper to J. For Wellhausen, J and E reflected the folk religion of the kingship period; they were witnesses to the first stage in the evolution of the Israelite faith. Levin also considers J a representative of popular religion, but this time no longer during the monarchy, since his J now advocates the concerns and the ideology of the Judean diaspora during the exilic period. For Noth, J's only contribution to the formation of the Pentateuch was the addition of the primeval history, to which Noth even declared: "The entire weight of the theology of J rests upon the beginning of its narrative."[68] Whereas Budde

---

65. According to Van Seters, the Torah was produced by the priestly caste (*Pentateuch*, 213); on the other hand, he argues that P can also be found in the book of Joshua (186–87).

66. John Van Seters, "The So-called Deuteronomistic Redaction of the Pentateuch," in *Congress Volume: Leuven, 1989* (ed. J. A. Emerton; VTSup 43; Leiden: Brill, 1991), 58–77.

67. Levin, *Jahwist*, 399–408.

68. Noth, *History of Pentateuchal Traditions*, 238.

attributed to the Yahwist a "nomadic ideal," the Yahwist of von Rad celebrates on the contrary the accomplishment of the promise of the land under the reigns of David and Solomon. Accordingly, one of the most important texts found in J for von Rad is the blessing of Gen 12:1–3,[69] which indicates to him that "The Yahwist bears witness to the fact that history is directed and ordered by God." He explains, With "David's great feats ... [came] ... almost overnight ... the fulfillment of God's ancient decrees" formulated in the land promises made to the patriarchs.[70] Whereas von Rad thought that the Yahwist wrote Gen 12:1–3 on the basis of older accounts, Levin argues on the contrary that the Yahwist was the inventor of the promises to the patriarchs.[71] But unlike von Rad, who saw in the land promises the legitimation of the "Solomonic empire," Levin's Yahwist is legitimating Jewish life outside the land, especially in presenting the patriarchs as strangers in the land in which they are living. Van Seters and Rose describe the message of J as universalistic. In addition, Rose's J sounds very Protestant since he insists on God's absolute sovereignty and on humankind's intrinsic sinfulness.[72]

Yet there is one aspect shared by all of these descriptions of J's message or theological program, namely, the almost systematic tendency to elucidate it primarily, if not sometimes exclusively, on the basis of the patriarchal narratives. This observation brings us to one last issue in the scholarly discussion on J.

4. THE YAHWIST AND THE LINK BETWEEN PATRIARCHS AND EXODUS

It is a well-known fact that the entire Documentary Hypothesis, including the notion of a Yahwistic document, was essentially elaborated through analyses of the book of Genesis. Significantly, in spite of the various conceptions of J over the past two centuries that have been surveyed in this paper, the book of Genesis has remained the basis for the study of J. The recent reconstruction of the Yahwistic history by Christoph Levin reveals that 82 percent of the J document is concentrated on Genesis. Given such a concentration of J, one wonders whether the so-called Yahwist should not be limited to Genesis, as was already suggested by Winnett and more recently by Kratz.[73] This alternative did

---

69. Noth agrees with von Rad that Gen 12:1–3 is a passage formulated by J, but he considered this text as much less important for J's theology (see *History of Pentateuchal Traditions*, 237 with n. 622).

70. Von Rad, "Problem," 71 and 73, English edition.

71. Levin, *Jahwist*, 412.

72. Martin Rose, *Une herméneutique de l'Ancien Testament : Comprendre – se comprendre – faire comprendre* (MdB 46; Genève: Labor et Fides, 2003), 376–77.

73. Reinhard G. Kratz, *Die Komposition der erzählenden Bücher des Alten Testaments: Grundwissen der Bibelkritik* (Uni-Taschenbücher 2157; Göttingen: Vandenhoeck & Ruprecht, 2000),

not encounter much success, however, since the other important feature of J on which almost all his defenders agree is that he was the artisan of the first Penta- or Hexateuch; more specifically, J is generally seen as the first document or author who combined the traditions on the patriarchs with those of Moses.[74] But in this regard, one should recall that Noth, while writing his commentary on Numbers, was actually quite aware of this issue. He admitted that if one were to analyze the composition of the book of Numbers without the model of the Documentary Hypothesis, "we would think not so much of 'continuous' sources as of an unsystematic collection of innumerable pieces of tradition of very varied content."[75]

As we have already seen, the ideological hiatus between the patriarchal narratives and the exodus story has been taken into account from the beginning of historical-critical exegesis. In 1899 Willy Staerk paid attention to the difference between the patriarchal and the exodus traditions and demonstrated that outside the Hexateuch these traditions were not connected before the seventh or sixth century B.C.E. He also argued that, even if the Jehowist did combine both traditions, he did not suppress their different, if not conflicting, conceptions of Israel's claim to the land in Genesis and in the rest of the Hexateuch.[76] Kurt Galling confirmed the original independence of the exodus and the patriarchs. He attributed to the first Yahwist (which he identifies with the "lay document," or L) the creation of the patriarchal narratives as a universalistic prologue to the Moses story. But once J was dated in the tenth century, scholars became less interested in the gap between the patriarchs and the exodus. The main concern was to describe the literary profile or the theology of J; the issue of the pre-Yahwistic traditions underlying this document was not a major concern.

However, this issue became significant once again when the Yahwist of von Rad and Noth came under attack. For Rendtorff, the hiatus between the two major themes was a strong argument against the classical documentary theory. The hiatus was also emphasized by Albert de Pury; according to him, the Jacob and the Moses stories were two different origin myths, as can be seen in particular in Hos 12. The combination of both myths was probably later than the composition of the Deuteronomistic History, which has no interest in the patriarchal tradition.[77] For these scholars who relocated the Yahwist from Solomon's

---

249–330. Kratz limits J to Gen 1–36*; he labels "E" the original exodus-story running from Exod 1* to Josh 12*.

74. A notable exception is Noth, for whom this blending happened already before J.

75. Martin Noth, *Numbers* (trans. J. D. Martin; OTL; Philadelphia: Westminster, 1968), 4.

76. Staerk, *Studien* I, 50–51.

77. See especially Albert de Pury, "Le cycle de Jacob comme légende autonome des origines d'Israël," in Emerton, *Congress Volume*, 78–96; idem, "Hosea 12 und die Auseinandersetzung um die Identität Israels und seines Gottes," in *Ein Gott allein? JHWH-Verehrung und biblischer Mono-*

reign to the Babylonian exile, J was still the one who elaborated the literary connection between Genesis and Exodus, but in this new perspective the traditions of the patriarchs and the exodus were necessarily independent until the sixth century.

In regard to the current debate about the formation of the Pentateuch, one should agree with David Carr's statement: "The main literary-critical division in the pre-P Pentateuch materials is not between a J and an E source.... [It] may be between the Moses story and its backward extension through the composition of an early form of Genesis."[78] The importance of this division has recently led Erhard Blum to modify his theory about the formation of the Pentateuch, since he envisages now that the Pre-priestly "D composition" did not comprise Genesis and began with the story of Moses' birth and call.[79] There is indeed a growing consensus about the relatively "late" origin of the combination of Genesis and the following books, but the question of the "author" of this combination is still open. Was the Priestly writer the first to link the patriarchs with the exodus (see already Winnett and now especially K. Schmid, Gertz, Otto, Witte)?[80] Did the Deuteronomists create this link (Ska[81])? Or was there a seventh-century (Zenger) or an exilic (Kratz) "Jehovistic" redactor?[82] Or should one still retain the traditional solution attributing this link, and together with it the first edition of the Pentateuch, to a "Yahwist"? In our view, the last solution is

---

theismus im Kontext der israelitischen und altorientalischen Religionsgeschichte (ed. W. Dietrich and M. A. Klopfenstein; OBO 139; Fribourg: Universitätsverlag; Göttingen: Vandenhoeck & Ruprecht, 1994), 413–39; idem, "Le choix de l'ancêtre," *TZ* 57 (2001): 105–14. See further Thomas Römer, "Deuteronomy in Search of Origins," in *Reconsidering Israel and Judah: Recent Studies on the Deuteronomistic History* (ed. G. N. Knoppers and J. G. McConville; SBTS 8; Winona Lake, Ind.: Eisenbrauns, 2000), 112–38; Bernhard Lang, "Väter Israels," *Neues Bibel Lexikon* 3 (2001): 989–93; and Folker V. Greifenhagen, *Egypt on the Pentateuch's Ideological Map: Constructing Biblical Israel's Identity* (JSOTSup 361; Sheffield: Sheffield Academic Press, 2002).

78. David M. Carr, "Genesis in Relation to the Moses Story: Diachronic and Synchronic Perspectives," in *Studies in the Book of Genesis: Literature, Redaction and History* (ed. A. Wénin; BETL 155; Leuven: Leuven University Press; Peeters, 2001), 273–95.

79. Erhard Blum, "Die literarische Verbindung von Erzvätern und Exodus: Ein Gespräch mit neueren Forschungshypothesen," in Gertz et al., *Abschied vom Jahwisten*, 119–56.

80. Winnett, "Re-examining the Foundations"; Schmid, *Erzväter und Exodus;* Jan Christian Gertz, *Tradition und Redaktion in der Exoduserzählung: Untersuchungen zur Endredaktion des Pentateuch* (FRLANT 186; Göttingen: Vandenhoeck & Ruprecht, 1999); Eckart Otto, *Das Deuteronomium im Pentateuch und Hexateuch: Studien zur Literaturgeschichte von Pentateuch und Hexateuch im Lichte des Deuteronomiumsrahmens* (FAT 30; Tübingen: Mohr Siebeck, 2000), 261–64; Markus Witte, *Die biblische Urgeschichte: Redaktions- und theologiegeschichtliche Beobachtungen zu Genesis 1,1–11,26* (BZAW 265; Berlin: de Gruyter, 1998).

81. Ska, *Introduction à la lecture du Pentateuque*, 280–88.

82. Zenger, *Einleitung in das Alte Testament*, 100–105; Kratz, *Komposition der erzählenden Bücher des Alten Testaments*.

the less attractive one. Nicholson, who defends the traditional view, argues: "We are bound to ask what idea pre-exilic Israel can have of its own history if it had not yet joined together its memories of Abraham, Isaac, and Jacob with those of Moses and the exodus."[83] To this we respond: we are first bound to ask if the Pentateuch offers any sort of indication for a thoroughgoing Yahwistic document connecting Genesis with Exodus at a pre-Priestly stage.

---

83. Nicholson, *Pentateuch in the Twentieth Century,* 130.

THE SO-CALLED YAHWIST AND THE LITERARY GAP BETWEEN GENESIS AND EXODUS*

Konrad Schmid

The Documentary Hypothesis with its four elements J, E, P, D has reached nearly a canonical status within Hebrew Bible scholarship in the twentieth century. The Documentary Hypothesis is based on the assumption that there are three similar narrative accounts of Israel's history between the creation, the ancestors, and the exodus to the conquest of the land: J, E, and P. The story-line of the Pentateuch was determined to be very old: the so-called Yahwist (J) adapted the structure of the narrative from the creeds of ancient Israel, and the structure of the narrative accounts of E and P were mere epigones or imitations of J. However, in the last thirty years serious doubts have arisen concerning this model.

Since the work of Rolf Rendtorff[1] and others a very common and simple observation on the narrative structure of the Pentateuch has gained increasing acceptance: the different narrative parts of the Pentateuch—the primeval history, the patriarchal stories, and the exodus story—stand more or less on their own. They seem to be much more autonomous literary units in their original form than parts of a long story from the creation to the conquest of the land. So one may ask: Did the older sources, J and E, really exist?

The weakness of the so-called Elohistic source (E) has long been recognized.[2] Its different parts do not form a continuing narrative account. They are mere fragments. One might think of some texts in Gen 20–22 of something like

---

*English translation by Anselm C. Hagedorn (Berlin).

1. Rolf Rendtorff, *Das überlieferungsgeschichtliche Problem des Pentateuch* (BZAW 147; Berlin: de Gruyter, 1977); English translation: *The Problem of the Process of Transmission in the Pentateuch* (trans. J. J. Scullion; JSOTSup 89; Sheffield: JSOT Press, 1990).

2. Cf. Paul Volz and Wilhelm Rudolph, *Der Elohist als Erzähler: Ein Irrweg der Pentateuchkritik? An der Genesis erläutert* (BZAW 63; Giessen: Töpelmann, 1933).

an E source,[3] but beyond this it is difficult to postulate an overarching Elohistic work from the ancestors in Genesis to a conclusion somewhere in the book of Numbers.[4]

The Yahwist (J) has also come under controversial discussion as well in the recent years.[5] Which texts should be assigned to J? Does J belong to the period of the Solomonic kingdom, to the eighth century, or to the Babylonian exile? Where is its literary end? This is not the place to unravel the debate, but it becomes more and more clear that J as a coherent redactional work can only be detected in the book of Genesis. The J hypothesis was developed from the texts in the book of Genesis, and it never really fit the other books of the Pentateuch. Martin Noth, for example, wrote at the outset of his commentary on Numbers: "If one takes the book of Numbers for itself, one would not explain it by 'continuing sources.' "[6]

Limiting J to the book of Genesis means at the same time that one leaves the usual definition of J behind, in which J was understood to be the main ordering thread of the pre-Priestly Tetrateuch. A Yahwistic work that is limited only to the book of Genesis no longer matches the fundamental criteria of this hypothesis. Therefore, it seems appropriate to argue for a "farewell to J."[7] This

---

3. However, Gen 22 seems clearly to be a redactional text; see Konrad Schmid, "Die Rückgabe der Verheißungsgabe: Der 'heilsgeschichtliche' Sinn von Genesis 22 im Horizont innerbiblischer Exegese," in *Gott und Mensch im Dialog: Festschrift O. Kaiser* (ed. M. Witte; BZAW 345/1; Berlin: de Gruyter, 2004), 271–300.

4. The main argument for E proposed by Axel Graupner, *Der Elohist: Gegenwart und Wirksamkeit des transzendenten Gottes in der Geschichte* (WMANT 97; Neukirchen-Vluyn: Neukirchener, 2002), 4, 7–8, is the coincidence of the Yнwн-/Elohim syndrome with textual doublets in the Pentateuch. The observation as such is true for some evident cases (e.g,. Gen 1 and 2–3; Gen 6–9; Gen 15 and 17; Exod 3–4 and 6), but these cases lead to the distinction between P and non-P-texts (and not between J and E).

5. See especially Jan Christian Gertz et al., eds., *Abschied vom Jahwisten: Die Komposition des Hexateuch in der jüngsten Diskussion* (BZAW 315; Berlin: de Gruyter, 2002).

6. Martin Noth, *Das vierte Buch Mose: Numeri* (3rd ed.; ATD 7; Göttingen: Vandenhoeck & Ruprecht, 1977), 7 (translation mine, original text: "Nimmt man das 4. Mosebuch für sich, so käme man nicht leicht auf den Gedanken an 'durchlaufende Quellen', sondern eher auf den Gedanken an eine unsystematische Zusammenstellung von zahllosen Überlieferungsstücken sehr verschiedenen Inhalts, Alters und Charakters ['Fragmentenhypothese']. Aber es wäre eben, wie schon bei der Inhaltsangabe gezeigt wurde, unsachgemäß, das 4. Mosebuch zu isolieren. Es hat im alttestamentlichen Kanon von Anfang an zu dem größeren Ganzen des Pentateuch gehört; und auch die wissenschaftliche Arbeit an diesem Buch hat immer wieder nur bestätigen können, dass es in diesem größeren Zusammenhang gesehen werden muss. Es ist daher gerechtfertigt, mit den anderwärts gewonnenen Ergebnissen der Pentateuchanalyse an das 4. Mosebuch heranzutreten und die durchlaufenden Pentateuch-'Quellen' auch in diesem Buche zu erwarten, selbst wenn, wie gesagt, der Sachverhalt im 4. Mosebuch von sich aus nicht gerade auf diese Ergebnisse hinführt").

7. See Gertz et al., *Abschied vom Jahwisten*.

might sound radical for some ears, but it is a scholarly fact that this perception is gaining more and more acceptance at least in the European context.[8]

This paper will address the following three observations that lead to the abandonment of the J hypothesis in the sense of a pre-Priestly Tetrateuch. They all have to do with the literary gap between Genesis and Exodus (1) more generally, there is a certain lack of narrative affinity between these two books; (2) more specifically, the sparse redactional bridges between Genesis and Exodus are mostly late, that is, presupposing P; (3) the findings in P itself show quite clearly that the connection of the patriarchal narratives and exodus is a new creation of its author or authors.

1. The Lack in Narrative Affinity between Genesis and Exodus

The narrative movement from Genesis to Exodus is clear, but scholars have long recognized that there is not a smooth transition from one book to the other. Rather, we encounter a decisive break that cannot simply be explained by referring to the oral prehistory of the material as proposed by Gerhard von Rad[9] and Martin Noth (who at the same time clearly recognized the relative independence of the main themes in the Pentateuch).[10] Instead, this break is of a literary nature and thus requires a literary explanation within the framework of the formation of the Pentateuch as a written text. All this is not necessarily new, but the importance and the depth of this caesura has thus far been underestimated by assuming that this break was already bridged by the Yawhist in the tenth century B.C.E. and by the Elohist in the eighth century B.C.E. The following observations do not yet prove specifically the lack of a pre-Priestly connection between Genesis and Exodus, but they set the stage for the following arguments.

(1) The chronology of the transition from the patriarchal period to the exodus gives a first hint concerning the discontinuity between these blocks of literature. P presupposes and integrates a tradition that reckons with a stay of the Israelites in Egypt that lasted for centuries (Exod 12:40–41 [P]: 430 years).[11]

---

8. See Kenton L. Sparks, *The Pentateuch: An Annotated Bibliography* (Grand Rapids: Baker, 2002), 32.

9. Gerhard von Rad, "Das formgeschichtliche Problem des Hexateuchs," in idem, *Gesammelte Studien zum Alten Testament* (TB 8; Munich: Kaiser, 1958), 9–86; English translation: "The Form-Critical Problem of the Hexateuch," in idem, *The Problem of the Hexateuch and Other Essays* (trans. E. W. Trueman Dicken; Edinburgh: Oliver & Boyd, 1966; repr., London: SCM, 1984), 1–78.

10. Martin Noth, *Überlieferungsgeschichte des Pentateuch* (Stuttgart: Kohlhammer, 1948); English translation: *A History of Pentateuchal Traditions* (trans. B. W. Anderson; Eaglewood Cliffs, N.J.: Prentice Hall, 1972; repr., Atlanta: Scholars Press, 1981).

11. LXX and Sam. are fully aware of this problem and try to harmonize Exod 12:40–41 with Exod 1:8 and 2:1 by stating that the 430 years in Exod 12:40–41 have to be applied to the staying

This stands in contrast to the information in Exod 1:8,[12] which mentions a change in generation after Joseph, and in Exod 2:1 (cf. 6:20), in which Moses is a grandson of Levi on his maternal side—if read in the light of the Genesis tradition (which originally might not be presupposed in Exod 2:1). The extended chronology in P does not reflect a tight literary connection between Genesis and Exodus but merely the knowledge of a formerly independent exodus story, which would have included the notion of a very long oppression of the Israelites in Egypt.

(2) The story of Joseph adds further doubts regarding a continuing *Grundschicht* in Genesis–Exodus, as the J hypothesis would suggest. The narrative goes to great pains to explain why and how Israel ended up in Egypt. However, it does not succeed in creating a wholly plausible transition from the patriarchs to the exodus: the book of Genesis depicts Joseph as an honored man serving at the Egyptian court under a pharaoh who was favorable to him while also picturing the Israelites as nomads. Yet the same Israelites appear in the beginning of the book of Exodus as badly treated conscript laborers, a status normally reserved for prisoners of war, under a pharaoh who is now a cruel despot and who wants to exploit and contain them. This complete change in circumstances and setting of the narrative is only explained by a brief transitional note in Exod 1:6–8 that mentions the death of Joseph and his generation. This text, moreover, introduces a new pharaoh who is no longer acquainted with Joseph, even though his position of leadership had made him the second most prominent man in the state (Gen 41:37–46). Is that the narrative style of a continuous story? One gets the impression that two already-fixed and separate literary blocks were joined together, rather than a single narrative in which events moves organically from Genesis to Exodus. The unevenness of the literary relationship between Genesis and Exodus leads to the more precise conclusion that the statement in Exod 1:8, "Now there arose a new king over Egypt, who did not know Joseph," is a narrative device that contextualizes the story of Joseph because otherwise the story of the exodus cannot be told. This means at the same time that the Joseph story was not shaped to bridge the gap between Genesis and Exodus. Only by means of later redactional insertions could the story of Joseph fulfill this function, as is evident in Gen 50:14.[13] The forefathers of Israel dwell in the land of Canaan

---

of Israel in Canaan and Egpyt. See Jeremy Hughes, *Secrets of the Times: Myth and History in Biblical Chronology* (JSOTSup 66; Sheffield: Sheffield Academic Press, 1990), 33–36.

12. See Konrad Schmid, *Erzväter und Exodus: Untersuchungen zur doppelten Begründung der Ursprünge Israels innerhalb der Geschichtsbücher des Alten Testaments* (WMANT 81; Neukirchen-Vluyn: Neukirchener, 1999), 69–73.

13. Cf. Konrad Schmid, "Die Josephsgeschichte im Pentateuch," in Gertz et al., *Abschied vom Jahwisten*, 83–118, 103–4.

in Gen 50, and it is only by means of the one verse (Gen 50:14) that they are brought back to Egypt to set the stage for the exodus.[14]

(3) In a comparable way, the several promises to the patriarchs, which are obviously the most important redactional pieces of cohesion in Genesis,[15] do not imply that they originally focused on the exodus. Among the many promises of the land in Genesis, only one passage (Gen 15:13–16, cf. 50:24) states that the descendants of the patriarchs would have to leave Canaan before the promise of the land would be fulfilled in a second immigration. The other promises in Genesis do not share this view. On the contrary, it is quite alien to them, as the formulation "to you and to your descendants" indicates.[16]

In addition, the non-P texts containing promises (the traditional J texts) concerning the increase of descendants do not point to the story of the exodus. The same absence of a literary connection can be noticed in the non-P story in Exodus. The statement about Israel becoming a great people does not refer back to the prominent non-Priestly promises of increase at the beginning of the patriarchal narrative (e.g., Gen 12:2; 13:13).[17] The comparison of the promise of descendants to Abraham in Gen 12:2 and the statement of Pharaoh in Exod 1:9 illustrates the absence of a clear relationship between the two bodies of literature.

Gen 12:2	Exod 1:9
And I will make you into a great people (לגוי גדול).	And he [Pharaoh] spoke to his people: "Behold, the people (עם) of the children of Israel are more (רב) and mightier (ועצום) than we."

On the other hand, it is all the more remarkable that the connections on the P-level are very tight.

---

14. See the contribution of Jan Christian Gertz in this volume.

15. See esp. Erhard Blum, *Die Komposition der Vätergeschichte* (WMANT 57; Neukirchen-Vluyn: Neukirchener, 1984).

16. Cf. the chart in Rendtorff, *Das überlieferungsgeschichtliche Problem*, 42.

17. Christoph Levin, *Der Jahwist* (FRLANT 157; Göttingen: Vandenhoeck & Ruprecht, 1993), 45–46 regards Exod 1:9 (גוי גדול) as the fulfillment of Gen 12:2 (עם [...] רב ועצום) despite the incongruencies in the formulations.

Gen 1:28

> Be fruitful (פרו), and multiply (ורבו), and fill (ומלאו) the earth (את הארץ).

Gen 9:7

> And you, be fruitful (פרו), and multiply (ורבו); increase abundantly (שרצו) in the earth, and multiply (ורבו) therein.

Gen 17:2

> And I will multiply (וארבה) you exceedingly (במאד מאד).

Exod 1:7

> And the children of Israel were fruitful (פרו), and increased abundantly (וישרצו), and multiplied (וירבו), and waxed (ויעצמו) exceeding mighty (במאד מאד); and the land (והארץ) was filled (ותמלא) with them.

If the non-Priestly substance of the patriarchal and exodus narrative was really written by the same author, it would be very difficult to explain why he did not correlate the promise to become a great people with its fulfillment, as it is done in P. Therefore it is much more likely that Gen 12:2 and Exod 1:9 were written by different authors rather than to assume that we have here a Yahwistic bridge between Genesis and Exodus.

(4) Finally, literature outside the Pentateuch also points to the fundamental separation between the patriarchs and the exodus. The Psalms provide especially strong evidence for the separation between the patriarchs and the exodus. In his research on the historical motifs in the Psalms, Aare Lauha realized already in 1945 that the sequence patriarchs–exodus is not presupposed.[18] Johannes Kühlewein has come to the same conclusion in 1973, writing:

> Außer im späten Ps 105 finden die Väter in keiner Geschichtsreihe des Psalters Erwähnung. Vergleichen wir Ps 80,9–12; 135,8–12 oder anerkannt späte Reihen wie Ps 78 oder 106, ja selbst 136, der mit dem Bericht von der Erschaffung der Welt einsetzt, nirgendwo ist die Geschichte der Erzväter auch nur angedeutet. Das ist gewiß nicht zufällig und auch nicht allein daraus zu erklären, daß es sich bei den genannten Texten um "freiere Abwandlungen der Gattung (des geschichtlichen Credo)" handelt. Sehr viel näher legt sich die Annahme, daß der urspr. Einsatz der Geschichtsreihen die Exodus- oder die Schilfmeertra-

---

18. *Die Geschichtsmotive in den alttestamentlichen Psalmen* (AASF Series B 16/1; Helsinki: Helsinki University Press, 1945), 34–35.

dition war, während die Überlieferung von den Vätern erst im Laufe der Zeit damit verbunden und dem bereits Bestehenden vorgeschaltet wurde.[19]

The prophetic books reinforce the conclusion from the Psalms. Hosea 12 places Jacob and Moses ("a prophet") in opposition to each other. The contrast is especially striking, and the chapter has been interpreted in detail by Albert de Pury with results that support the assumption of a fundamental separation of the Jacob and the Moses story.[20] Furthermore, one could mention texts such as Amos 3:11; Mic 7:20; Ezek 20:5; 33:24, which seem to imply the same thing, but limited space does not allow a detailed discussion here.[21]

2. The Redactional Links between Genesis and Exodus

Thus far the general remarks have shown only what appears to be quite obvious, namely, that the current connection between Genesis and Exodus is not of an organic nature but rather a secondary construction. On the basis of these observations, one can already argue the case for a different main redaction of the pre-Priestly material in Genesis, on the one hand, and in Exodus, on the other hand. In other words: J in Genesis and J in Exodus are different J's.

For the *more strict* version of the thesis of a "farewell" to the Yahwist that assumes that there has never been a *pre-Priestly* connection between Genesis and Exodus, we must look closer at the concrete redactional connections between Genesis and Exodus and investigate their exact literary-historical place and date.

If one limits the study to the explicit literary connections that refer either backwards or forwards within the two books, only a few texts deserve closer consideration. Besides the fringes of the books in Gen 50–Exod 1, one has mainly to examine Gen 15:13–16 in the book Genesis and Exod 3:1–4:18 in the book of Exodus.[22]

---

19. Johannes Kühlewein, *Geschichte in den Psalmen* (Calwer theologische Monographien 2; Stuttgart: Calwer, 1973), 158.

20. See "Osée 12 et ses implications pour le débat actuel sur le Pentateuque, " in *Le Pentateuque: Débats et recherches* (ed. P. Haudebert; LD 151; Paris: Cerf, 1992), 175–207; idem, "Erwägungen zu einem vorexilischen Stämmejahwismus: Hosea 12 und die Auseinandersetzung um die Identität Israels und seines Gottes," in *Ein Gott allein? JHWH-Verehrung und biblischer Monotheismus im Kontext der israelitischen und altorientalischen Religionsgeschichte* (ed. W. Dietrich and M. A. Klopfenstein; OBO 139; Fribourg: Universitätsverlag; Göttingen: Vandenhoeck & Ruprecht, 1994), 413–39; and the summary in Schmid, *Erzväter und Exodus*, 82–84.

21. See Schmid, *Erzväter und Exodus*, 84–89.

22. See in more detail ibid., 56–78.

David Carr has, furthermore, detected linguistic and factual allusions to Exodus—similar "patterns" in Genesis and Exodus, so to speak—in texts such as Gen 12:10–20; 16; and 18. He argues for a literary continuation of the patriarchal narrative into the story of Moses before P on the basis of such common literary patterns.[23] Of course, it is quite obvious that Gen 12:10–20 and 16:1–16[24] reflect the story of the exodus (the case of Gen 18 is more difficult to decide). However, such references do not constitute obvious cross-references within the same literary work—as is the case with texts such as Gen 15:13–16 and 50:24, which explicitly point ahead to the exodus—but can equally be allusions to or between different "books" (or, more precisely, "scrolls"). On the basis of this argument, I limit my study to explicit cross-references in order to address the question of the history of redaction of the literary connections between the patriarchs and the exodus.

On the other hand, the methodological inquiry that I am proposing has been criticized by Christoph Levin. His redactional interpretation of the Yahwist admittedly has clarified the literary-historical understanding of the relation between tradition and redaction in the book of Genesis, but Levin lets his Yahwist continue far beyond Genesis into the book of Numbers (although in a very limited number of texts [only ca. 17 percent of his J]). He also disputes whether the explicit cross-references between Genesis and Exodus (which he generally regards as late) have to be interpreted as the work of a post-P author:

> [D]ie späten Querverbindungen, auf die man sich bezieht, sind nur der Stuck auf dem längst vorhandenen Gebäude, nicht die Tragbalken, die die Konstruktion zusammenhalten. Der Stuck liegt außen und fällt ins Auge. Das verleiht den Beobachtungen die Evidenz. Für die Statik kommt es indessen auf die Tragbalken an. Sie sieht man nicht auf den ersten Blick. Man muß das ganze Gebäude vermessen."[25]

It is possible, of course, that later cross-references accentuate already-existing connections. However, if one follows Levin's assumption (which tends to violate the principle of Ockham's razor), then the circumstantial evidence for the "supporting beams" identified would need to be very clear. In the case of Levin's J that remains doubtful: Levin

---

23. David M. Carr, "Review of Konrad Schmid, *Erzväter und Exodus,*" *Bib* 81 (2000): 579–83; idem, "Genesis in Relation to the Moses Story: Diachronic and Synchronic Perspectives," in *Studies in the Book of Genesis: Literature, Redaction and History* (ed. A. Wénin; BETL 155; Leuven: Leuven University Press; Peeters, 2001), 273–95, 274 n. 4; see also, idem, *Reading the Fractures of Genesis: Historical and Literary Approaches* (Louisville: Westminster John Knox, 1996), 185–87, 192–94.

24. See, e.g., Thomas Römer, "Isaac et Ismaël, concurrents ou cohéritiers de la promesse? Une lecture de Genèse 16," *ETR* 74 (1999): 161–72.

25. Christoph Levin, "Das israelitische Nationalepos: Der Jahwist," in *Große Texte alter Kulturen: Literarische Reise von Gizeh nach Rom* (ed. M. Hose; Darmstadt: Wissenschaftliche Buchgesellschaft, 2004), 63–85, here 72–73.

focuses on four overarching "signs of systematic closure" ("Merkmale ... planvoller Geschlossenheit"): (1) the selection of the sources used by Levin's J ("Alle Erzählungen mit einer Ausnahme spielen außerhalb des Landes Israel und Juda" [73]); (2) language; (3) the perception/picture of history; and (4) the theme of blessing. Now, already the open-endedness of Levin's Yahwist ("Ein regelrechter Abschluß fehlt" [65]) implies a problem for any proof of a systematic conception. In addition, the characteristic features for identifying the "supporting beams" are without exception not of a stringent but of a tentative nature. Most problematic is the first sign, since the important exception, namely, the narrative of Abraham, which obviously plays on Israelite and Judean territory (73), now must be regarded as the exception to prove the rule. According to Levin, the land of Israel had been artificially transformed into foreign territory by the distinction between Israelites and Canaanites in Gen 12:6 [Levin: J]) so that now even Abraham lives in a foreign land. The assumption that the Yahwistic work narrates the story of an existence as strangers ("Geschichte einer Fremdlingherrschaft" [73]) seems a rather forced interpretation of the pre-Priestly account of Abraham and does not recognize that the perspective of the patriarchs as strangers in the land is a distinguishing feature of the Priestly source (see §3[2] below). The overarching sign of "language" addresses an important point, but in the case of Levin's J it cannot be used as a "supporting beam" for his redactional-historical reconstruction (cf. Levin himself: "Allerdings darf man das Kriterium des sprachlichen Stils nicht mechanisch handhaben; die Redaktion hängt einerseits von ihren Quellen ab und hat andererseits den später noch hinzugekommenen Text beeinflusst" [75–76]). Similarly problematic is the argument focusing on the perception of history and the topic of blessing: considerations concerning those topics may be used to illustrate Levin's synthesis of his J hypothesis, but to use them as support for this hypothesis makes the argument circular. In addition, already the Documentary Hypothesis had to admit that the theological program of J, developed in Gen 12:1–3, does not really reoccur in the following text of J: "Im folgenden hat er [der Jahwist] sich dann fast ausschließlich an das überkommene Gut der Pentateucherzählung gehalten, ohne ändernd oder erweiternd in dessen Substanz einzugreifen. Es genügte ihm, im Eingang eindeutig gesagt zu haben, wie er alles weitere verstanden wissen wollte."[26] The topic of blessing is not really helpful to prove the redactional unity of J from Genesis to Numbers.

If, then, the possibilities considered for a closer determination of the author do not yield any clear results ("Was läßt sich über den Verfasser feststellen, der das jahwistische Werk geschaffen hat? Es gibt eine Reihe von Indizien. Sie ergeben indessen kein einheitliches Bild" [81]), the initial suspicion seems to be justified: the supporting beams identfied cannot support the building.

I will refrain from discussing the texts in great detail, since this will be done in other contributions by Jan Christian Gertz (on Gen 50–Exod 1) and Thomas

---

26. Noth, *Überlieferungsgeschichte des Pentateuch,* 258.

Dozeman (on Exod 3–4), and limit myself to the most evident observations on Gen 15 and Exod 3–4, which seem to support a post-P date for these texts.

Traditional scholarship on the Pentateuch has long recognized that Gen 15 is a text *sui generis*.[27] Some label the text as the beginning of the Elohistic source. Already within the Documentary Hypothesis this assumption is hardly convincing, since Gen 15 never uses "Elohim" but always speaks of YHWH. Others decided to split the text in Yahwistic and Elohistic parts, but that remained equally unconvincing. Thus, suspicion arose that Gen 15 has nothing to do with either J or E. However, due to the doublet in Gen 17, it cannot be part of P either.

A number of recent studies regard the whole of Gen 15 as a post-Priestly document (Thomas Römer;[28] John Ha;[29] Konrad Schmid;[30] Christoph Levin;[31] Eckart Otto;[32] see also Erhard Blum[33]), although this conclusion is not without debate.[34] Older scholarship already recognized that Gen 15:13–16, which

---

27. See Schmid, *Erzväter und Exodus*, 172 n. 6–10.

28. "Gen 15 und Gen 17: Beobachtungen und Anfragen zu einem Dogma der 'neueren' und 'neuesten' Pentateuchkritik," *DBAT* 26 (1989/90): 32–47.

29. *Genesis 15: A Theological Compendium of Pentateuchal History* (BZAW 181; Berlin: de Gruyter, 1989).

30. *Erzväter und Exodus*, 172–86.

31. *Der Jahwist*, 151; idem, "Jahwe und Abraham im Dialog: Gen 15," in Witte, *Gott und Mensch im Dialog*, 237–57.

32. *Das Deuteronomium im Pentateuch und Hexateuch* (FAT 30; Tübingen: Mohr Siebeck, 2000), 219–20.

33. "Die literarische Verbindung von Erzvätern und Exodus: Ein Gespräch mit neueren Endredaktionshypothesen," in Gertz et al., *Abschied vom Jahwisten*, 119–56, 143–44.

34. See Jan Christian Gertz, "Abraham, Mose und der Exodus: Beobachtungen zur Redaktionsgeschichte von Gen 15," in idem et al., *Abschied vom Jahwisten*, 63–81. He detects a basic layer in Gen 15:1*, 2a, 4–10, 17–18 that contains critical allusions to the exodus and Sinai (esp. vv. 7, 17–18) and has most likely been written within the frame of a patriarchal narrative that stands in competition with the Exodus tradition. By inserting Gen 15:11, 13–16, a post-P redaction later transformed Genesis into a prologue to Exodus. Gertz's literary and theological analysis is certainly possible even if the connection of vv. 10, 12 is not very elegant and the priestly allusions in vv. 7, 17–18 either have to be qualified (Gertz thinks it is possible that Gen 15:7 is not influenced by 11:28 but vice versa that the place name "Ur-Kasdim" has been added to 11:27–32 because of 15:7 ["Abraham, Mose und der Exodus," 72–73]) or neglected (the qualification of the promise of the land as covenant is otherwise only known to P; see Schmid, *Erzväter und Exodus*, 182 with n. 66). In addition to that, we have to ask whether the complexity of Gen 15—rightly stressed by Gertz—and here especially the "addition" of vv. 13–16 cannot be explained without using literary-critical operations; rather, the verses seem to show the attempt to harmonize quite disparate blocks of tradition with equally disparate theologies within the frame of a new concept. Tensions within the text not only indicate literary growth but can also be determined by the matter of things; especially in Gen 15, a text that now clearly links Genesis and Exodus, we can expect a complex train of thoughts within a single text.

looks ahead to the oppression of the Israelites in Egypt and the exodus, pre-supposes P based on its language: רכשׁ ("possession") in Gen 15:14 and שׂיבה טובה ("good old age") in 15:15 are quite typical expressions of P's language.[35]

> 15:13–15: Then Yнwн said to Abram: "Know for certain that your offspring will be sojourners in a land that is not theirs and will be servants there, and they will be afflicted for four hundred years. (14) But I will bring judgment on the nation that they serve, and afterward they shall come out with great possessions (רכשׁ). (15) As for yourself, you shall go to your fathers in peace; you shall be buried in a good old age (שׂיבה טובה)."

If the only explicit reference in Genesis that looks ahead to Exodus is a post-P text, what, one may ask, forces us to assume a pre-Priestly connection of Genesis and Exodus? In the light of the fundamental divergence of the material in the two books, such an assumption does not seem very likely.

The findings in Exod 3–4 point in a similar direction. Here also traditional source criticism realized that Exod 3:1–4:18 interrupts the flow of the narrative of the exodus story. Noth, for example, regarded the chapters as an addition to J.[36] The reason for that was both simple and obvious. Prior to Noth, Wellhausen and Rudolph already saw that there is a close connection between Exod 2:23aα and 4:19,[37] a connection that is now interrupted by the P insertion in Exod 2:23aβ–25 and the call of Moses in 3:1–4:18. Like Exod 2:15–23aα, Exod 4:19 is situated in Midian and originally seems to have followed 2:23aβ immediately.[38] The Septuagint explicitly stresses this connection of 2:23aα and 4:19, since it repeats 2:23aα again before 4:19:

> *And it came to pass in process of time, that the king of Egypt died* (< MT). And Yнwн said to Moses in Midian, "Go, return into Egypt, for all the men are dead who sought your life." (Exod 4:19 LXX)

---

35. רכשׁ occurs next to Gen 15:14 in Gen 12:5; 13:6; 31:18; 46:6 (all P); cf. also Gen 14:11–12, 16, 21; Num 16:32; 35:5; Ezra 1:4, 6; 8:21; 10:8; 2 Chr 21:14, 17; 32:29; שׂיבה טובה occurs next to Gen 15:15 in 25:8 (P; cf. also Judg 8:32; 1 Chr 29:28); cf. Ha, *Genesis 15*, 94–95; Levin, "Jahwe und Abraham im Dialog," 249–50.

36. *Überlieferungsgeschichte des Pentateuch*, 31–32 n. 103.

37. Julius Wellhausen, *Die Composition des Hexateuchs und der historischen Bücher des Alten Testaments* (3rd ed.; Berlin: Reimer, 1899), 71; Volz and Rudolph, *Der Elohist als Erzähler*, 6–7 (W. Rudolph); for more recent views, see Schmid, *Erzväter und Exodus*, 189 n. 112.

38. For older opinions disputing such findings, see Schmid, *Erzväter und Exodus*, 189 n. 114; for more recent ones, see Blum, "Die literarische Verbindung," 123 n. 20.

In addition, the name used for Moses' father-in-law distinguishes Exod 3:1–4:18 from its context: in 3:1 and 4:18 he is called Jethro, while in 2:18 his name is Reguël.

That this addition either in whole or in part must be dated after P seems the most likely option to me. The same has been argued by Hans-Christoph Schmitt,[39] Eckart Otto,[40] Jan Christian Gertz,[41] and (for Exod 4) Erhard Blum.[42] In Exod 3 it is remarkable that the crying of the Israelites in Exod 3:7, 9 to which Yhwh hearkens has previously only been reported in Exod 2:23b (P) and that this passage seems to be presupposed here.[43] If we move on to Exod 6, the priestly counterpart to the call of Moses in Exod 3–4, we realize that this text does not seem to know Exod 3–4,[44] a fact that is surprising only if one clings to a pre-Priestly dating of Exod 3–4. Rather, Exod 3–4 integrates the problems that Exod 6 unfolds in a narrative way after the call of Moses: the narrative account of the Israelite people not listening to Moses in Exod 6 is stated as a problem by Moses in Exod 3, even though he has not yet talked to the Israelites. In addition, Exod 3 changes the location of the call of Moses to the holy mountain, which appears to be a secondary setting for the commission of Moses from its given setting in the land of Egypt in Exod 6.

If the explicit connection of Genesis and Exodus in Gen 15 and Exod 3–4 is a post-Priestly composition, the assumption is not far that Genesis and Exodus were not connected on a pre-Priestly level. Looking at P itself further supports this view. P indicates that significant conceptual work was undertaken to join these two blocks of tradition.

---

39. "Redaktion des Pentateuch im Geiste der Prophetie," *VT* 32 (1982): 170–89, 186–89.

40. "Die nachpriesterschriftliche Pentateuchredaktion im Buch Exodus," in *Studies in the Book of Exodus: Redaction—Reception—Interpretation* (ed. M. Vervenne; BETL 126; Leuven: Leuven University Press; Peeters, 1996), 61–111, 101–11.

41. *Tradition und Redaktion in der Exoduserzählung: Untersuchungen zur Endredaktion des Pentateuch* (FRLANT 186; Göttingen: Vandenhoeck & Ruprecht, 2000), 233–327.

42. Blum, "Die literarische Verbindung," 123–27.

43. The references to Gen 16:11; 18:20–21; 19:13—passages showing that the hearkening of Yhwh can be reported without previously narrating the crying—only demonstrate the possibility of an alternative, but more complicated explanation; see Rainer Kessler, "Die Querverweise im Pentateuch: Überlieferungsgeschichtliche Untersuchung der expliziten Querverbindungen innerhalb des vorpriesterlichen Pentateuchs" (Th.D. diss., University of Heidelberg, 1972), 183; Gertz, *Tradition und Redaktion*, 186–87; Blum, "Die literarische Verbindung," 124–25.

44. See Schmid, *Erzväter und Exodus*, 198 n. 156–58.

3. The Connection of the Patriarchs with the Exodus in P

It is commonly accepted that the Priestly source remains a well-defined body of literature in pentateuchal criticism and that the source extends into the books of Genesis and Exodus. The extent of the Priestly source can clearly be demonstrated by its special language, its overall structure, and the manifold literary references between its texts. We can neglect the question of the literary character of P—source or redaction[45]—as well as the problem of its literary end, since it is only important for our current enterprise to state that P runs from the book of Genesis into the book of Exodus. To the best of my knowledge, this is not disputed by any of the scholars who accept the hypothesis of Priestly literature in the Pentateuch.

Within the framework of traditional source criticism, the extension of P in Genesis, Exodus, and beyond has not been a point of debate—because the presentation of history in P was thought to be an imitation of both J and E. But this assumption seems highly unlikely. As its inner argumentation shows quite clearly, P could not take over the connection of the patriarchal narrative to the story of the exodus from an older tradition but obviously placed two originally independent corpora of tradition for the first time in a logical sequence.

(1) First and foremost, we must look at the crucial passage in the Priestly report of the call of Moses in Exod 6:2–8:[46]

A   I am YHWH

B   And I appeared unto Abraham, unto Isaac, and unto Jacob, as El Shadday

A'   But my name is YHWH

B'   I have not revealed myself to them

According to this statement, P advocates a progressive theory of revelation that distinguishes between two stages. God has revealed himself to the patriarchs

---

45. See ibid., 54 with n. 33 (bibliography).

46. The grammatical problems of the verse have frequently been discussed (see especially W. Randall Garr, "The Grammar and Interpretation of Exodus 6:3," *JBL* 111 [1992]: 385–408); generally the half-verse 3b is interpreted as a sentence with a double subject (ושמי/יהוה). I think a simpler solution should be preferred according to the parallelism in 6:2–3 as identified above (A, B, A', B') and as indicated by the accentuation (*zaqeph qaton* after ושמי יהוה) probably also preferred by the Masoretes: "My name is YHWH; I did not reveal myself to them." Most likely the use of the language was influenced by Ezekiel (ידע niphal in the first-person singular in the Hebrew Bible only used of God [except in Exod 6:3, only Ezek 20:5, 9; 35:11; 38:23]; Exod 6 shows further references to Ezekiel [see Bernard Gosse, "Exode 6,8 comme réponse à Ézéchiel 33,24," *RHPR* 74 (1994): 241–47; Erhard Blum, *Studien zur Komposition des Pentateuch* (BZAW 189; Berlin: de Gruyter, 1990), 236 n. 31]); this would add further support to the proposed translation.

as El Shadday, but now he announces that his name is Yʜwʜ. This theory is strictly retained in the whole text of the Priestly source with the notable and much debated exception in Gen 17:1, a text that most likely serves to provide additional information for the reader and does not concern Abraham. For the patriarchs God introduces himself as El Shadday; for Moses and his generation he is Yʜwʜ.

This theory is so well known among exegetes that one hardly ever bothers to ask why P makes such a distinction. Sometimes it has been argued that P adopts the theological concept of E, since E uses a similar change from Elohim to Yʜwʜ in Exod 3, but this does not explain the use of El Shadday. And on a methodological level it is hardly convincing to use a problematic hypothesis such as E to explain literary problems of other texts.

If we ask about the internal logic of P, there is little reason to separate the period of the patriarchs from the one of the exodus. For P, the time of Moses is that of the fulfilment of the promises to Abraham,[47] and a qualitative separation of the two is far from natural for P. Admittedly, the revelation of the name of Yʜwʜ becomes necessary for the cult that originates with Moses.[48] The name Yʜwʜ serves the purpose of cultic address and so forth. But at the same time this theory of a progressive revelation of God's name in stages also becomes obviously necessary to combine two divergent blocks of tradition. So P still shows that it regarded the patriarchal narrative as something like the "Old Testament of the Old Testament."[49]

Thus, Exod 6:2–8 supports the view already found in the non-P material of Genesis–Exodus: in its concept of history P newly combines two blocks of tradition that have a quite different literary and theological origin and profile. This combination needs a new logical and theological argument, which P provides in Exod 6:2–8. This shows quite clearly that P was unable to utilize an already-known sequence of the epochs of the history of Israel that could simply be reproduced with a slightly different focus; rather, P had to create this sequence from scratch. The fusing of the divergent concepts of God is a remarkable accomplishment by P.

---

47. See already Walther Zimmerli, "Sinaibund und Abrahambund: Ein Beitrag zum Verständnis der Priesterschrift," *TZ* 16 (1960): 268–80; repr. in idem, *Gottes Offenbarung: Gesammelte Aufsätze zum Alten Testament* (TB 19; Munich: Kaiser, 1963), 205–17, here 212; following him Bernd Janowski, *Sühne als Heilsgeschehen: Traditions- und religionsgeschichtliche Studien zur priesterschriftlichen Sühnetheologie* (2nd ed.; WMANT 81; Neukirchen-Vluyn: Neukirchener, 2000), 9.

48. See Blum, *Studien zur Komposition des Pentateuch*, 295–96.

49. Robert W. L. Moberly, *The Old Testament of the Old Testament: Patriarchal Narratives and Mosaic Yahwism* (OBT; Minneapolis: Fortress, 1992).

(2) Equally remarkable is P's introduction and qualification of the patriarchs as "strangers" in the land of Canaan: Only in the Priestly texts of Genesis are the Patriarchs labeled "strangers" (גרים)[50] (Gen 17:8; 23:4;[51] 28:4; 35:27; 36:7; 37:1; cf. the retrospective in Exod 6:4). This was already noted by Gerhard von Rad, but he concluded that the same concept was already present in J, even though J did not use the same terminology.[52] This is, however, simply eisegesis. Rather, it becomes apparent that the labeling of the patriarchs as "strangers" (גרים) who could not acquire any land[53] is only necessary if—in contrast to the non-Priestly promise of the land—the descendants of the patriarchs had to leave the holy land first in order to take possession of it again after the exodus from Egypt several centuries later. The depiction of the patriarchs as strangers in Canaan and its literary confinement to the Priestly texts is clear only within the assumption that Genesis and Exodus were distinct bodies of literature before P.

---

50. The substantive גרים is only found in P in Genesis–Exodus (cf. *THAT* 1:409 [Robert Martin-Achard]); on the expression ארץ מגרים in P and its translation, see Blum, *Die Komposition der Vätergeschichte*, 443; Matthias Köckert, "Das Land in der priesterlichen Komposition des Pentateuch," in *Von Gott reden: Beiträge zur Theologie und Exegese des Alten Testaments: Festschrift S. Wagner* (eds. D. Vieweger and E.-J. Waschke; Neukirchen-Vluyn: Neukirchener, 1995), 147–62, 156 with n. 30 (see also Michaela Bauks, "Die Begriffe מורשה und אחזה in Pᵍ: Überlegungen zur Landkonzeption der Priestergrundschrift," *ZAW* 116 [2004]: 171–88). A bit more differentiated but not necessarily opposing is the findings regarding the verb גור. It occurs in Genesis in Priestly and non-Priestly texts (Gen 12:10; 19:9; 20:1; 21:23; 26:3; 32:5; 35:27; 47:4). Here 35:5 belongs to P, 19:9 refers to Lot in Sodom, 20:1 refers to Abraham in Gerar, 35:2 refers to Jacob at Laban's place; 47:4 refers to Joseph's brother in Egypt, and in 21:23 Abimelech is talking to Abraham. Only Gen 26:3 is a non-Priestly statement; here God states that Isaac has "dwelled as a stranger" in Gerar, but Gerar was foreign territory during the period of monarchy (see, e.g., *BHH* 1:547–48 [Karl Elliger]).

51. On the discussion whether Gen 23 belongs to P, see Blum, *Die Komposition der Vätergeschichte*, 441–46 (differently, Thomas Pola, *Die ursprüngliche Priesterschrift: Beobachtungen zu Literarkritik und Traditionsgeschichte von Pᵍ* [WMANT 70; Neukirchen-Vluyn: Neukirchener, 1995], 308–09). Gerhard von Rad concluded as far as Gen 23 was concerned that at the time of their death the patriarchs were already heirs and no longer strangers (*Die Priesterschrift im Hexateuch: Literarisch untersucht und theologisch gewertet* [BWANT 65; Stuttgart: Kohlhammer, 1934], 51; see also Pola, *Die ursprüngliche Priesterschrift*, 309).

52. *Die Priesterschrift im Hexateuch*, 69.

53. See *ThWAT* 1:985 (Ulrich Kellermann); on the legal status of the גר, see 983–90; Christoph Bultmann, *Der Fremde im antiken Juda: Eine Untersuchung zum sozialen Typenbegriff 'ger' und seinem Bedeutungswandel in der alttestamentlichen Gesetzgebung* (FRLANT 153; Göttingen: Vandenhoeck & Ruprecht, 1992), 17–22, 34–212, who describes the status according to the different legal corpora in the Hebrew Bible; Markus Zehnder, *Umgang mit Fremden in Israel und Assyrien: Ein Beitrag zur Anthropologie des "Fremden" im Licht antiker Quellen* (BWANT 168; Stuttgart: Kohlhammer, 2005).

Synoptic Overview of the Attributions to P in Genesis 37–Exodus 1

	Wellhausen[55]	Noth[56]	Elliger[57]	Lohfink[58]	Levin[59]	Donner[60]	de Pury[61]	Carr[62]	Seebass[63]	Kratz[64]	Lux[65]
37	2	1, 2a*, b	1–2	1–2	1, 2a*, b	1–2	1	2	2a*	2	1, 2a
41	(46a)	46a	46a	46a	46a	46a		(46a)	46a		46a
45								19–21	19b–21a*		
46	6–7(, 8–27)	6–7(, 8–27)	6–7	6–7	6–7	6–27	6–7(, 8–27)	*5–7, 8–27	6–7[66]	6–27	6–7(, 8–27)
47	5, 6a, 7–11, 27b, 28	27b, 28		27b, 28	27–28	5a*, 6a, 7–11, 27b, 28	27*, 28(, 29–31)	11, 27b, 28	(5, 6a, 7–10), 5b, 6–11, 28	27–28	5*, 6a, 7–11, 27b, 28
48	3–6(, 7)	3–6	3–6	3–6		3–6		3–6[67]	3–6		3–7
49	(28,)29–33	1a, 29–33	1a, 28b–33	1a, 28b–33	1a, 28b*, 29–33a*, b	1a, 28b, 29–33	1a, 29f(30–31), 32–33	1a, 29–33	29–33	1a, 29–33	1a, 28b, 29–33*
50	12–13	12–13	12–13	12–13	12–13, 22b	12–13	12–13	12–13, 22–23, 26a	12–13	12–13	12–13
Exod 1	1–7, 13–14	1–7, 13–14	1–7, 13–14	1–5, 7, 13–14	13–14		1–6a, 7, 13–14	1–5, 7, 13–14		13–14	

(3) Finally, we must examine the concrete literary form of the Priestly tran-sition from the period of the patriarchs to the exodus.[54] There is a considerable consensus about what texts in Gen 37–50 have to be attributed to P.

At the same time, there seems to be a similar consensus that we can find nothing but fragments of the original Priestly presentation of the story of Joseph.[68] This opinion is mainly based on the attribution of the full verse of Gen 37:2 to P.

---

54. There are several problems with the study of the priestly texts in Gen 37–50 by Rüdiger Lux, to this point the most detailed ("Geschichte als Erfahrung: Erinnerung und Erzählung in der priesterschriftlichen Rezeption der Josefsnovelle," in *Erzählte Geschichte: Beiträge zur narrativen Kultur im alten Israel* [ed. R. Lux; BTS 40; Neukirchen-Vluyn: Neukirchener, 2000], 147–80). He introduces a textual basis that he calls a critically secured minimum ("kritisch gesichertes Mini-mum"), which is surprising since we simply do not have—on a methodological level—either critical secured minima or maxima. Even a minimalist set of texts (in comparison to other exegetes, Lux's text is certainly no minimalist) can contain wrong attributions. Lux remarks on these texts: "Die Durchmusterung der Stellen legt den Schluß nahe, dass es sich hier nicht um Fragmente einer ursprünglich eigenständigen Josefserzählung handelt, sondern eher um eine redaktionelle Bearbei-tung derselben im Geiste von P" (151). *Tertium non datur?* He states on such a third possibility: "Der fragmentarische Charakter von P in der Josefsnovelle ist allerdings noch kein hinreichender Grund, P insgesamt den Status einer selbständigen Quellenschrift abzusprechen und in ihr eine redaktionelle Bearbeitungsschicht zu sehen" (151 n. 14). However, it is exactly that which his obser-vations seem to imply.

55. *Die Composition des Hexateuchs,* 51–52.

56. *Überlieferungsgeschichte des Pentateuch,* 18.

57. "Sinn und Ursprung der priesterlichen Geschichtserzählung," *ZTK* 49 (1952): 121–43 in idem, *Kleine Schriften zum Alten Testament* (ed. H. Gese and O. Kaiser; TB 32; Munich: Kaiser, 1966), 174–98, 174.

58. Norbert Lohfink, "Die Priesterschrift und die Geschichte," in *Congress Volume: Göttingen, 1977* (ed. J. A. Emerton; VTSup 29; Leiden: Brill, 1978), 183–225 = idem, *Studien zum Pentateuch* (SBAB 4; Stuttgart: Katholisches Bibelwerk, 1988), 213–53, 222 n. 29.

59. *Der Jahwist,* 262, 271, 285, 305, 309, 315.

60. Herbert Donner, *Die literarische Gestalt der alttestamentlichen Josephsgeschichte* (SHAW; Heidelberg: Winter, 1976), 7 n. 3 = idem, *Aufsätze zum Alten Testament aus vier Jahrzehnten* (BZAW 224; Berlin: de Gruyter, 1994), 76–120, 77 n. 3.

61. Albert de Pury, "Le cycle de Jacob comme légende autonome des origines d'Israël," in *Con-gress Volume: Leuven, 1989* (ed. J. A. Emerton; VTSup 43; Leiden: Brill, 1991), 78–96, 82.

62. *Reading the Fractures of Genesis,* 271.

63. Horst Seebass, *Genesis III: Josephsgeschichte (37,1–50,26)* (Neukirchen-Vluyn: Neukirch-ener, 2000), 211.

64. Reinhard Gregor Kratz, *Die Komposition der erzählenden Bücher des Alten Testaments: Grundwissen der Bibelkritik* (Uni-Taschenbücher 2157; Göttingen: Vandenhoeck & Ruprecht, 2000), 243, 281.

65. "Geschichte als Erfahrung," 147–80, 150–51.

66. Missing on page 211 but not disputed on page 122 as P (on page 117: 5b–7).

67. Missing in the chart on page 271.

68. See Noth, *Überlieferungsgeschichte des Pentateuch,* 13–14; Levin, *Der Jahwist,* 271.

These are the generations of Jacob (אלה תלדות יעקב). Joseph, being seventeen years old, was pasturing the flock with his brothers. He was a boy with
the sons of Bilhah and Zilpah, his father's wives. And Joseph brought a bad
report of them to their father.

This is the only specific mention of Joseph in the common P texts in Gen 37–50.
If, however, one follows the proposal by Albert de Pury and limits the Priestly
parts of this verse to אלה תלדות יעקב, one arrives at an acceptable and complete description of the *eisodos* within P without an account of Joseph[69] but with
an Israelite stay in Egypt of 430 years summarized later in Exod 12:40–41.[70]

(37:1–2) Jacob lived in the land of his father's sojournings, in the land of
Canaan. (2) These are the generations of Jacob.

(46:6–7) And they took their livestock and their goods, which they had gained
in the land of Canaan, and came into Egypt—Jacob and all his offspring with
him, (7) his sons, and his sons' sons with him, his daughters, and his sons'
daughters. All his offspring he brought with him into Egypt.

---

69. Cf. also Rendtorff, *Das überlieferungsgeschichtliche Problem*, 113–15. John Van Seters in his
response to this contribution has raised severe criticism against such a hypothesis. This criticism,
however, does not address the central issues. (1) There are some minor corrections to be made concerning Van Seters's objections. He writes: "Following the introduction in 37:1–2aα, 'Jacob lived
in the land of his father's sojourning, in the land of Canaan. These are the generations of Jacob,' we
expect some narrative account of Jacob's sons in Canaan" [see below, 148]. An examination of the
toledot-formula, for example, in Gen 2:4a and 36:1 shows that such an expectation is unwarranted.
In addition, Van Seters also objects to the continuation of Gen 37:1–2aα in the plural formulation of 46:6–7. The syntax in 46:6–7 is unusual but by no means impossible; the plural subject
is explicitly given in 46:6b: "Jacob and all his offspring with him." Finally, Van Seters makes the
reader believe that I am not attributing Exod 1:1–5 to P (with reference to my *Erzväter und Exodus*,
30) and that therefore in my reconstruction of P Exod 1:13–14 would have immediately followed
Gen 50:13, with the result that an *eisodos* account would be lacking in P. This is a misreading of the
argumentation in *Erzväter und Exodus*, 30 n. 177, where I am pointing to the difficulties of considering Exod 1:1–5 as a P text without concluding that Exod 1:1–5 could not be attributed to P.
In the meantime, I would be ready to follow Jan Christian Gertz's argument to identify Gen 50:14
as P (see the contribution of Gertz in this volume), despite Van Seters's criticism of Gertz. (2) Van
Seters's interpretation of the P texts in Gen 37 to Exod 1 assumes his notion of P as a redactional
layer and not as an independent source. Although this hypothesis has become attractive to many
recent interpreters, the theory is becoming increasingly difficult to maintain. Already the sequence
in Gen 1–3 or in Gen 6–9 indicates clearly that P cannot be conceived purely as a redaction. I must
refrain from pointing out further arguments here, and I refer instead to Klaus Koch, "P—kein
Redaktor! Erinnerung an zwei Eckdaten der Quellenscheidung," *VT* 37 (1987): 446–67, and more
recently to Gertz, *Tradition und Redaktion*.

70. See recently Gertz, *Tradition und Redaktion*, 58 with n. 126 (bibliography).

(47:27–28) Thus Israel settled in the land of Egypt, in the land of Goshen. And they gained possessions in it, and were fruitful and multiplied greatly. (28) And Jacob lived in the land of Egypt seventeen years. So the days of Jacob, the years of his life, were 147 years.

(49:1a) Then Jacob called his sons (49:29–33) and he commanded them and said to them, "I am to be gathered to my people; bury me with my fathers in the cave that is in the field of Ephron the Hittite, (30) in the cave that is in the field at Machpelah, to the east of Mamre, in the land of Canaan, which Abraham bought with the field from Ephron the Hittite to possess as a burying place. (31) There they buried Abraham and Sarah his wife. There they buried Isaac and Rebekah his wife, and there I buried Leah—(32) the field and the cave that is in it were bought from the Hittites." (33) When Jacob finished commanding his sons, he drew up his feet into the bed and breathed his last and was gathered to his people.

(50:12–13) Thus his sons did for him as he had commanded them, (13) for his sons carried him to the land of Canaan and buried him in the cave of the field at Machpelah, to the east of Mamre, which Abraham bought with the field from Ephron the Hittite to possess as a burying place.

The assumption of such a small literary bridge between the patriarchs and the exodus in P converges now with a generally recognized aspect of the internal analysis of the Joseph story, namely, that it was not composed—as argued by Martin Noth—as the literary joint between patriarchs and exodus. Rather, the plot and the connecting literary devices show that the story was originally attached to the patriarchal narrative before it was transformed into the connecting link, as a secondary literary development.[71] Thus the connection of the patriarchs and the exodus made by P—without an elaborated Joseph story— indicates that it does not presuppose a pre-Priestly connection of the patriarchs and the exodus in an earlier composition of the story of Joseph. Otherwise, one would have to expect that P also had a Joseph story.

4. CONCLUSION

How can one summarize these observations and considerations? (1) The history of research aptly demonstrates that the hiatus between Genesis and Exodus was always recognized (see esp. Kurt Galling[72] and Martin Noth[73]) but only fully

---

71. See Schmid, "Die Josephsgeschichte im Pentateuch."

72. *Die Erwählungstraditionen Israels* (Giessen: Töpelmann, 1928).

73. *Überlieferungsgeschichte des Pentateuch.*

utilized after the classic theory of an old Hexateuch (J) started to dissolve in the 1970s.

(2) Both the narrative substance of the book of Genesis as well as its reception outside the Pentateuch supports the suspicion that this text was not written from the beginning as a prelude to the book of Exodus.

(3) Explicit literary connections between Genesis and Exodus appear only in Priestly texts or texts that presuppose P.

(4) P itself shows that it creates something new by joining the patriarchal narrative with the exodus. This is accomplished with a progressive revelation by stages of the divine name and the newly created qualification of the patriarchs as "strangers." In addition, P does not seem to know the Joseph story as a bridge between Genesis and Exodus.

(5) A pre-Priestly connection between Genesis and Exodus cannot be proven and does not seem likely.

5. Consequences for the History of Religion and Theology

The redaction-historical separation of Genesis and Exodus before P has fundamental consequences for our understanding of the history of religion and theology of the Hebrew Bible. First, it is obvious that a farewell to the Yahwist has to abandon the thesis so popular in the twentieth century that the religion of ancient Israel was based on salvation history (*Heilsgeschichte*). That such a view can no longer be maintained has been made clear by the numerous archaeological finds discovered and published in the past years.[74] One must envisage the religion of Israel differently than the biblical picture suggests. The polemics of the Deuteronomists are probably closer to the preexilic reality in ancient Israel than the normative-orthodox statements in the Bible that promulgate a monotheism based on salvation history.[75]

Without the Yahwist, the paradigm of a clear discontinuity between ancient Israel and its neighbors can no longer be maintained. This paradigm of discontinuity developed in the wake of dialectical theology. It presupposed that Israel

---

74. See, e.g., Othmar Keel and Christoph Uehlinger, *Göttinnen, Götter und Gottessymbole: Neue Erkenntnisse zur Religionsgeschichte Kanaans und Israels aufgrund bislang unerschlossener ikonographischer Quellen* (5th ed.; QD 134; Freiburg: Herder, 2001); and Christoph Hardmeier, ed., *Steine—Bilder—Texte: Historische Evidenz außerbiblischer und biblischer Quellen* (Arbeiten zur Bibel und ihrer Geschichte 5; Leipzig: Evangelische Verlagsanstalt, 2001); Friedhelm Hartenstein, "Religionsgeschichte Israels—ein Überblick über die Forschung seit 1990," *VF* 48 (2003): 2–28.

75. See Manfred Weippert, "Synkretismus und Monotheismus: Religionsinterne Konfliktbewältigung im alten Israel," in idem, *Jahwe und die anderen Götter: Studien zur Religionsgeschichte des antiken Israel in ihrem syrisch-palästinischen Kontext* (FAT 18; Tübingen: Mohr Siebeck, 1997), 1–24.

occupied from the beginning a very special place in the ancient Near East. But if there has been no early (i.e., Solomonic) or at least monarchic (Josiah) conception of a salvation history that began with the creation and ends with the conquest of the land—be it as a detailed historical work or simply as a short creed[76]—Israel must be seen in continuity rather than discontinuity with its neighbors. The paradigm of discontinuity is not a peculiarity of ancient Israel but rather a characteristic feature of Judaism of the Persian period, which projected its ideals back into the Hebrew Bible. This insight is not really new and also remains possible if one advocates a late dating of the Yahwist (or its equivalents) closer to the environment of the Deuteronomistic literature.

We arrive at a new perspective, however, if we realize that the patriarchal narrative and the story of the exodus stood next to each other as two competing concepts containing two traditions of the origin of Israel with different theological profiles. Even behind the carefully crafted final form of the Pentateuch the different conceptions remain apparent:[77] the patriarchal narrative is constructed mainly autochthonous and inclusive, while the story of the exodus is allochthonous and exclusive.[78] Of course, such a polar opposition can only serve as a model, but it points nevertheless to a basic difference between the two blocks of tradition. To be more precise, the patriarchal narrative constructs a picture of the origin of Israel in its own land—a fact that is especially prominent in the specific formulations of the promises of the land that do not presuppose that there will be several centuries between promise and fulfilment.[79] At the same time, the patriarchal story is both theologically and politically inclusive: the different gods can—without any problems—be identified with YHWH, and the patriarchs dwell together with the inhabitants of the land and make treaties with them. In contrast, the story of the exodus stresses Israel's origin abroad in Egypt and puts forward an exclusive theological argument: YHWH is a jealous god who does not tolerate any other gods besides him, and the Israelites shall not make peace with the inhabitants of the land.

These divergent concepts cannot be fully grasped theologically if one regards them from the beginning as part of the same logical literary order—an

---

76. See Jan Christian Gertz, "Die Stellung des kleinen geschichtlichen Credos in der Redaktionsgeschichte von Deuteronomium und Pentateuch," in *Liebe und Gebot: Studien zum Deuteronomium: Festschrift L. Perlitt* (ed. R. G. Kratz and H. Spieckermann; FRLANT 190; Göttingen: Vandenhoeck & Ruprecht, 2000), 30–45.

77. See Albert de Pury, "Le cycle de Jacob," 78–96; idem, "Osée 12;" idem, "Erwägungen zu einem vorexilischen Stämmejahwismus."

78. In more detail Schmid, *Erzväter und Exodus*, 122–29, 159–64.

79. The promise is addressed to the patriarch himself and to his descendants. See the chart in Rendtorff, *Das überlieferungsgeschichtliche Problem*, 42.

order that, to my mind, is secondary. Rather, the patriarchal narrative and the story of the exodus existed next to each other (and not following each other) as two competing stories of the origin of Israel.

THE JACOB STORY AND THE BEGINNING
OF THE FORMATION OF THE PENTATEUCH

Albert de Pury

The Jacob story—as it is preserved, *grosso modo,* in Gen 25–35—does not play a very obvious role in the structure of the present Pentateuch. Surely, the Pentateuch mentions Jacob as the ancestor who first can claim the name of "Israel" (Gen 32:29; 35:10) and it acknowleges him as the father of the twelve eponymous tribes of Israel. Both facts are narrated, but barely reflected upon, except perhaps in the Joseph story, and the father Jacob looks like a somewhat minor figure, jammed as he is between such giants as Abraham and Moses. Moreover, in spite of the presence of two intriguing theophanies, his story is deprived of major theological landmarks comparable to the convenants with Abraham (Gen 15; 17) or Moses (Exod 3–4; 6; 19–24). Finally, Jacob appears ever again as trickster, and he does not reach the spiritual and moral grandeur of the other two dominating figures. At first sight, it is difficult to see what has been the role, place, and function of the Jacob story in the formation of the Pentateuch, both in structural and genetic perspective. Yet there are, as we shall see, some important insights to be gained if the birth of the Pentateuch is questioned from this angle. First, let us just recall some of the major stages in history of research.

1. THE JACOB STORY IN TWENTIETH-CENTURY RESEARCH

In the debate around the formation of the Pentateuch, the Jacob story of Gen 25–35 has never played a prominent role.[1] During the nineteenth century, artisans of the Documentary Hypothesis, including Wellhausen, were interested mainly in determining and separating the literary strands—J, E, and P—and in

---

1. For a more detailed presentation, see Albert de Pury, "Situer le cycle de Jacob: Quelques réflexions, vingt-cinq ans plus tard," in *Studies in the Book of Genesis: Literature, Redaction and History* (ed. A. Wénin; BETL 155; Leuven: Leuven University Press; Peeters, 2001), 213–41, here 213–21.

establishing between them a relative chronology. And in this respect, the Jacob story did not pose any particular problems: it was very easy to separate the P-version from the JE-version, and even within the remaining bulk of the cycle, the critics were quite confident they could separate J from E when it came to such episodes as Gen 27; 28:10–22; 30–31; 32–33; and 35. The chronological order did not raise any difficulty either: P was manifestly a shortened, moralized,[2] and streamlined version of the long and colorful JE version! Genesis 25–35 indeed served as a welcome pillar to the emerging Documentary Hypothesis.

What strikes us when we look back at these late-nineteenth-century inquiries is that the questions that today would seem paramount to us were *not* asked, and apparently *could not* be asked. One did *not* try, for instance, to know what could have been the literary project of this or that author, or what his literary horizon was. Nor did one ask where the author might have found the matters he was setting up in his story. The presupposition was that each "author" of a literary strand, each "writer," was simply reproducing in his particular way the global pentateuchal narrative that in some sense was just thought to be in existence "somewhere out there." The problem was not so much the historicity of the patriarchal tales, since many critics did not hide their general skepticism as to the historical content of these tales. What could not be grasped was that the entire history and prehistory of Israel's origins had to be understood—whatever its historical content—as a construct of the mind, as the purposeful and expanding founding legend of a collective identity, and that this *construct* as such was the historical phenomenon that had to be investigated and historically situated. As the commentaries of August Dillmann[3] or Heinrich Holzinger[4] illustrate it, nineteenth-century commentators on Genesis thought they had finished their task when they had attributed the last verse of the biblical text to one of the extant sources or subsources of the Documentary Hypothesis.

In the beginning of the twentieth century, one important step forward was taken by Hermann Gunkel.[5] He suggested that behind the episodes of the Jacob cycle, as of the rest of Genesis, one still could see the raw material from which it had been made of: folk tales, fairy tales, local anecdotes, or etiologies. As a consequence, he concluded that the cycle (*Sagenkranz*) as a whole had been secondarily crafted and assembled from previously self-contained *Einzelsagen* and

---

2. The change of motivation for Jacob's departure to Haran between Gen 27:41–45 JE and Gen 26:34–35; 27:46; 28:1–5 P was indeed used as a "textbook case" demonstrating the validity of Welhausen's "Newer Documentary Hypothesis."

3. August Dillmann, *Die Genesis* (6th ed.; Leipzig: Hirzel, 1892).

4. Heinrich Holzinger, *Genesis* (KHC 1; Leipzig: Mohr Siebeck, 1898).

5. Hermann Gunkel, *Genesis übersetzt und erklärt* (6th ed.; HKAT 1/1; Göttingen: Vandenhoeck & Ruprecht, 1964; repr., 1977); English translation: *Genesis* (trans. M-E. Biddle; Macon, Ga.: Mercer University Press, 1997); idem, "Jacob," *Preussische Jahrbücher* 176 (1919): 339–62.

Märchen. He thought that thematic groupings of small units—for example, an anthology of Jacob/Esau stories, a cycle of transjordanian Jacob stories, or a cycle of Cisjordanian "cultic legends"—could probably be construed as intermediary stages on the way to the full cycle of Jacob. With Gunkel, the focus thus had shifted from the literary to the preliterary level of the stories. This perspective was to be taken up in the 1930s by Albrecht Alt[6] and Martin Noth.[7] Alt was the first to point out that the geographical contexts of the Abraham and the Jacob stories were not the same, and he concluded that the roots of the Abraham tradition were to be sought in southern Palestine, whereas the Jacob tradition was anchored rather in the Ephraimite north and in Transjordan.[8] That divergence as to their geographical setting showed that these two patriarchal cycles had different local orgins (*Haftpunkte*) and therefore came probably from different groups or were, at least, transmitted by different circles. And this observation paved the way to understand the patriarchal cycles as tribal traditions that did possibly not concern the whole of Israel from the beginning. Gerhard von Rad, for his part, concentrated his interest on the writer whom he considered as the main collector and editor of patriarchal lore: the Yahwist, whom he dated in the Solomonic era.[9] The Yahwist was credited with conceiving a narrative tradition beginning with the creation and early history of humankind (Gen 2–11*), leading to an elaborate history of the promise to the patriarchs (Gen 12–50*), and finding its climax in the story of the Israelites brought out of Egypt under Moses and conquering the land (Exodus*; Numbers*; Joshua*).

In my doctoral thesis, written between 1969 and 1972 but published in 1975,[10] I concentrated on the problem of the coherence or noncoherence of the Jacob cycle and, first and foremost, of the story of Gen 28:10–22, which seemed to constitute its nodal point. I tried to show, for instance, that in Gen 28 the promise of the land, understood as a promise of sedentarization, and the local cult etiology were not necessarily heterogeneous elements that had to be attrib-

---

6. Cf. in particular Albrecht Alt, "Der Gott der Väter: Ein Beitrag zur Vorgeschichte der israelitischen Religion" (1929), in idem, *Kleine Schriften zur Geschichte Israels* (Munich: Beck, 1959), 1:1–78.

7. Martin Noth, *Überlieferungsgeschichte des Pentateuch* (Stuttgart: Kohlhammer, 1948; repr., Darmstadt: Wissenschaftliche Buchgesellschaft, 1960).

8. Alt, "Gott der Väter," 48–61.

9. Gerhard von Rad, *Das formgeschichtliche Problem des Hexateuch* (BWANT 4/13 ; Stuttgart: Kohlhammer, 1938), reprinted in G. von Rad, ed., *Gesammelte Studien zum Alten Testament* (2nd ed.; TB 8; Munich: Kaiser, 1961), 9–86. English translation: "The Form-Critical Problem of the Hexateuch," in idem, *The Problem of the Hexateuch and Other Essays* (trans. E. W. Trueman Dicken; Edinburgh: Oliver & Boyd, 1966; repr., London: SCM, 1984), 1–78.

10. Albert de Pury, *Promesse divine et légende cultuelle dans le cycle de Jacob: Genèse 28 et les traditions patriarcales* (ÉB; Paris: Gabalda, 1975).

uted to different stages of the story's diachronic development and that the Jacob cycle as a whole was best explained not as the progressive redactional agglutination of unconnected anecdotes but rather as a narrative *gesta* that had its own logic and its own dynamic. The Jacob cycle thus appeared to me as a structure whose basic outline was given from the outset, in spite of the admitted variability of its components, a process somewhat alike to what we can observe in the transmission history of the Gilgamesh Epic or the *Odyssey.* The Jacob cycle, thus, had to be read as the founding saga of the "sons of Jacob" or "sons of Israel," which I presumed to be some kind of proto-Israelite Recent Bronze or early Iron I tribal conglomerate in the mountains of Ephraim and in Transjordan.[11] But in my analysis and dating of the texts, I remained completely dependent on the still prevailing Documentary Hypothesis: a tenth-century Yahwist, a ninth- or eighth-century Elohist, and a sixth-century Priestly writer.

By the time my thesis appeared in print, the Documentary Hypothesis had practically collapsed. Critics such as John Van Seters,[12] Hans Heinrich Schmid,[13] and Rolf Rendtorff[14] had shown the unlikelihood of a Solomonic Yahwist and, even more basically, of a preexilic emergence of a pentateuchal project.[15] Of course, especially in the line of Rendtorff, that did not signal the end of all preexilic narrative, and Erhard Blum[16] produced, in 1984, an imposing analysis

---

11. See also my review of Thomas L. Thompson, *The Historicity of the Patriarchal Narratives* (1974) and John Van Seters, *Abraham in History and Tradition* (1975), *RB* 85 (1978): 589–618.

12. John Van Seters, *Abraham in History and Tradition* (New Haven: Yale University Press, 1975).

13. Hans Heinrich Schmid, *Der sogenannte Jahwist. Beobachtungen und Fragen zur Pentateuchforschung* (Zürich: Theologischer Verlag, 1976).

14. Rolf Rendtorff, *Das überlieferungsgeschichtliche Problem des Pentateuch* (BZAW 147; Berlin: de Gruyter, 1977); English translation: *The Problem of the Process of Transmission in the Pentateuch* (trans. J. J. Scullion; JSOTSup 89; Sheffield: JSOT Press, 1990).

15. For an overview of that "crisis," see the contributions of Albert de Pury and Thomas Römer in *Le Pentateuque en question* (ed. A. de Pury and T. Römer; 3rd ed.; MdB 19; Genève: Labor et Fides 2002), 9–80, and especially of Thomas Römer, vii–xxxix. See also Albert de Pury, "Yahwist ('J') Source," *ABD* 6 (1992): 1012–20; and Römer's analysis in *Introduction à l'Ancien Testament* (ed. Thomas Römer et al.; MdB 49; Genève: Labor et Fides 2004), 63–113.

16. Erhard Blum, *Die Komposition der Vätergeschichte* (WMANT 57; Neukirchen-Vluyn: Neukirchener, 1984). At the origin of the Jacob tradition, Blum sees some isolated stories (Gen 28* [without promise or vow]; 25:27–28*; 27*; 31:46–53*). The first Jacob cycle (die "Jakoberzählung," comprising Gen 25:21–24*; 27*; 28*; 29:2–30*; 30:25–43*; 31:17–32*, 44–53* but not the encounter at Penuel nor the second meeting with Esau, would have been composed under the reign of David or Solomon. That ensemble would have undergone an important reinterpretation and extension under Jeroboam I, the vow now being added to the Bethel story, as well as the second meeting with Esau and the Penuel episode. That "Kompositionsschicht" would then have led to a third phase, the "Jakobsgeschichte," which would have integrated a first version of the Joseph story and thus established the link with the Moses story.

of the patriarchal narratives that maintained the attribution to the Davidic era of the first stages of the literary growth of a Jacob story yet unconnected with the Moses story. Blum, however, did not enter into the perspective of the Jacob story as a tribal *gesta* and remained under the spell of the priority of the Gunkelian *Einzelsage*.

For me, the turning point came, partly at least, with Thomas Römer: he became my assistant in 1984, and I had to chaperone his doctoral thesis in which he took up John Van Seter's suggestion of 1972 that the fathers (the אבות) in Deuteronomy and the Deuteronomistic literature did *not* refer to the patriarchs of the book of Genesis—in spite of the seven passages in Deuteronomy (Deut 1:8; 6:10; 9:5, 7; 29:12; 30:20; 34:4) that explicitly, but secondarily, identify the אבות with the patriarchal triad. In his thesis, *Israels Väter*, which appeared in 1990, Thomas Römer showed convincingly that for Deuteronomy and the Deuteronomistic literature, Israel's history began in Egypt.[17]

Initially, Römer believed that this could and would prove that there existed no preexilic Jacob story at all and that consquently the Jacob cycle was, as was already being suggested by other authors (Bernd Diebner[18] and Martin Rose[19]), a postexilic construction reflecting the experiences of the Judean returnee community having to import their wives from the Golah. But when I asked him whether the Deuteronomists' apparent absence of knowledge could not be decoded as a very obvious *refusal* of knowledge, Römer agreed that that possibility, still remote in his eyes, could not be completely ruled out.

There were several signs, as I saw it, that pointed to the conclusion that the Deuteronomists—at least those who were behind Deuteronomy, Joshua, and 1–2 Kings—not only had very well known the Jacob tradition, but that they had vehemently rejected it, to the point of excluding and silencing it absolutely. There is only one passage in which the Deuteronomists obviously refer back to Jacob: Deut 26:5–9. When offering the firstfruit, the Israelite is instructed to say:

---

17. Thomas Römer, *Israels Väter: Untersuchungen zur Väterthematik im Deuteronomium und in der deuteronomistischen Tradition* (OBO 99; Fribourg: Universitätsverlag; Göttingen: Vandenhoeck & Ruprecht, 1990).

18. Bernd J. Diebner and Hermann Schult, "Die Ehen der Erzväter," *DBAT* 8 (1975): 2–10; idem, "Alter und geschichtlicher Hintergrund von Gen 24," *DBAT* 10 (1975): 10–17.

19. Martin Rose, *Deuteronomist und Jahwist: Untersuchungen zu den Berührungspunkten beider Literaturwerke* (ATANT 67; Zürich: Theologischer Verlag, 1981); idem "L'itinérance du Iacobus pentateuchus: Réflexions sur Genèse 35, 1–15," in *Lectio Difficilior Probabilior? L'exégèse comme expérience de décloisonnement: Mélanges offerts à Françoise Smyth-Florentin* (ed. T. Römer; DBAT.B 12; Heidelberg: Wiss.-theol. Seminar, 1991), 113–26.

> My father was an Aramaean about to perish [ארמי אבד אבי]. He went down into Egypt with a few people and lived there and became a great nation, powerful and numerous! (Deut 26:5)

There is no trace of romanticism in this allusion to Jacob: no one is evoking here a wandering nomad! It is rather the exact expression of this "not-wanting-to-know" that characterizes the Deuteronomist's attitude toward Jacob: (1) this father is not mentioned by name, probably because his name is detestable; (2) this father is not an Israelite but an Aramaean, in other words, a foreigner; (3) this father is about to perish; he has no future; and (4) it is his offspring only, the offspring that has come to Egypt, that will become "Israel."[20] For the Deuteronomy/Deuteronomistic tradition, the history of Israel thus indeed begins in Egypt. This is not because the bearers of that tradition did not know of the existence of a Jacob ancestry but because for them Israel's real "ancestor" is not the father (Jacob) but the prophet (Moses).

That scenario became for me the point of departure of a new inquiry. The story of a mere literary persona does not provoke such a negative and even violent reaction unless it is perceived as a danger or a menace to something held dear. Could it not be—that was my next question—that the Jacob cycle represented in fact, not just a saga relating the origins of some proto-Israelite group, as I had suggested in my thesis, but an autonomous legend of Israel's origins, that is, a legend that was meant to stand for itself as a founding story of *Israel* and that required neither a prehistory (Abraham) nor a posthistory (Moses and the exodus)?

2. The Jacob Story as an Autonomous Legend of Origins

Did the Jacob story originally function as an autonomous founding legend of the people of Israel? That thesis can be construed, it seems to me, on the basis of four different literary compositions: (1) the non-Priestly account of the Jacob stories as preserved in the non-P sections of Gen 25–35; (2) the poem of Hos 12; (3) the Jacob story in its P version; and (4) the analogy of the Moses legend (Exod 2–4, non-P).

2.1. The non-P Jacob Story in Genesis 25–35

The non-P (previously called J/E) version of the Jacob story is structured as a triptych, followed by an epilogue that combines various endings and beginnings. Summarily, the Jacob story can be presented in the following way:

---

20. See Albert de Pury, "Le cycle de Jacob comme légende autonome des origines d'Israël," in *Congress Volume: Leuven, 1989* (ed. J. A. Emerton; VTSup 43; Leiden: Brill, 1991), 78–96, 83.

1. Jacob and Esau (first act)

The origin of the conflict and its consequences

Gen 25:19–26   Birth of Jacob and Esau. They struggle within the womb of their mother.

Gen 25:27–34   Esau sells his birthright to Jacob.

Gen 27:1–40   The blessing destined for Esau is fraudulently acquired by Jacob.

Gn 27:41–45   Esau vows revenge. Jacob flees.

Gn 28:10–22   Jacob's encounter with Yhwh (or 'El?) in Bethel (Jacob's Dream)

2. Jacob and Laban

The rise of Jacob

Gen 29:1–14   Jacob arrives at Laban's abode

Gen 29:15–30   Jacob's marriages

Gen 29:31–30:24 Birth of Jacob's children

Gen 30:25–43   Jacob acquires wealth

Jacob's struggle for the independence of his clan

Gen 31:1–21   Deliberations and departure of Jacob and his clan.

Gen 31:22–42   Laban catches up with them; argument

Gen 31:43–32:1   The conflict is resolved. A treaty is concluded.

3. Jacob and Esau (second act)

Solving the conflict with Esau

Gen 32:2–22   Preparing for the confrontation with Esau

Gen 32:23–33   Nightly struggle with an אלהים at the Jabbok. Jacob is blessed and bestowed with the name Israel.

Gen 33:1–17   Meeting Esau; reconciliation.

Epilogue: The ending(s) of the Jacob story and the beginning(s) of the story of the sons of Jacob

Gen 33:18–20   Jacob's arrival in Shechem; altar-building; recognition of אל אלהי ישראל (= ending 1)

Gen 34:1–31   Dinah sequestered. Raid against the Shechemites (beginning 1)

Gen 35:1–5, 7   Jacob and his clan return from Shechem to Bethel (originally to settle there; see v. 1); altar-building; recognition of אל בית אל (= ending 2).

Gen 35:16–20   Birth of Benjamin and death of Rachel (beginning 2)

Gen 35:21–22   Incest of Rueben (beginning 3)

The core of the Jacob story lies evidently in part 2 (Gen 29–31), but these chapters presuppose or announce at least some elements of both parts 1 and 3. The hero is an outcast, a refugee who has been admitted to a foreign clan.

Elements of part 1 are necessary to explain why the hero is on the run. Thanks to his charm and talents, thanks also to his astuteness, the hero gets to marry the daughters of the sheikh, becomes the father of those who will engender the eponymous tribes of Israel, acquires great wealth, and, finally, with the complicity of his wives, succeeds—and that is the decisive breakthrough!– to break loose from the Aramean's clan and to be recognized solemnly as a separate, autonomous clan. After that, there remain only the various obstacles that the hero will have to overcome before reaching his destination—be it Shechem (Gen 33:20) or Bethel (Gen 35:1–5.7)—and installing his clan or nation-to-be in its legitimate northern Israelite territory!

The legend is autonomous in so far as it defines everything a founding legend has to define: the group's origins and complex composition (four mothers of different status), its relationships with its "brothers" or neighbors (Esau/Edom, Laban/Aram, perhaps the Shechemites, etc.), its territorial claims, its cult places (Shechem and/or Bethel, perhaps also Mahanaim and Penuel), its genealogical hierarchy.

The milieu, the chronological setting, and the historical context of such a group remains to be determined. What kind of groups, political entities, or ethnical communities are likely to define their identity through a genealogical legend, such as we have in Gen 25–35*? Is it a tribal society at a prestate level, could it be a kingdom such as the kingdom of Israel (but where is the king?), or is it, after all, a religious community such as the emerging Judaism in postexilic times? We can, of course, make suppositions about the original provenance of the Jacob legend, or of the Moses legend, but it will be difficult to go beyond suppositions. What we should be able to ascertain, however, is at what historical period, and perhaps in what circles, these legends were still alive and functioning as autonomous legends. We are thus looking for traces of a possible precanonical life of these legends; we are calling for witnesses.

So far, we have founded our argument mainly on the internal logic of the non-P Jacob story. But are there some other witnesses that would allow us to corroborate, from the outside, the existence of the Jacob story as an autonomous legend of origin? As I have tried to show elsewhere,[21] there can be adduced three separate witnesses to the existence, in preexilic times, of an autonomous Jacob story and to its function. The first, and the most striking, of these witnesses is the poem of Hos 12.

---

21. See mainly "Situer le cycle de Jacob: Quelques réflexions, vingt-cinq ans plus tard," in Wénin, ed., *Studies in the Book of Genesis*, 213–41.

2.2. The Jacob Story as It Is Reflected in Hosea 12

The interpretation of Hos 12 is a complex and much-discussed topic, and there is no room here to go into many details.[22] A few points can, nevertheless, rapidly be made:

(1) In this poem, Hosea—or the presumed author of Hos 12—reproaches his (presumed) listerners/readers of northern Israel (or "Ephraim," the remnant of it after the debacle of 734) to be the close and naive reincarnation of their ancestor Jacob. Evoking quite a few episodes of the ancestor's life, the poet underlines Jacob/Ephraim's instability,[23] his quarrelsome and violent nature,[24] his fake toughness (Jacob/Ephraim takes aggressive postures but begs and weeps as soon as he is confronted[25]), or his hypocrisy—in fact Jacob/Ephraim is even more corrupt than the Canaanite, that is, the Phoenician merchant proverbially known for his biased scales![26] Jacob is seen in Hos 12 as a pitiful character who, although having been "found" by 'El in Bethel, remains to the end a bitter failure.

(2) The author of Hos 12 progressively builds up a contrast between the ancestor (Jacob) and the prophet (Moses). The climax comes in verses 13–14:

(13) ויברח יעקב שׂדה ארם ויעבד ישׂראל באשה ובאשת שמר

(14) ובנביא העלה יהוה את ישׂראל ממצרים ובנביא נשמר

13: Jacob fled to the plains of Aram / Israel served for a woman / Yes, for a woman he had made himself a keeper!

---

22. On that subject, see my following articles: Albert de Pury, "Osée 12 et ses implications pour le débat actuel sur le Pentateuque," in *Le Pentateuque: Débats et recherches, XIVe Congrès de l'ACFEB (Angers 1991)* (ed. P. Haudebert; LD 151; Paris: Cerf, 1992), 175–207; idem, "Las dos leyendas sobre el origen de Israel (Jacob y Moisés) y la elaboración del Pentateuco," *Estudios Bíblicos* 52 (1994): 95–131; idem, "Erwägungen zu einem vorexilischen Stämmejahwismus: Hosea 12 und die Auseinandersetzung um die Identität Israels und seines Gottes," in *Ein Gott allein? JHWH-Vereh-rung und biblischer Monotheismus im Kontext der israelitischen und altorientalischen Religionsgeschichte* (eds. W. Dietrich and M. A. Klopfenstein; OBO 139; Fribourg: Universitätsverlag; Göttingen: Vandenhoeck & Ruprecht, 1994), 413–39.

23. Hos 12:2a, 13a.

24. Hos 12:2a, 4a, 4b.

25. Hos 12:5 (reading ויכל בכה ויתחנן לו [ ] וישׂר אל; "But El [ ] imposed himself /and (only by) weeping did he (Jacob) 'make it' / and he (Jacob) begged for his mercy!").

26. Hos 12:8–9 ("8: Canaan holds in his hands dishonest scales; he loves to defraud. 9a: But Ephraim says: 'I only enriched myself! I found myself a fortune! 9b: And in all my acquisitions one will not (be able to) find with me (i. e. to prove) (one instance of) crookedness that would be a transgression!' ").

14: But through a prophet has Y_HWH_ brought Israel up from Egypt / Yes,
through a prophet has it (Israel) been kept!

The prophet, of course, is Moses, but if he is designated by his function and
not by his name, it can only mean that it is the function that here is at stake.
Hosea, himself a prophet and affirming his belonging to the line of prophets
(see v. 11), does not oppose two personalities of Israel's past but two conceptions
of Israel's identity. The first conception, quite conventional and symbolized by
the "woman," is genealogical: Israel/the Israelite is born from the tribal ancestor.
The other conception could be called prophetical or "vocational": Israel/the Israelite is the one who has been called by Moses, who has listened to Moses's voice
and has followed him out of Egypt. The "woman" of verse 13, therefore, does
not present Jacob as a "womanizer" but as a "patriarch": she is the mother of the
tribes. But for Hos 12, the only real "ancestor" is the prophet, the one who has
called Israel into existence. No other biblical passage illustrates it more clearly:
the Jacob story and the Moses story originally represent not two consecutive
chapters in Israel's history but *two rival legends* of Israel's origins! The poem of
Hos 12 as a whole must be understood as a plea for the legitimate legend, for
the right "ancestor," for Israel's true identity: in other words, Israel is invited to
choose its ancestor![27]

(3) In the course of his poem, the author of Hos 12 alludes to quite a series
of episodes in Jacob's life. It has been much debated how these allusions relate
to the Jacob stories as we know them from Gen 25–35. Some think that Hos
12 presupposes a completely different story of Jacob, and William D. Whitt has
gone so far as to say that it is Genesis that depends on Hos12 and that the Jacob
cycle has been spun out of the prophetic poem.[28] Whitt suspects, for example,
that the motif of Jacob's two wives—Leah and Rachel—is based on an erroneous
understanding of the double באשה in Hos 12:13b. In that verse, says Whitt,
we have only one woman, as in verse 14 we have only one prophet. I have tried
to look at the matter from all angles and have come to the conclusion that in
its substance, the Hosean allusions presuppose a Jacob story quite close to the
one we know from Genesis.[29] In fact, it is quite surprising that the five verses of

27. Albert de Pury, "Le choix de l'ancêtre," *TZ* 57 (2001): 105–14; idem, "Choisir l'ancêtre.
Jacob, Moïse et Abraham comme figures d'une identité collective dans l'Ancien Testament," in *Le
fait religieux: Cours de la chaire UNESCO de religions comparées 1999–2002* (ed. A. Charfi; Tunis:
Edition Sahar, 2005), 39–59.

28. William D. Whitt, "The Jacob Traditions in Hosea and their Relation to Genesis," *ZAW*
103 (1991): 18–43.

29. De Pury, "Situer le cycle de Jacob," 227–35.

Hos 12 that are concerned with Jacob are able to allude to more than a dozen episodes or features we know from the Genesis Jacob:

+ the twin birth (v. 4a; Gen 25:21–26)
+ the etymology of the name *Jacob* (v. 4a; Gen 25:26; 27:36)
+ the pushing aside of the brother (v. 4a; Gen 25:21–26; 25:29–34; 27:1–45)
+ the struggle with a divine adversary (v. 4b; Gen 32:23–33)
+ the etymology of the name *Israel* (v. 5a; Gen 32:19)
+ the ambiguous victory of the patriarch (v. 5a; Gen 32:27, 30–31)
+ the unsolicited theophany in Bethel (v. 5b; Gen 28:10–22; 35:1, 7)
+ the promise of safe return and of divine protection (v. 7; Gen 28:15, 21; 31:13)
+ the acquisition of wealth by doubtful means (v. 9; Gen 30:25–31:19)
+ the cairns of stones in Galeed (v. 12b; Gen 31:46–54)
+ Jacob's flight to Aram (v. 13a; Gen 27:43–45; 29:1; in P: Gen 28:2, 6–7)
+ the voluntary service for a woman (v. 13b; Gen 29:15–30)
+ the keeping of herds for a woman (v. 13b; Gen 30:25–42)

All parts of the Jacob story, including the two theophanies, find themselves reflected in Hos 12. The evocation of the various episodes obviously does not follow the chronological order of the Genesis story, but, as we shall see, that does not imply a reference to a differently structured narrative.

(4) Much of the debate has been aimed at the date of the oracle collections of the book of Hosea and of Hos 12 in particular. Martti Nissinen[30] and others have proposed to bring that date down to postexilic times.[31] Of course, in the absence of material evidence and of Carbon-14 dates, anything is conceivable in biblical exegesis. But if the substance of Hosean tradition is removed from the preexilic period, nothing is explicable any longer. To me, a strong argument for the antiquity of the Hosean oracle collections has been formulated by Grace I. Emmerson:[32] the Judaean annotations—in Hos 12, they are easily identified in

30. Martti Nissinen, *Prophetie, Redaktion und Fortschreibung im Hoseabuch: Studien zum Werdegang eines Prophetenbuches im Lichte von Hos 4 und 11* (AOAT 231; Kevelaer: Butzon & Bercker; Neukirchen-Vluyn: Neukirchener, 1991).

31. Cf. along the same lines, Thomas Römer, "Osée," in idem et al., *Introduction à l'Ancien Testament*, 383–98.

32. Grace I. Emmerson, *Hosea: An Israelite Prophet in Judean Perspective* (JSOTSup 28; Sheffield: JSOT Press, 1984), 56–116, 158–59.

verses 1b and 6, especially in 1b!—are themselves quite obviously preexilic. That feature of a still preexilic Judaean rereading practically locks up the whole of the Hosean collections in the time of the monarchy. The book of Hosea, in its substance, has probably been put to writing soon after the fall of the kingdom of Israel, perhaps in conjunction with the book of Amos.[33]

That means that between 720 and 700 B.C.E. the Jacob cycle also must have had an (at least) oral existence. It may also have existed in written form, but Hos 12 shows that the Jacob stories were present in the minds and memory of the poet's listeners or readers. Hosea 12 is indeed one of the only biblical texts that allow us to observe directly the functioning of oral tradition. The Jacob story does not have to be retold by the Hosean poet, and the allusions to that story do not have to respect the sequential order of the episodes in the narrative: obviously it suffices for his audience to hear one word or one allusion to make the connexion, immediately, with the well-known story.

2.3. The Jacob Story as Told in the Work of P^g

The Priestly Work (P^{g}[34]) is the only element of the Wellhausen system to have survived the storm that has struck pentateuchal studies since the 1970s. Even if some important scholars such as Rendtorff and Van Seters consider P a redactional layer, reworking and reinterpreting an older text without suppressing it, the mere fact that the P elements can be isolated rather easily and then joined together without practically any loss suggests very strongly that P^g was originally indeed an independent and autonomous work, standing for itself (so David Carr,[35] Eckart Otto, Thomas Pola, and many others). The well-known and much-discussed problem pertains to the question of the work's end. Does P^g extend to the death of Moses (Deut 34:1, 5, 7–9) or even to the death of Joshua (Josh 18:1; 24:29b)? Thomas Pola,[36] Erich Zenger,[37] and Eckart Otto[38] have

---

33. See Jörg Jeremias, "Die Anfänge des Dodekapropheton: Hosea und Amos," in *Congress Volume: Paris, 1992* (ed. J. A. Emerton; VTSup 61; Leiden: Brill, 1995), 87–106; idem, *Hosea and Amos: Studien zu den Anfängen des Dodekapropheton* (FAT 13; Tübingen: Mohr Siebeck, 1996).

34. By the siglum P^g, we designate the *Priestergrundschrift*, the original work before its junction with other pentateuchal material (or, more precisely, the introduction into the frame formed by P^g, of other material, be it older or younger) and before its supplementation by secondary material (narrative or legislative) redacted in the priestly style or thematic.

35. David M. Carr, *Reading the Fractures of Genesis: Historical and Literary Approaches* (Louisville: Westminster John Knox, 1996), 43–140.

36. Thomas Pola, *Die ursprüngliche Priesterschrift: Beobachtungen zur Literarkritik und Traditionsgeschichte von P^g* (WMANT 70; Neukirchen-Vluyn: Neukirchener, 1995).

37. Erich Zenger, "Priesterschrift," *TRE* 27 (1997): 435–46.

38. Eckart Otto, "Forschungen zur Priesterschrift," *TRu* 62 (1997): 1–50.

given very strong arguments to opt for a short original Priestly work (P^g) extending only to the building of the sanctuary in the desert. Pola sees its end in Exod
15:22; 16:1; 19:1; 24:15b–18a; 25:1, 8a, 9; 29:45–46; 40:16, 17a, 33b. For the
part of P^g in Genesis, the attributions are subject to much less controversy. There
is, it seems to me, an emerging consensus that P^g at least—that is, the original
Priestergrundschrift—was an independent, well structured, and carefully crafted
literary work. As Konrad Schmid has argued, P^g may even represent the first
"history of the origins" that set out to englobe in its project the creation of the
universe and humankind (Adam to Noah and his sons), the history of the patriarchs (Abraham to Jacob), and the history of the birth of the people of Israel
and of Moses' call (Moses to Sinai).[39] As far as P^g's Jacob story is concerned, we
will again have to limit ourselves to a few remarks:[40]

The structure of P^g is as follows:

Part 1: History of Humankind

Gen 1:1–2:4a	Creation of heaven and earth and humankind
Gen 5:1–32	Linear genealogy from Adam to Noah
Gen 6:9, 11–22; 7:6, 11, 13–16abα, 17–21, 24	The flood
Gen 9:1–17, 28–29	God's *berit* in favor or Noah, humanity, and all living beings
Gen 10:1–7, 20, 22–23, 31–32	Segmented genealogy of the sons of Noah: Table of Nations

Part 2: History of the Abrahamides

Gen 11:10–28a.	Linear genealogy from Shem to Abra(ha)m
Gen 11:29–32; 12:4b, 5	Transmigration of the Abrahamic clan to Harran and Canaan
Gen 13:6, 11b, 12	Separation from Lot
Gen 16:3, 15–16	Birth of Ishmael
Gen 17:1–13, 15–27	Theophany to Abra(ha)m of Yнwн under the name El Shaddai. Institution of a double ברית: first in favor of Abraham

39. Konrad Schmid, *Erzväter und Exodus: Untersuchungen zur doppelten Begründung der Ursprünge Israels innerhalb der Geschichtsbücher des Alten Testaments* (WMANT 81; Neukirchen-Vluyn: Neukirchener, 1999).

40. For a more extensive treatment of that matter, see Albert de Pury, "Der priesterschriftliche Umgang mit der Jakobsgeschichte," in *Schriftauslegung in der Schrift: Festschrift O.H. Steck* (ed. R. G. Kratz et al.; BZAW 300; Berlin: de Gruyter, 2000), 33–60.

and his multinational descendants (vv. 1–14. "a mass [המון] of peoples," v. 5). The land of Canaan is given to them, and they all must have their sons circumcised on the eighth day; then in favor of the yet-to-be-born son of Sarah and of his particular descendants (vv. 15–21): they are called to "live before the face of 'Yhwh'" (cf. v. 18!). The circumcision is accomplished by Abraham and Ishmael (vv. 23–27).

Gen 19:29	Salvaging Lot
Gen 21:1b–5	Birth of Isaac
Gen 23:1–20	Death of Sarah; acquisition of the cave of Machpelah
Gen 25:7–10	Death of Abraham; his burial by Ishmael and Isaac
Gen 25:13–17	List of the twelve sons of Ishmael
Gen 25:20	Marriage of Isaac and Rebekah
Gen 26:20	Birth of <Jacob and Esau>
Gen 26:34–35;	Esau's marriages with the daughters of Het; disappointment of Rebekah. Jacob sent to Laban to get a wife for himself; marriage of Esau with a daughter of Ishmael.
Gen 35:6aα, 11–15	Jacob arrives in Luz (Bethel) and receives promise of numerous descendants ("an assembly [קהל] of peoples") and of the land. He raises a *massebah*. (…)
[lacuna]	Jacob's stay with Laban and marriage to Laban's daughters; birth of the sons of Jacob [These elements were probably left out because the non-P Jacob story told them much along the same lines.]
Gen 31:18*; 35:9–10	The return of Jacob and his family. While he is on his way, God gives him the name *Israel.*
Gen 35:27–29	Arrival of Jacob in Mamre; death of Isaac; burial of Isaac by Esau and Jacob in the cave of Machpelah
Gen 36:40–43	List of the eleven chiefs of Esau
Gen 37:1	Jacob settles in Canaan.
Gen 46:6–7; 47:27b–28	Jacob and his sons descend to Egypt [no Joseph story!]
Gen 49:1a, 28bβ, 29–33	Jacob blesses his sons and asks them to bury him in the cave of Machpelah. Death of Jacob.
Gen 50:12–12	Jacob's sons bury him in the cave of Machpelah.

Part 3: History of the vocation of the sons of Israel

Exod 1:1–5a	List of the twelve sons of *Israel* who came to Egypt with their father [one must reinstitute the mention of Joseph]
Exod 1:7–2:25*	The oppression of Israel in Egypt
Exod 6:2–12	The call of Moses; the revelation of the name of Yhwh
Exod 7:1–5	Aaron is adjoined to Moses.
Exod 7:6–11:10*	Pleading before Pharaoh; the plagues of Egypt
Exod 12:37a–13:20*	Leaving Egypt

Exod 14:1–29*   Crossing the sea; Pharaoh's army is engulfed into the sea.

Exod 15:22; 16:1;   Arrival at Sinai; Yʜwʜ calls Moses from the mountain.
19:1; 24:15b–18a

Exod 25:1, 8a, 9;   Yʜwʜ orders Moses to build a sanctuary. Moses completes the
29, 45–46; 40:16, work.[41]
17a, 33b

If, within Pᵍ's global project, we single out the sequence that corresponds to the life of Jacob, we notice that Pᵍ's Jacob story has the same skeletal structure as the non-P Jacob cycle, although with a completely different narrative substance, all "problematic" episodes having disappeared. The birth of Jacob and Esau engenders no conflict between the twins, and the departure of Jacob is motivated only by his parents' fear that he might follow Esau's example in marrying a daughter of Het. The stay of Jacob in Paddan-Aram is alluded to, but its actual recounting is missing. These few verses, apparently, have been lost when the non-P story was introduced into the Pᵍ matrix. The verses telling the return of Jacob from Paddan-Aram to his father's abode in Canaan have been preserved, but in an obviously perturbed state. As Gunkel already had argued in his commentary of 1910,[42] the scene of Gen 35:6.9–15 in the Masoretic Text results from the conflation of two different theophanies: the theophany of Bethel (Gen 35:6aα, 11–15); and the divine encounter at Penuel (31:18; 35:9–10). In the original Pᵍ text, the first theophany (v. 6aα, 11–15) had its place before the lacuna and the second one after the lacuna. When we replace the verses in their original order (as has been done in the above outline), we see that Pᵍ's Jacob story bears the same strucure as the older, non-P story.

We can conclude from these observations that the author of Pᵍ knew the Jacob story well but deliberately purged it of all that seemed incompatible with his understanding of the behavior of God's chosen partners. For our purpose, that means that Pᵍ does indeed attest the existence of an older Jacob story that included at least one episode about Jacob and Esau, the theophany in Bethel, the stay with Laban, the encounter at Penuel, and Jacob's return to his father. But that does not mean that Pᵍ knew the Jacob story as already connected to stories about Abraham and Isaac or as serving as prelude to the story of Israel in Egypt. In the time of Pᵍ, the Jacob story still could have had its autonomous status.

---

41. The end of Pᵍ, according to the proposal of Pola, *Die ursprüngliche Priesterschrift*, 213–98.
42. Gunkel, *Genesis übersetzt und erklärt*, 384–87; cf. de Pury, "Der priesterschriftliche Umgang," 46–48.

2.4. The Jacob Story as Reflected in the Story of Moses' Youth (Exodus 2–4)

In 1987 Ronald Hendel drew attention to the fact that the story of Moses' youth has surprising similarities to the Jacob story.[43] Both Moses and Jacob are forced to flee after a transgression committed during a conflict. Both seek refuge outside their land and end up meeting girls at the well. Both find shelter in the families of these girls, and both become the sons-in-law of the sheikh who has welcomed them to his abode. In both cases, the decision to come back—brought about by, among other factors, an intervention of God—is a turning point in the mission of the hero. From that point on, both Moses and Jacob have to confront various ordeals and overcome countless obstacles before they finally reach home and can start with their mission proper. Among the ordeals, the hero in both stories is attacked during the night by his divine patron (Gen 32:23–33; Exod 4:24–26).

These similarities suggest that the story of Exod 2–4 may have been influenced in part by the Jacob story. If indeed there was a rivalry between the Jacob and the Moses stories as the founding legend of Israel, the aim of the Exodus narrator could have been to present Moses as a kind of new Jacob. Of course, there also are in the story of Moses' birth and youth elements that fully belong to the situation of the qualification of a prophet or that reflect the credentials of a charismatic leader: the endangered birth, the education received in the very seraglio of the enemy court, the discovery of the people's oppression, the solitude in the desert, the call and the prophet's numerous objections, the ordeal. But the irony is that the very feature that is constitutive of the Jacob story and makes it into a genealogical legend of origins—the hero getting a wife or wives and begetting a son or sons—remains a blind motif in the Moses story. Moses begets a son, of course, but this son plays no role whatsoever in the subsequent story or in the definition of Mosaic Israel's collective identity. This is a clear sign that the structure shown by Hendel is "natural" or primary in the Jacob story, whereas it is "artificial" or secondary in the Moses story. It is in that sense that the Moses legend, which has often been dated to the Assyrian period,[44] can serve as a witness to the existence of an old and autonomous Jacob story and, probably, to its rival status as founding legend of Israel.

What Hos 12 shows us, too, is that the Moses legend of origins was carried, within eighth-century Israelite society, by prophetic circles. Even in its definitive literary elaboration, the story of "Mosaic Israel" bears the traits of a prophetic

---

43. Ronald S. Hendel, *The Epic of the Patriarch: The Jacob Cycle and the Narrative Traditions of Canaan and Israel* (HSM 42; Atlanta: Scholars Press, 1987).

44. See Thomas L. Thompson, *The Literary Formation of Genesis and Exodus 1–23* (vol. 1 of *The Origin Tradition of Ancient Israel;* JSOTSup 55; Sheffield: JSOT Press, 1988).

Utopia. The antitribal and antigenealogical taint of the Moses story, manifest in the evocation of the archaic Levites in Exod 32:25–29; Deut 33:8–11 or, in adverse perspective, Gen 49:5–7, suggests that some of the prophetic guilds functioned as brotherhoods. For the sociological roots of "Jacobian Israel," represented by the Jacob legend, they must be sought, most probably, in the tribal elites, that is, in the formerly feudal land aristocracy of northern Israel and Transjordan.

How long did these rival legends remain separate, both on the conceptual and on the literary level? That remains an open question. The Deuteronomists of Deut 26:5–9 apparently know that those who will become the actors of the Mosaic legend of origins are the descendants of that wretched Aramean they refuse to name, of Jacob.[45] So it is probable that the *idea* that the Israelites called into being by Moses were none other than the descendants of Jacob had already made its way and was not an invention of P^g. But that does not preclude the possibility, and indeed the probability, that P^g was the first writer to have ventured to link together both stories on a *literary* level and to make out of the Jacob legend a prelude to the Moses story within a comprehensive literary project, thus in a way reconciling two stories that had been considered incompatible by prophetic and Deuteronomistic circles.

3. P^g, the Jacob Story, and the Formation of the Pentateuch

If we come back to the the work of P^g as a whole, as it appears in the synopsis above, two further remarks must be made. First, for P^g—compared with the Deuteronomy/Deuteronomistic tradition—history does not begin in Egypt but starts with the creation of heaven and earth, at the beginning of time and space. Whereas the animal world in all its variety and the human species, with its unique, kingly vocation, appear on the stage of the universe in the first act, and whereas all nations—the offspring of Shem (representing, probably, in the eyes of P^g the inhabitants of the Achaemenid Empire), but also the offspring of Ham (in the south) and of Japheth (in the north and the west), settle the entire surface of the earth and the isles of the sea, each "according to their clans, their languages, their countries, and their nations" (Gen 10:5, 20–21, 31, 32a) in the final scene of part 1, the people of Israel appear on the stage only in the final act, at the beginning of part 3![46] This alone shows that in the world of humans

---

45. The descent of Jacob and his retinue to Egypt (without mention of the story of Joseph) is mentioned also in 1 Sam 12:8 and Josh 24:4. In Gen 46:27, the descendants of Jacob are numbered seventy, which is also the number of the "fathers" arriving in Egypt according to Deut 10:22. All these passages are recognized to be later than the first Deuteronomist, and also later than P^g.

46. On P^g and the table of nations, see Albert de Pury, "Sem, Cham et Japhet: De la fraternité à l'esclavage?" in *Koryphaiô andri: Mélanges offerts à André Hurst* (ed. A. Kolde et al.; Genève: Droz, 2005), 495–508.

the sons of Israel are not meant to be just another nation but that they will have a mission of their own within the community of nations. Israel's fundamental and perhaps only mission is to build and keep the sanctuary (מקדש and משכן, Exod 25:8a, 9) that will allow Yhwh to reside among the sons of Israel and, through them, among humankind.

Second, Pᵍ's Jacob story is completely embedded in the story of the Abrahamides and does not bear its own theological weight. With the exception of the change of name (Gen 35:10), the words spoken by God to Jacob (Gen 35:11–12; cf. 28:3–4) are a mere repetition of those addressed to Abraham. The ברית, with all its inherent promises (Gen 17:1–8: the multinational offspring, begetting kings [i.e., forming states], the right to live in the land of Canaan, the promise to be "their God") and obligations (Gen 17:9–13: the circumcision), is founded with the multinational Abraham, not with the "national" ancestor Jacob. For the final, canonical book of Genesis, as well as for traditional Jewish and Christian exegesis, these promises are understood, of course, to have been "refocused" at each generation on a specific branch of the genealogical tree— Isaac and not Ishmael, Jacob and not Esau!—but within Pᵍ there is not a single text that would found, justify, or even presuppose this progressive narrowing of the list of beneficiaries of the ברית. Pᵍ knows of no expulsion of Hagar and Ishmael, of no phasing out of Esau. In his view, both Ishmael and Esau remain in the land, and quite legitimately so: they are present at their father's burial in the cave of Machpelah (Gen 25:9; 35:29), and their descendants doubtlessly share the task with the descendants of Jacob of maintaining in Hebron the patriarchal mausoleum as a place of common pilgrimage. Again, the only specific task of the sons of Israel will be to "live before the face of 'Yhwh,'" that is, to take care of the cult and to be the "priests of humanity," since that is the only role denied by God to Ishmael (Gen 17:18).[47] In the project of Pᵍ, the specific vocation of the sons of *Israel* unfolds in part 3, starting in Exod 1:1. Within part 2, Jacob and his sons have as their only, modest function to be the link between the Abrahamic community of nations and the "sons of Israel" who finally emerge to their proper destiny in the Moses story. On that point at least, Pᵍ stays in some sense close to the Deuteronomistic view: for him, too, Israel's specific history starts in Egypt!

These observations should lead us, if I see it correctly, to the following conclusions.

(1) The author of Pᵍ is not a minor redactor trying to correct or emend, or even to reformulate, an existing literary work: he is a conceptor, an architect,

---

47. For that interpretation of Gen 17 and the role of Abraham for Pᵍ, see Albert de Pury, "Abraham, the Priestly Writer's 'Ecumenical' Ancestor," in *Rethinking the Foundations: Historiography in the Ancient World and in the Bible: Essays in Honour of John Van Seters* (ed. S. L. McKenzie and T. Römer; BZAW 294; Berlin: de Gruyter, 2000), 163–81.

and a creator. He, the first, has conceived the project to write, not so much a history of the origins of Israel, but a history of God's universal project. The role of Israel in this project is pivotal but also surprisingly discreet: Israel will allow Yнwн to take his abode among humankind, in a location and according to a model that are not even defined yet. For the time being, that משכן has a virtual existence, somewhere out there in the Sinai, but the aim—not yet formulated—is to rebuild the temple and therewith to guarantee the permanence of the wonderful world order founded in Gen 1 and 9 and the regional order inaugurated in Gen 17. The author of P^g is definitely an individual and not a school, even though the later elaboration of the so-called Priestly legislation is surely the work of a school.

(2) What is the date or the historical insertion of P^g? It has been recognized for over a century that P^g is not imaginable before the exile. As a growing number of scholars see it, he is not imaginable before the beginning of the Persian era either. Just like Deutero-Isaiah, he manifestly has been touched by the "euphoria" of the advent of Cyrus. Many traits of his work could be shown to be in "dialogue" with the ideology of Cyrus, most notably his favorable view of the diversity of nations, cultures, ... and forms of religion. P^g is the one biblical author who admits some kind of history and geography of religion: according to him, Yнwн has not revealed his name—that is, his intimate name, his cult name—to others than the sons of Israel through Moses (Exod 6:2–3), but that does not mean that the great ancestors of humankind (or of parts of humankind) like Noah or Abraham did not know the real, true, and only God. Geographically, that implies that the other contemporary humans—Ishmaelites, Edomites, ... even these sons of Het (Gen 23:6!) whose daughters one should not marry!—recognize the one and only God. That novel theological paradigm, so different from the Deuteronomists' conventions and even from Deutero-Isaiah's, is a direct adaptation of the Achaemenid doctrine (perceptible already in the Cyrus Cylinder). P^g is also the author who seems to have "invented" the linguistic convention to use the appellative "god" as a divine name (i.e., without article or determinative), that is, to designate the universal god as אלהים, or to call "the god" "God" (with a majuscule initial).[48] Genesis 1, which could be read as the charter of the new worldview bears as a whole the mark of the Cyrus era.[49]

---

48. See Albert de Pury, "Gottesname, Gottesbezeichnung und Gottesbegriff: 'Elohim als Indiz zur Entstehungsgeschichte des Pentateuch," in *Abschied vom Jahwisten: Die Komposition des Hexateuch in der jüngsten Diskussion* (ed. J. C. Gertz et al.; BZAW 315; Berlin: de Gruyter, 2002), 25–47.

49. See Albert de Pury, "Genesis 1 in Its Historical Context and Today's Ecological Concerns," in *Listening to Creation Groaning* (ed. L. Vischer; John Knox Series 16; Geneva: Centre International Réformé John Knox, 2004), 61–74.

That gives us for P^g a *terminus a quo* of 539 B.C.E., the entry of Cyrus into Babylon. For the *terminus ad quem,* we cannot, in my view, go beyond the end of Cyrus's reign, and that for several reasons: the pharaoh remains in the work of P^g the only real enemy. Egypt was indeed the only major power to have stayed outside the huge empire Cyrus had just founded. Cyrus had planned to conquer Egypt, but the task was carried out, five years after his death, by his successor Cambysses (530–522), between 525 and 522. Starting with Darius (522–486), the Persian king invested himself so thoroughly into his new role of pharaoh[50] that a hostile portrait of the pharaoh could no longer have been envisaged by a pro-Persian author. Another telling sign could be the extraordinary concern of P^g for the formation of a kind of fraternity or "ecumenism" between the populations of southern Palestine by their inclusion into an Abrahamic genealogy. When one knows that the Edomites and Ishmaelites had profited from the collapse of the Assyrian and Babylonian Empires to penetrate and settle precisely these southern marshes of Palestine at the end of the seventh and beginning of the sixth century, one cannot but wonder to see them treated with such benevolence. The reason is probably that as long as Egypt was not integrated into the Persian commonwealth, the south of Palestine remained a "sensitive border region." Cultivating an Edomite-Ishmaelite-Judean entente must have responded to Persian interests, and P^g is manifestly playing into the Persians' hands. The last argument pertains to the perspectives of the reconstruction or reinstallation of the temple of YHWH in Jerusalem. Many commentators have been intrigued by P^g's vagueness about any concrete measures in that sense: neither the model—Pola is certainly right in considering the transformation of the מקדש of Exod 25:8–9 into a transportable tabernacle as a secondary, post-P^g development[51]—nor the location are elaborated in any way. This can only mean that great precautions still had to be taken not to rush the Persian authorities nor to provoke Samaritan opposition. Such precautions would no longer have been necessary after 520. We are therefore led to situate P^g's work under the reign of Cyrus, let us say between 535 and 530,[52] a span of a decade at most, which is, for biblical standards, a surprisingly narrow window.

(3) This setting of a fairly early date, considering today's more radical tendencies, for the composition of P^g enables us to understand the huge impact

---

50. Cf. Pierre Briant, *Histoire de l'empire perse: De Cyrus à Alexandre* (Paris: Fayard, 1996), 490–93; English translation: *From Cyrus to Alexander: A History of the Persian Empire* (trans. P. T. Daniels; Winona Lake, Ind.: Eisenbrauns, 2002), 481–84.

51. Cf. Pola, *Die ursprüngliche Priesterschrift,* 312–18.

52. These arguments have been brought forward in de Pury, "Der priesterschriftliche Umgang," 39–40 but with an unfortunate slip in the dates of the end of the reign of Cyrus. Read 535–30 instead of 530–525!

that this, as such rather concise, work was to have on the start of the processus that led to the formation of the Pentateuch. In the books of Genesis and Exodus, the often meager thread of the Priestly narrative constitutes a sort of watershed, at which the exegete will have to determine what is earlier and what is later than P^g. Every time the question will be: What does P^g presuppose; on what does he look back? And to what does P^g give rise? What reaction does he provoke? It seems to me, as we have seen, that P^g does presuppose both the Jacob and the Moses story, but in a still unconnected state. P^g of course does not reproduce these literary works, but he formulates them anew and, by integrating them into his big project, gives both of them a new turn. For the rest, notably for the *Urgeschichte* (Gen 1–11*)[53] and for the Abraham story (Gen 12–25*),[54] the situation is different: all extant non-P text material seems to presuppose P, or even to have been provoked by it.

The figure of Abraham as such was probably that of a local intertribal and intercommunal ancestor, hero, or saint, linked to his "cave" or "rock"[55] in Hebron, a *genius loci* that enjoyed great popularity not only among Judeans but also among the inhabitants of the desert fringes who visited the Hebron market. If P^g chose this interethnic figure of the local folklore to make out of him the father of all the desert and mountain people of southern Palestine, he doubtless responded not only to Persian interests but also to local demand. But let us remember that for the circle of Ezekiel, the Abrahamic "melting pot" had provoked only anger and disgust![56] Here again P^g acts as creator. Before him Abraham had not yet been integrated into a unified genealogy of Israel's ancestors. It is clear also that the motif of Abraham's immigration from Mesopotamia has been taken from the Jacob tradition and imposed on Abraham by P^g. All the non-P stories of Gen 12–25 presuppose the framework created by P^g.

Let us conclude by coming back, one last time, to the Jacob story and its fate at the outset of the formation of the Pentateuch. We can propose the following scenario. (a) The extant non-P Jacob story in Gen 25–35* is, in its substance, a preexilic and originally north Israelite patriarchal *gesta*, representing one of ancient Israel's major legends of origins. Notwithstanding this claim,

---

53. See, e.g., Eckart Otto, "Die Paradieserzählung Genesis 2–3: eine nachpriesterschriftliche Lehrerzählung in ihrem religionshistorischen Kontext," in *"Jedes Ding hat seine Zeit...": Studien zur israelitischen und altorientalischen Weisheit. Festschrift D. Michel* (ed. A. A. Diesel et al.; BZAW 241; Berlin: de Gruyter, 1996), 167–92; Markus Witte, *Die biblische Urgeschichte: Redaktions- und theologiegeschichtliche Beobachtungen zu Genesis 1,1–11,26* (BZAW 265; Berlin: de Gruyter, 1998).

54. See de Pury, "Genèse 12–36," in Römer et al., *Introduction à l'Ancien Testament*, 134–56, 150–53.

55. See Isa 51:1.

56. See Ezek 33:23–39.

it may very well be that some elements or whole episodes of today's Genesis Jacob story are less old or have replaced older versions of that particular episode. Doubts have been voiced concerning the "Bethel layer" or the birth story of Jacob's sons: Do they belong in their present form to the oldest form of the Jacob *gesta*?[57] Perhaps not. But the possible lateness of this or that feature of the present non-P Jacob story does not invalidate, however, the claim that the Jacob *gesta*, as a whole, is old and functioned as a tribal or national legend of origin.

(b) In the wake of the rejection by prophetic circles of the Jacob tradition, as illustrated by the poem of Hos 12, the Jacob legend of origin has been subjected to what amounts to a *damnatio memoriae*. The Deuteronomists do not want to know the Jacob legend and do not mention it in their historical works, with the notable exception of Deut 26:5–9, a passage that precisely confirms the will to silence the Jacob tradition.

(c) Conceiving and building his own work, P^g sets out to situate the founding of Israel's mission within a history of God's work in the world, where history of humankind and the history of the regional Abrahamic *oikoumene* play a major role. Within that project, P^g takes over the mere structure of the old Jacob story and uses it as a narrative and genealogical link between parts 2 and 3 of his work. However, he does not take over the narrative substance of the old Jacob story, which he surely dislikes as much as the Deuteronomists do. Nevertheless, thanks to his symbolic reintegration of the contested father figure, he sets the stage for a later reintegration of the full and unadulterated old Jacob story.

(d) In the wake of the choice of the P^g work as blueprint and framework for the Pentateuch-to-be, the redactors responsible for the compilation, enriching, and completion of the successive editions of the Pentateuch will introduce in it countless new stories or other elements. But in a few cases, some of these "new" stories may in fact have been traditional, recuperated stories, older than P^g. This is certainly the case with the non-P Jacob story. Here, thanks to these redactors, one of the really old—and for the afterworld unforgettable—Israelite legends was saved from *damnatio* and oblivion. Why was that old story recuperated? We do not know. It may have been antiquarian interest. But it may also be that very soon in the fifth century, the theological climate turned away from P^g's peaceful "humanism" and readopted a more nationalistic and combative view of Israel's place in the world. In that context, the scenes of Jacob despoiling Esau or cheating on Laban might have been considered much less offensive. And in any case, from an emotional and esthetic point of view, the non-P Jacob makes for better literature than the P^g Jacob: the Pentateuch would not have been the same without it!

---

57. On that question, see de Pury, "Situer le cycle de Jacob," 237–40.

THE TRANSITION BETWEEN THE
BOOKS OF GENESIS AND EXODUS*

Jan Christian Gertz

I realize I am not saying anything new when I describe the recent discussion about saying farewell to the Yahwist as multifaceted—almost so multifaceted as the various Yahwists presented by scholars of the last decades. The points disputed by the advocates of the Yahwist hypothesis are familiar. Texts ascribed to the Yahwist are generally considered to be multilayered, yet a consensus in explaining this widely acknowledged point is, however, not in sight. Disunity surrounds also the extent and dating of the Yahwist's work, and it is perhaps here that the differences are the most apparent. A similar polyphony in past research surrounds the characterizations of the Yahwist and his work. On the one end, there are those who still speak of a salvation-historical account drafted by a theologian from Solomonic times; on the other end, there are those who argue for a work composed by an anti-Deuteronomic redactor in the exilic period who aimed to explain the origins of the Diaspora. Still others describe the work as an account of Israel's history written by a post-Deuteronomistic author. With respect to all the disputed points, we are not dealing with peripheral details. To the contrary, the debate concerns our fundamental understanding of the nature of the literary work.

Yet it is perhaps fairer and more helpful for the ongoing discussion when one focuses on the minimal consensus among the proponents of the thesis of the Yahwist, rather than emphasizing the dissension. This minimal consensus consists in the basic agreement that there is a running narrative thread of pre-Priestly material in the Tetrateuch.[1] By way of this thread, the Yahwist purportedly con-

---

*The original wording of the lecture has been maintained. In order to respond to at least some of the responses, I have added "5. The First Connection between the Patriarchal Cycles and the Exodus Narrative in P." I am grateful to Dr. Jacob Wright for help in translating the manuscript.

1. What follows does not relate to a specific version of the Yahwist thesis but rather to the minimal consensus specified above—regardless of the question whether the respective advocate of the thesis subsumes the pre-Priestly Pentateuch under the term "Yahwist."

nected the essential components of the various accounts into the transmitted sequence of historical events.[2] Although the end of the pre-Priestly narrative is disputed, there is a consensus that the pre-Priestly Tetrateuch created by the Yahwist comprised at least three sections: the primordial history in Gen 1–11; the patriarchal cycles (including the story of Joseph); and the exodus narrative.[3] A good place to begin testing the thesis of the Yahwist is thus in the literary seams between these three sections of texts.

1. Explicit or Implicit Cross-references: How Does One Establish the Unity of the Yahwist?

One can investigate the connections between the various sections of the pentateuchal narrative on various levels. Opponents of the Yahwist thesis like to focus on the *explicit* cross-references between the narrative sections.[4] Here the situation is fortunately very clear. For some texts, like the final form of Gen 15, there is no room for doubt that they have the entire Pentateuch in view and that they secondarily integrate larger narrative units that originally did not belong together. Yet all in all there is a very small number of these redactional passages, and an increasing number of scholars consider them to be the youngest additions to the Pentateuch. Thus, I would accept the widespread view that the prolepsis of the exodus in Gen 15:13–16 represents a post-Priestly supplement to the primary stratum of Gen 15, which itself is very late.[5] An analysis of the explicit cross-references produces, therefore, unfavorable results for the thesis of the Yahwist.

Consequently, proponents of the thesis of the Yahwist prefer an alternative approach. They treat the explicit cross-references as late attempts to augment the coherency of the preexistent narrative.[6] In order to maintain the thesis,

---

2. See Christoph Levin, *Der Jahwist* (FRLANT 157; Göttingen: Vandenhoeck & Ruprecht, 1993), 9: "Es *muß* im vorpriesterschriftlichen Material des Tetrateuchs ein redaktioneller Faden vorhanden sein, der einen beträchtlichen Teil des unterschiedlichen Stoffs erstmals zu der vorliegenden Abfolge des heilsgeschichtlichen Geschehens verknüpft hat."

3. Representative is the view of Otto Kaiser, *Die erzählenden Werke* (vol. 1 of *Grundriss der Einleitung in die kanonischen und deuterokanonischen Schriften des Alten Testaments;* Gütersloh: Gütersloher Verlagshaus, 1992), 63.

4. Thus Konrad Schmid, *Erzväter und Exodus: Untersuchungen zur doppelten Begründung der Ursprünge Israels innerhalb der Geschichtsbücher des Alten Testaments* (WMANT 81; Neukirchen-Vluyn: Neukirchener, 1999).

5. For further bibliographical references, see Jan Christian Gertz, "Abraham, Mose und der Exodus: Beobachtungen zur Redaktions-geschichte von Gen 15," in *Abschied vom Jahwisten: Die Komposition des Hexateuch in der jüngsten Diskussion* (ed. J. C. Gertz et al.; BZAW 315; Berlin: de Gruyter, 2002), 63–81.

6. See David M. Carr, "Genesis in Relation to the Moses Story: Diachronic and Synchronic Perspectives," in *Studies in the Book of Genesis: Literature, Redaction and History* (ed. A. Wénin;

they emphasize the *implicit* cross-references as well as conceptual and linguistic characteristics that represent the point of departure for postulating a unified literary work. To be sure, the discussion shows that it is much more difficult to attain unanimity in interpreting this textual evidence. Thus, the way one assesses the linguistic peculiarities of the Yahwist, which have often been catalogued,[7] depends upon one's general approach. This applies even for the way one interprets the allusions in the motifs. I would like to mention at least one example: Gen 12:10–20 evinces a strong similarity to the accounts of the plagues in Exod 7–11.[8] Does this text constitute a prolepsis of the exodus within a literary work comprising the patriarchal narratives and the exodus account,[9] or does it represent an attempt to reclaim the exodus tradition for an independent corpus of patriarchal narrative?

The difficulties are due not least to a procedure in which a thesis—in this case, the existence of the Yahwist—is postulated experimentally in order to verify or—less often—to falsify it on the basis of its heuristic value for extremely complex literary evidence. Such a procedure seems unavoidable, yet it requires a cross-examination that does not presuppose the thesis in question. In our case, this means that the Yahwist thesis must prove its validity in the literary seams connecting the various sections of the pentateuchal narrative. In consideration of the emphases in current research, I will concentrate my attention on the transition from the patriarchal narratives to the exodus account.

BETL 155; Leuven: Leuven University Press; Peters, 2001), 273–95, esp. 276–83; Christoph Levin, "Das israelitische Nationalepos: Der Jahwist," in *Große Texte alter Kulturen: Literarische Reise von Gizeh nach Rom* (ed. M. Hose; Darmstadt: Wissenschaftliche Buchgesellschaft, 2004), 63–85. See these works for the following discussion.

7. A prominent example is the "Lexikon des Jahwisten" in Levin, *Jahwist,* 399–408.

8. Gen 12:17 shares the term נגע ("stroke") in common with Exod 11:1. The paragraph Exod 11:1–3 presupposes the integration of the Priestly document into the non-Priestly exodus narrative. See Levin, *Jahwist,* 335–39; Jan Christian Gertz, *Tradition und Redaktion in der Exoduserzählung: Untersuchungen zur Endredaktion des Pentateuch* (FRLANT 186; Göttingen: Vandenhoeck & Ruprecht, 2000), 176–77. If Gen 12:17 depends upon Exod 11:1, then it also presupposes the integration of P into the non-Priestly exodus narrative. See Levin, *Jahwist,* 141–42. It is, however, conceivable that author of Exod 11:1 drew upon נגע, which is not used elsewhere in the account of the plagues in Exod 7–11, from Gen 12:17 in order to refer the reader back to Gen 12:10–20.

9. Carr, "Genesis in Relation," 278–79, and Levin, *Jahwist,* 141–42, view Gen 12:10–20 as a prolepsis of the exodus. Carr ascribes Gen 12:10–20 to the texts that combine Genesis and the Moses story at the pre-Priestly level, whereas the text is, according to Levin, later than the connection between P and the Yahwist. That Abraham, in the present form of the text, anticipates the path taken by God's people is quite evident. Nevertheless, this may not have been always the intended interpretation, inasmuch as Gen 12:10–20 is part of a series of texts that relegate the historical importance of Moses and the exodus in favor of Abraham.

2. The Transition from the Patriarchs and Joseph to Moses in the Priestly Document

On the level of P, the patriarchal narratives and the exodus account are connected by means of a tight and well-formed link. This is demonstrated by a glance at the commission of Moses in Exod 2:23aβ–25; 6:2–7:7*: God's revelation to Moses is explicitly placed in continuity with the patriarchal period. According to P, God's intervention in Egypt to save his people is the direct consequence of his "covenant" with Abraham, Isaac, and Jacob. Simultaneously, this text singles out the promise of an enduring divine relationship from the various pledges to the patriarchs in Gen 17*, and this promise is then honored in the announcement of Yhwh's dwelling amidst Israel in Exod 29:45–46 (P). Insofar as it has correlated the creation account and the beginning of the Sinai pericope,[10] P has interwoven the themes of creation, the patriarchs, the exodus, and Sinai into an intricate fabric.

For the sections of the pentateuchal narrative that P has so masterfully integrated, it appears that P presupposed the basic substance of the non-Priestly material. However, it does not follow from this generally accepted conclusion that the sequence and connection of the material already existed in the sense of a pre-Priestly Tetrateuch—unless one cannot imagine P being capable of such a profound intellectual accomplishment.

I would like to elaborate on this point by briefly examining the Joseph story. According to the usual division of the sources, P does not provide a version of the non-Priestly novella of Joseph and his brothers as we know it today. Instead, the succinct narrative in P concentrates on the *eisodos* of the clan of Jacob. Although this story is told quite succinctly, it is much more detailed than the non-Priestly Joseph novella. It seems, therefore, that P was cognizant of the connection between Joseph and Egypt. The extent and purpose of this connection is, however, an unsettled issue.

3. The Joseph Novella and the Post-Priestly Supplements to Genesis 50

In examining the non-Priestly texts, we are voyaging into terra incognita. Nevertheless, it is widely acknowledged that the patriarchal narratives and the story of the exodus were originally transmitted separately.[11] This also applies to

---

10. For the structural parallels between Gen 1:1–2:3 and Exod 24:15b–18aα; 25–31; 35–40, see Jon D. Levenson, "The Temple and the World," *JR* 64 (1984): 275–98, 286–89; Bernd Janowski, "Tempel und Schöpfung: Schöpfungstheologische Aspekte der priesterschriftlichen Heiligtumskonzeption," *JBT* 5 (1990): 37–69, 46–67.

11. For older English literature, see, e.g., Frederick V. Winnett, *The Mosaic Tradition* (Near and Middle East Studies 1; Toronto: University of Toronto Press, 1949); idem, "Re-examining

the Joseph novella. Already Martin Noth argued that the latter was conceived specifically for the transition from the patriarchal narrative to the story of the exodus.[12] Yet this thesis is undermined not only by the often noted friction between the Joseph novella and the story of the exodus but also by the problem that the Joseph novella does not concentrate single-mindedly enough on the *eisodos,* which supposedly represents this work's overarching theme. Indeed, the theme appears at times to constitute a subsidiary objective of the novella. The approaching exodus is the subject of only several passages: the paragraph in Gen 46:1–5*, which is usually ascribed to a redactional hand;[13] the conclusion of the book in 50:22–26; and the notice in 48:21, which depends upon this conclusion.

The actual *eisodos* is portrayed only in one verse in the Joseph novella: Gen 50:14. One cannot help but notice that after this verse the narrative in 50:15–21 switches gears, so to speak, by depicting the reconciliation of Joseph and his brothers. The presentation of the brothers finding out about the death of their father in verse 15 is simply out of place directly after the presentation of Joseph and his brothers returning to Egypt at the conclusion of the extended funeral ceremonies. Verse 15 "seems to envisage a different situation at the death of Jacob from the preceding verse."[14] Thus, verse 14b attempts to resolve the chronological confusion with the gloss "after he buried his father," which is absent in the LXX. In order to account for the literary evidence, scholars have argued that the entire reconciliation scene in Gen 50:15–21 or the burial of Jacob in Canaan has been added.[15] The problem with this radical solution is that both of these paragraphs are inseparably integrated into the rest of the Joseph novella. The same cannot be said for Gen 50:14*. Within the non-Priestly text,

---

the Foundations," *JBL* 84 (1965): 1–19; John Van Seters, "Confessional Reformulation in the Exilic Period," *VT* 22 (1972): 448–59; Norman E. Wagner, "Pentateuchal Criticism: No Clear Future," *Canadian Journal of Theology* 13 (1967): 225–32.

12. Martin Noth, *Überlieferungsgeschichte des Pentateuch* (3rd ed.; Darmstadt: Wissenschaftliche Buchgesellschaft, 1966), 226–32.

13. For a different take on this text, see Hermann Gunkel, *Genesis* (HKAT 1/1, Göttingen: Vandenhoeck & Ruprecht, 1901), 481–82; Erhard Blum, "Die literarische Verbindung von Erzvätern und Exodus: Ein Gespräch mit neueren Endredaktionshypothesen," in Gertz et al., *Abschied vom Jahwisten,* 119–56, here 131–32; Schmid, *Erzväter und Exodus,* 62–63. These scholars do not see a reference to the exodus here. For a diachronic analysis of Gen 46:1–5*, see Gertz, *Tradition und Redaktion,* 273–81.

14. Donald B. Redford, *A Study of the Biblical Story of Joseph (Gen 37–50)* (VTSup 20; Leiden: Brill, 1970), 31.

15. See, e.g., Levin, *Jahwist,* 310–11, as well as Ludwig Schmidt, *Literarische Studien zur Josephsgeschichte* (BZAW 167; Berlin: de Gruyter, 1986), 212–13, who ascribes Gen 50:1–11, 14* to the Yahwist and Gen 50:15–21* to the Elohist.

the return is connected to the narrative progression solely—and poorly—by means of Gen 50:8b. Whereas verse 8a speaks of the "all the household of Joseph and his brothers and the house of his father," the notice in verse 8b presents the little ones and the cattle remaining in Egypt. It appears to be a secondary and rather unsuccessful attempt to provide a reason for the repeated trip to Egypt. On the basis of these observations, Konrad Schmid has recently proposed that Gen 50:14a (as well as 50:7b, 8b) is redactional. According to his thesis, the reconciliation scene in 50:15–21 originally followed directly after 50:11 (50:12–13 belongs to P).[16] The second part of this solution seems to me quite plausible. It is undeniable that the depiction of the brothers becoming aware of their father's death and the consequences of it, as well as the reconciliation of the brothers, is well suited to the situation of a burial. If Gen 50:14* does not belong to the primary stratum of the Joseph novella, then this work originally concluded with an account of the clan of Jacob back in Canaan.

Who, then, is responsible for Gen 50:14*? The friction between verses 14a and 15 as well as the attempt to smooth out this friction by means of the gloss in 14b indicate that the Joseph novella has undergone expansions. In general, redactors adapt themselves to the traditions that they are transmitting; we would thus expect a purely redactional notice of return after verse 21. Accordingly, Gen 50:14* belongs to a source. Because this verse is isolated within the non-Priestly text, I would assign it to P, in which a corresponding notice is missing after verses 12–13.[17] There are no linguistic reasons to reject this proposal.[18] On the other hand, it would be strange if precisely the Priestly Joseph story, which treats solely the *eisodos*, did not contain such a notice. Moreover, the redactional process in Gen 50 becomes much clearer if verse 14* is ascribed to P.

We may now turn to Gen 50:14, 15–22. The information with respect to the place of Joseph and his father's house in Egypt as well as Joseph's age in verse 22 has been ascribed to P by an increasing number of scholars, who point out the correspondence of this information to Gen 47:27–28.[19] As far as the notice

---

16. See Konrad Schmid, "Die Josephsgeschichte im Pentateuch," in Gertz et al., *Abschied vom Jahwisten*, 83–118. For a critical assessment of the isolation of v. 14, see John Van Seters, review of Konrad Schmid, *Erzväter und Exodus: Untersuchungen zur doppelten Begründung der Ursprünge Israels innerhalb der Geschichtsbücher des Alten Testaments*, Review of Biblical Literature (2000), n.p. Online: http://www.bookreviews.org/pdf/231_245.pdf; and his contribution in this volume.

17. See Walter Dietrich, *Die Josephserzählung als Novelle und Geschichtsschreibung: Zugleich ein Beitrag zur Pentateuchfrage* (BTS 14; Neukirchen-Vluyn: Neukirchener, 1989), 44 n. 118.

18. This applies especially for the change from "his (Jacob's) sons" (vv. 12–13) to "Joseph…, he and his brothers" (v. 14a), which provides a segue from the burial of the father to death notice in v. 22b that necessarily concentrates on Joseph.

19. See Dietrich, *Josephserzählung als Novelle und Geschichtsschreibung*, 44 n. 118; Erhard Blum, *Studien zur Komposition des Pentateuch* (BZAW 189; Berlin: de Gruyter, 1990), 364 n. 14.

on Joseph's age is concerned, this conclusion is merited. Yet for verse 22a one should consider whether it does not represent a graphic *Wiederaufnahme* of 14a connecting it to Gen 50:15–21.

14a   וישב יוסף מצרימה הוא ואחיו וכל־העלים אתו לקבר את־אביו
22a   וישב יוסף במצרים הוא ובית אביו

If so, verse 22a would be part of the redaction responsible for the integration of P and the non-Priestly Joseph novella. This redaction would have attached the original end of the non-Priestly Joseph novella to the *eisodos* notice of P and woven it together with P by means of the *Wiederaufnahme* of verse 14a (P) in verse 22a. In this manner, the important finale of the non-Priestly Joseph novella would take place in Egypt and would function in the final redaction of the text—just as it is already in P—as the transition to the exodus narrative.

The evidence in Gen 50:22b–26 substantiates our findings. As already mentioned, verse 22b belongs to P. From the information on Joseph's age, a later redactor drew the conclusion in verse 23 that Joseph lived to see the third generation of his descendants.[20] In verse 26a, the original narrative strand of P resumes with the notice on Joseph's death.[21] Whether 26a belongs to P is still an open question. The problem is complicated by the slight aberrations in the formulation of the notice on Joseph's age and the repetition in the conclusion to the notice of his death. We can easily explain both on the assumption that non-Priestly material is once again to be read together with P.[22] However, in contrast to the preceding paragraph, this text does not represent a piece of the non-Priestly Joseph novella but rather purely redactional material. Although the paragraph in Gen 50:24–26 is a mixture of Priestly (v. 26a) and non-Priestly texts (vv. 24–25, 26b), on the level of the transmitted context it seems to be unified. This text reports not only Joseph's final words to his brothers but also his death, age, and (preliminary) burial. With regard to its form, we notice a chiastic correspondence of the essential statements; this structure would topple if even one of these statements were removed:[23]

David M. Carr, *Reading the Fractures of Genesis: Historical and Literary Approaches* (Louisville: Westminster John Knox, 1996), 109–10, includes v. 26a. Rudolf Smend Sr., *Die Erzählung des Hexateuch auf ihre Quellen untersucht* (Berlin: Reimer, 1912), 108–9, argued that only the age notice in v. 22b stems from P. Levin, *Jahwist*, 315, adopts Smend's approach.

20. Levin, *Jahwist*, 316.

21. Blum, *Studien zur Komposition des Pentateuch*, 364, n. 14; Carr, *Reading the Fractures of Genesis*, 109–10.

22. Blum, *Studien zur Komposition des Pentateuch*, 364 and n. 14.

23. Following Norbert Lohfink, *Die Landverheißung als Eid: Eine Studie zu Gn 15*, (SBS 28; Stuttgart: Katholisches Bibelwerk, 1967), Erhard Blum, *Die Komposition der Vätergeschichte*

50:24	die/ visit	שבע/עלה + פקד יפקד/מות niphal
	+ bring up / swear	
50:25, 26a	swear /visit	מות/עלה + פקד יפקד/ hiphil שבע
	+ bring up/die	

Insofar as the author of this artistically composed paragraph employs the notice of Joseph's death in verse 26a, he is to be identified with the hand that reworked P in this passage. The paragraph has been composed verse for verse with a continuation in the exodus narrative and thus functions to bridge the time of Joseph to that of Moses. From all this, it follows that the text is post-Priestly.

Other observations support this conclusion; here there is space to mention only several of them.[24] After Gen 50:25, Joseph makes the Israelites swear to take his bones when they leave Egypt to settle in the promised land. Genesis 50:26b describes the necessary preparations for the fulfillment of the oath. The oath is then fulfilled in Exod 13:19 and Josh 24:32 with explicit references to Gen 50:25–26. Additionally, the notice in Josh 24:32 refers with the same wording to Gen 33:19, which reports that Jacob bought a piece of land in Shechem. Genesis 50:25–26 thus emerges in a literary complex whose two central features—the possession of land in Shechem and the transportation of Joseph's bones—are combined in Josh 24:32 and simultaneously have their point of departure there. One finds it difficult to deny the priority of this combination of the burial and the purchase of land, especially if Josh 24:32 presupposes an older burial tradition. Genesis 50:25–26. and Exod 13:19 treat the secondary technical problem of how the death of Joseph, which is certainly not original, is connected to the burial tradition in Shechem. Genesis 50:25–26 (and probably also 33:19) is thus formulated with Josh 24:32 in view. Moreover, the Old Testament often reports the fulfillment of pronouncements like Joseph's in Gen 50:25. It is therefore difficult to attribute Josh 24:32 to a late addition that depends upon Gen 33:19; 50:25–26; and Exod 13:19. Indeed, on the basis of their close conceptual and literary ties, these passages can be assigned to one and the same literary layer, or (Gen 33:19;) Gen 50:25-26; and Exod 13:19 may be dated after Josh 24:32. The fulfillment of Gen 50:25–26 in Exod 13:19 has been identified by

---

(WMANT 57; Neukirchen-Vluyn: Neukirchener, 1984), 256 (recently he has adopted a different approach; see his *Studien zur Komposition des Pentateuch*, 363, as well as "Die literarische Verbindung von Erzvätern und Exodus"); Hans-Christoph Schmitt, "Die Josephsgeschichte und das Deuteronomistische Geschichtswerk" (1997), in idem, *Theologie in Prophetie und Pentateuch* (BZAW 310; Berlin: de Gruyter, 2001), 295–308, here 296–97. More arguments for the unity of Gen 50:24–26 are provided by Gertz, *Tradition und Redaktion*, 361–63.

24. On this point, see Blum, *Studien zur Komposition des Pentateuch*, 363–64; Schmitt, "Die Josephsgeschichte," 295–300; Gertz, *Tradition und Redaktion*, 364.

various scholars as post-Priestly.[25] Since M. Noth, most scholars have viewed the conceptual goal and literary point of departure, Josh 24:32, as a post-Deuteronomistic supplement. V. Fritz has demonstrated the dependency of this verse on the burial traditions for Abraham in Gen 25:9 and Jacob in 50:13 as well as the depiction of Abraham purchasing the cave of Machpelah in Gen 23. These texts belong to P.[26] Accordingly, we should probably posit a post-Priestly origin for Gen 50:25–26—and presumably also for 33:19. The transition from the Joseph story to the exodus narrative in 50:24–26 proves to be a redactional supplement postdating the integration of the Joseph novella into P.

Now, it is of course conceivable that not only fragments of P but also non-Priestly remains of the Joseph novella have been transmitted in the post-Priestly paragraph Gen 50:24–26. In considering the various possibilities, Joseph's announcement of his death in Gen 50:24 appears as the only candidate. This notice demands a corresponding death notice. The line in verse 26a belongs, however, to P. Aside from this, verse 26 in its present form cannot be separated from the post-Priestly verse 25. Within a possible pre-Priestly context, verse 26 is accordingly precluded as a continuation to verse 24. What remains is the death notice in Exod 1:6, which has been repeatedly claimed for a pre-Priestly seguence from Joseph to Moses.[27] Yet Exod 1:6 connects better to the Priestly—if not post-Priestly—genealogy in Exod 1:1–5. The information on the death of Joseph and his brothers as well as the entire generation in Exod 1:6 presupposes their enumeration in Exod 1:1–5. That is also demonstrated by the likelihood that the generalizing statement on the death of the entire generation (יוסף וכל-אחיו) in Exod 1:6 has received its information from Exod 1:1b and 5a.[28] Conversely, the postulated direct sequence of Gen 50:24 (Joseph

---

25. See Gertz, *Tradition und Redaktion,* 207–9 (and the further bibliographical references there).

26. Of course one could argue that the idea of claiming land by burying ancestors in it is a widespread, cross-cultural idea. See Brian B. Schmidt, *Israel's Beneficent Dead: Ancestor Cult and Necromancy in Ancient Israelite Religion and Tradition* (FAT 11; Tübingen: Mohr Siebeck, 1994). Nonetheless, it is difficult to deny that the relevant texts in the Hexateuch must be assigned to P or an even younger stratum. Yet even when one does not follow Fritz in ascribing Josh 24:32 to a post-Priestly redaction, one must at least identify the verse with a redactional expansion of Josh 24, a Deuteronomistic text. This means that the verse must be a post-Deuteronomistic expansion. Thus one has achieved little for the attempt to ascribe Gen 50:25 to a Yahwist. What remains is only the necessity of claiming a Hexateuch perspective for this Yahwist.

27. Blum, *Studien zur Komposition des Pentateuch,* 364, sees this connection in Gen 50:24 and Exod 1:6, 7*, 8. (A fundamental revision of his own position is provided in Blum, "Die literarische Verbindung von Erzvätern und Exodus" 145–51.) Carr, "Genesis in Relation," 291–93, isolates the pre-Priestly link in 50:24–25 and Exod 1:6, 8.

28. See Schmitt, *Literarische Studien zur Josephsgeschichte,* 297, as well as Gertz, *Tradition und Redaktion,* 360 (with n. 42 and the bibliographical references provided there).

announces his death to his brothers and their exodus from Egypt) and Exod 1:6 (Joseph and his brothers die) does not lack a certain tragicomedy.

4. The Exodus-Narrative and the Post-Priestly Supplements to Exodus 1

Since we cannot discover a pre-Priestly bridge to the narrative of the exodus in Gen 50, we turn our attention in conclusion to the opposite bank, namely, Exod 1:6, 8–10. The repetition of the death notice for Joseph in Exod 1:6, as well as the genealogy of Israel's son in Exod 1:1–5, may be due to the division of the books. Yet it is also conceivable—in analogy to the transition from the time of conquest to the period of the judges (Josh 24:29 and Judg 2:8–10)—that the repetition of the death notice together with Gen 50:26 and Exod 1:8 marks the epochal transition from the patriarchal period to the time of Moses. Whatever the case may be, even here the genealogy in Exod 1:1–5 is presupposed by Exod 1:6, since it is difficult to imagine a direct sequence of both death notices.[29] Furthermore, verse 6 refers directly to 1b and 5a, as observed above.

With respect to Exod 1:8, one observes first that together with verse 6 the memory of the Joseph story and its *drammatis personae* has been consistently eradicated. The respect enjoyed by Joseph in Egypt and the servitude of the Israelites are mutually exclusive, and thus Joseph was removed with one stroke of the pen. Regardless of the redaction to which one ascribes this editorial activity, it constitutes solid evidence that the connection between the narratives in the books of Genesis and Exodus postdates the primary literary stratum of the texts. No one would dispute that Exod 1:8 belongs inseparably to Gen 50:24–26 (and possibly also Exod 1:[1–5,] 6). Genesis 50:24–26 has been formulated verse for verse for a continuation of the narrative in the book of Exodus. Conversely, Exod 1:8 presupposes a notice regarding Joseph's death, as indicated not least by the introduction of a new ruler as one "who did not know Joseph" (אֲשֶׁר לֹא־יָדַע אֶת־יוֹסֵף, v. 8b). We have classified Gen 50:24–26 as post-Priestly. It follows that Exod 1:8 is also post-Priestly, and this conclusion is confirmed by Exod 1:9–10. That the new Egyptian ruler notices the dangers posed by the Israelites connects smoothly to Exod 1:8, yet this depiction also refers beyond this verse. Conceptually, the fear on the part of the new ruler about the increasing numbers of the Israelites requires that Israel had already become a great nation. This is reported, however, solely in Exod 1:7—a verse (or at least it oldest layer) that clearly belongs to P. Accordingly, Exod 1:9–10 presupposes P.

---

29. For a different view, see John Van Seters, *The Life of Moses: The Yahwist as Historian in Exodus-Numbers* (Louisville: Westminster John Knox, 1994), 16–19.

Against this argument, D. M. Carr has objected that an author or narrator can also present new information on the lips of the *dramatis personae*.[30] Exodus 1:8–10 would then make sense without the help of P. Although that is certainly correct, it does not take the terminological parallels between verses 9 and 7 (P) seriously enough. Whereas the depiction of the servitude in verses 11–12 describes the growth of the Israelites with רבה "to become many" and פרץ "to spread" (v. 12), the Egyptian ruler refers in verse 9 to a "numerous and mighty" (רב ועצום) people. This statement is anticipated in verse 7 (P), and that is hardly coincidental. Scholars have treated the line "and they increased and became mighty" (וירבו ויעצמו) in verse 7 as secondary because of the evident correspondence to verse 9, which is usually attributed to the Yahwist. Yet the reasons presented for isolating a supplement within verse 7 are, in my view, unconvincing.[31] Another observation should be given greater weight: verse 9 plays a significant role for the thesis of the Yahwist. It is supposed to function as a hinge between the patriarchal promises and the exodus. Here Exod 1:9 is read as the fulfillment of the promise to Abraham in Gen 12:2, according to which he would become a great nation. For the present context, this reading is certainly possible and probably also intended, yet it is hardly Yahwistic. The connection between Gen 12:2 and Exod 1:9 is at most conceptual, since the formulation of Exod 1:9 עם רב ועצום is not the expected correspondence to the promise of a גוי גדול in Gen 12:2. For the only Yahwistic link between the patriarchal promises and the exodus from Egypt, one would have wished for a more explicit reference.

Our findings in Exod 1:1–10 confirm our interpretation of the evidence in Gen 50. This literary bridge between Genesis and Exodus has been built by P (Exod 1:[1–5,] 7, 13–14) and a younger hand (Exod 1:6, 8–10). Whether the beginning of the formerly independent non-Priestly narrative of the exodus is to be found in Exod 1:11 (J. C. Gertz), Exod 2:1 (D. M. Carr; C. Levin;

---

30. Carr, "Genesis in Relation," 291.

31. For the arguments, see Gertz, *Tradition und Redaktion*, 366–67. Scholars who eliminate וירבו ויעצמו base their decisions on the fact that this expression is not typical for P. One, however, overlooks that after the removal of these two words the language does not completely comport with the rest of P's notices for the growth of Israel. Perhaps P is not so monotonous as has been claimed. Whatever the case may be, if one treats these two words as secondary (even when there are not strong formal literary-critical arguments for this approach), one has still not achieved anything for the transition from the Yahwist to the exodus narrative. The relevant references for the putative expression are found in late Deuteronomistic passages (see Deut 7:1; 9:1; 26:5). Those who deny that the verse in its present form is the work of P must concede that it appears to be a composite of Priestly and Deuteronomistic language, which happens to be characteristic for those redactional layers that combined the Priestly document with the non-Priestly material. For a defense of this thesis, see Levin, *Jahwist*, 315, who ascribes v. 7 to a post-Priestly redactor.

K. Schmid), or Exod 3:1 (F. V. Winnett)[32] is a problem for itself and is not directly related to the discussion of the existence or nonexistence of a Yahwist.

5. The First Connection of the Patriarchal Cycles to the Exodus Narrative in P

In questioning the minimal consensus that there is a running thread in the pre-Priestly material of the Tetrateuch that included at least the primordial history, the patriarchal cycles (with the Joseph story), and the narrative of the exodus, many proponents of the thesis of the Yahwist raise the question whether P represents the first comprehensive literary source of the Tetrateuch. I have embraced the popular assumption that P presented an account extending from the primordial history to the Sinai pericope and have demonstrated in my study of the transitional texts Gen 50–Exod 1 that the oldest literary connection between the patriarchs/Joseph and Moses was constructed by P. Thus, as far as one can ascertain, P deserves the recognition for the intellectual feat of both sequentially arranging the patriarchal accounts and the story of the exodus into one and the same literary context and providing a conceptual basis for the sequence. In what follows, I will attempt to add precision to the thesis as a way of response to a methodological objection and several misunderstandings.

First, according to the methodological objection I have transferred the minimal consensus of the proponents of the hypothesis of the Yahwist to the P source. My proposal is said to be the *petitio principii* that "[t]here must be a Priestly thread in the Pentateuch to have created the coherence of the whole."[33] With respect to my assignment of the *eisodos* notice in Gen 50:14* to P, this disagreement cannot be immediately dismissed. Indeed, I have attributed the verse, which certainly appears to stem from some source, to P because it lacks a fitting place within the non-Priestly material and a similar notice is missing in P.[34] One may designate this argumentation as "highly speculative," yet in contrast to the hypothesis of the Yahwist no one would deny that the explicit cross-references in P indicate that this stratum includes both the patriarchal cycles and the exodus narrative. To be sure, the well-known correspondence between creation and Sinai, as well as the covenant theology as an overall concept from Noah to Moses by way of Abraham and Jacob, requires the assumption of a Priestly sequence from the patriarchs/Joseph to Moses. For this

---

32. See Gertz, *Tradition und Redaktion*, 381; Carr, "Genesis in Relation," 293–94; Levin, *Jahwist*, 317–20; Schmid, *Erzväter und Exodus*, 152–57; Winnett, *Mosaic Tradition*, 27–28; "Re-Examining the Foundations," 18–19.

33. This approach has been taken by Levin in his very prudent response. See also n. 2 above.

34. See §3 above.

reason, I would also refer to my suggestions for the Priestly texts in Gen 50 and Exod 1 as "controlled speculation," a discipline that has characterized (literary-) historical research from its inception.

Second, it is necessary to refine our thesis, especially when it comes to understanding the degree of originality of P's presentation of Israel's history. What we observe elsewhere applies also to literary history: powerful ideas, insights, and conceptions did not develop *ex nihilo* in ivory towers and then later take hold in the general consciousness. Even when their origins are occasionally difficult or impossible to determine, they represent the products of various ideas and discourses, which presuppose specific historical conditions, and they also establish themselves under contingent conditions and in unpredictable ways. Here I cannot elaborate on this basic conviction either in general or as it pertains to P; important is rather that we acknowledge a significant intellectual prehistory for P's arrangement of the patriarchs and Moses. With respect to the general historical and intellectual background, it suffices to point out that the subsequent formation of Judaism between the exile that began with the downfall of Samaria and the early Second Temple period, on the one hand, and the formation of the earlier Pentateuch, on the other, coincide both chronologically and conceptually and are mutually dependent. (Those who propose a late date for the Yahwist or who dismiss the thesis of the Yahwist altogether agree on this point.)

Intellectual discourses from formative Judaism have made themselves felt in the various conceptions of Israel's identity as the people of God. As prominent examples, one could cite the patriarchal cycles and narrative of the exodus, which were transmitted independently of each other, as well as (from a later time) the Priestly *unified* presentation of Israel's origins. Because of the paucity of our sources, we cannot reconstruct all the particulars of these discourses. Nevertheless, one observes that the historical sequence of the patriarchs and Moses was a hotly disputed topic in the exilic and postexilic periods. This is explicitly the case in those texts that are cognizant of the controversial conception in P as this source was still independently transmitted. Examples of these texts are "das kleine geschichtliche Credo" in Deut 26:1–11[35] as well as those non-Priestly passages in Genesis that transfer the central importance of Moses and the exodus to Abraham and the patriarchal period, such as Gen 15*[36] and perhaps also Gen

---

35. Jan Christian Gertz, "Die Stellung des kleinen geschichtlichen Credos in der Redaktionsgeschichte von Deuteronomium und Pentateuch," in *Liebe und Gebot: Festschrift for Lothar Perlitt,* (ed. R. G. Kratz and H. Spieckermann; FRLANT 190; Göttingen: Vandenhoeck & Ruprecht, 2000), 30–45.

36. For Gen 12:10–20, see nn. 8–9 above. For Gen 15, see Gertz, "Abraham, Mose und der Exodus." It should be emphasized, however, that allusions to P within the pre-Priestly substratum in

12:10–20. Other texts such as Gen 16:1–11*[37] grapple in a similar way with the story of the exodus, but they do not yet appear to be familiar with the Priestly conception. They belong to the prehistory of the connection between the patriarchal cycles and the narrative of the exodus just as much as the sharp contrast between the Jacob story and the tradition of the exodus in Hos 12[38] as well as the juxtaposition and mingling of the patriarchs and the exodus in Second Isaiah.[39] Against the background of this discussion, one must refine the thesis that P was the first to connect the patriarchal and the exodus stories inasmuch as P's contribution is restricted to *the first literary work* presenting the patriarchal story and the narrative of the exodus as successive episodes in the history of Israel's origins.

6. SUMMARY

The non-Priestly Joseph novella originally concluded with the reconciliation of the brothers at the grave of their father in the land of Canaan (Gen 50:1–5a, 5b*, 6–7a, 8a, 9–11, 15–21). At this stage of the text's literary development, there is no connection to the story of the exodus. P does not offer a parallel version to the Joseph novella as we know it; instead, the succinct narrative focuses on the *eisodos* of Jacob's sons to Egypt. Similarly, the depiction of the exodus in P resumes this narrative strand and embeds it into the encompassing presentation of Israel's history (Gen 50:12–14a, 22b, 26a; Exod 1:[1–5,] 7, 13–14; 2:23aβ–25; 6:2–7:7*). In this way, P provides the earliest (and almost uninterrupted?[40]) literary transition from the patriarchs and Joseph to Moses. The connection between the patriarchal stories and the narrative of the exodus was first introduced and conceptually established by P, a literary innovation that

---

Gen 15 should not be played down (see vv. 7, 17–18). If Gen 15* belonged to the latest material in the patriarchal narrative as it was still independently transmitted, its author was very probably familiar with the Priestly conception. The difference is that this author was writing for a different literary work.

37. Thomas Römer, "Isaac et Ismaël, concurrents ou cohéritiers de la promesse? Une lecture de Genèse 16," *ETR* 74 (1999): 161–72.

38. Albert de Pury, "Le cycle de Jacob comme légende autonome des origines d'Israël," in *Congress Volume: Leuven, 1989* (ed. J. A. Emerton; VTSup 43; Leiden: Brill, 1991), 78–96; and idem, "Osée 12 et ses implications pour le débat acuel sur le Pentateuque," in *Le Pentateuque: Débats et recherches, XIVe Congrès de l'ACFEB (Angers 1991)* (ed. P. Haudebert; LD 151; Paris: Cerf, 1992), 175–207; Reinhard G. Kratz, "Erkenntnis Gottes im Hoseabuch," *ZTK* 94 (1997): 1–24, esp. 16–17, 22–23.

39. Schmid, *Erzväter und Exodus*, 266–70.

40. That P's introduction of Moses may have been lost is considered by Gertz, *Tradition und Redaktion*, 251–52 with n. 84 (bibliography).

won the day in the subsequent traditions. Once it originated, all succeeding redactors were required to embrace this connection as the historically accurate and theologically intended sequence. Thus, the transition was embellished as P was integrated with the non-Priestly Joseph novella and the non-Priestly narrative of the exodus (Gen 50:8b, 22–26*; Exod 1:6, 8–10). This was necessitated not least by the failure of the independently transmitted non-Priestly stories to compete with a unified and continuous historical portrayal. To state our conclusion differently, the string holding the pearls of the non-Priestly pentateuchal narratives was furnished by P!

THE LITERARY CONNECTION BETWEEN
THE BOOKS OF GENESIS AND EXODUS
AND THE END OF THE BOOK OF JOSHUA*

Erhard Blum

The Documentary Hypothesis, which has been a hallmark in pentateuchal research for generations, has in the last thirty years been losing ground, especially in German research, where the hypothesis had originally been established in the early nineteenth century. Only one of its elements is still valid: the differentiation between Priestly (P) and non-Priestly material. All other components of the classical hypothesis now are controversial. This holds true regarding the differentiation between J and E as well as for the basic supposition of the existence of a non-Priestly source, starting with Gen 2 and ending either in the book of Numbers or in the first chapter of Judges.

To some extent this process of breakdown has been concealed, since there are scholars who still designate certain texts as J, even though they do not mean the Yahwist as posited by the Documentary Hypothesis. A prominent example is the Yahwist of Van Seters.[1] This work has no counterpart in an Elohistic source nor in an independent P-document (he considers the Priestly material a *redac-*

*This article was first published in Hebrew in Zipora Talshir and Dalia Amara, eds., *On the Border Line: Proceedings of a Conference in Honor of Alexander Rofé On the Occasion of His Seventieth Birthday* (Hebrew) (Beer-Sheva 18; Beer-Sheva: Ben-Gurion University of the Negev Press, 2005), 13–32. My thanks go to Mrs. Judith Seeligmann, Jerusalem, for the translation into English; to my colleague Prof. David Carr, New York, for additional assistance in editing; and to the editors for the publishing permission. See also Erhard Blum, "Die literarische Verbindung von Erzvätern und Exodus: Ein Gespräch mit neueren Endredaktionshypothesen," in *Abschied vom Jahwisten: Die Komposition des Hexateuch in der jüngsten Diskussion* (ed. J. C. Gertz et al.; BZAW 315; Berlin: de Gruyter, 2002), 119–56.

1. John Van Seters, *Abraham in History and Tradition* (New Haven: Yale University Press, 1975); idem, *Prologue to History: The Yahwist as Historian in Genesis* (Zürich: Theologischer Verlag, 1992; idem, *The Life of Moses: The Yahwist as Historian in Exodus-Numeri* (CBET 10; Kampen: Kok Pharos, 1994).

tional addition to what he designates as J). In fact, the Yahwist (J) of Van Seters contains all the texts that J.Wellhausen attributed to the combined J and E, that is to say, to the Jehovist (R^JE). Nevertheless, its character differs altogether from the older JE, since Van Seters regards his J as a uniform composition, the work of a single author, very similar to the *Histories* of Herodotus. Another example of a "new" J is the Yahwist as postulated by C. Levin,[2] who refers by this designation to a redactional stratum originating during the Babylonian exile. On the one hand, Levin's J holds texts from the book of Genesis previously attributed to E (e.g., Gen 22). On the other hand, this J contains only few passages from the books of Exodus and Numbers. In my opinion, these labelings are misleading, since they blur discontinuities with traditional research.[3]

In a way it was already H. Gunkel who unintentionally prepared the ground for the disintegration of J.[4] Gunkel observed that within the stories of the ancestors there are separate "story cycles," such as the story of Jacob-Esau-Laban or the novella about Joseph and his brothers, which in the main are self-contained, each of them having its own prehistory. He saw the origin of these narratives in an oral tradition existing before the documents of J and E. However, it can be argued that these cycles reflect units that existed in writing. It is for this reason that we can still delineate their outlines, whereas it is hardly ever feasible to reconstruct the contours of oral traditions. Moreover, evidence can be adduced that most of the pre-Priestly traditions concerning the patriarchs were collated into an independent (written) *composition,* having no primary connection with the exodus narratives.[5] In my opinion, this composition came into being during the days of the exile. F. Crüsemann has analogously demonstrated the literary independence of a pre-Priestly *Urgeschichte* (Gen 2–11), a hypothesis that has gained wide support.[6] It seems to me that in the books of Exodus and Numbers as well one can outline a basic and independent story cycle—a kind of *Vita Mosis.*[7]

---

2. Christoph Levin, *Der Jahwist* (FRLANT 157; Göttingen: Vandenhoeck & Ruprecht, 1993).

3. Even more misleading must be the labeling in Reinhard G. Kratz, *Die Komposition der erzählenden Bücher des Alten Testaments: Grundwissen der Bibelkritik* (Uni-Taschenbücher 2157; Göttingen: Vandenhoeck & Ruprecht, 2000), where "J" is used to indicate the pre-Priestly stratum in the book of Genesis and "E" for the pre-Dtr stratum in Exod 2–Josh 12 ("E" for "Exodus"!).

4. Hermann Gunkel, *Genesis* (3rd ed.; HKAT 1/1; Göttingen: Vandenhoeck & Ruprecht, 1910).

5. Erhard Blum, *Die Komposition der Vätergeschichte* (WMANT 57; Neukirchen-Vluyn: Neukirchener, 1984).

6. Frank Crüsemann, "Die Eigenständigkeit der Urgeschichte: Ein Beitrag zur Diskussion um den 'Jahwisten,'" in *Die Botschaft und die Boten: Festschrift H. W. Wolff* (ed. Jörg Jeremias and Lothar Perlitt; Neukirchen-Vluyn: Neukirchener Verlag, 1981), 11–29.

7. Erhard Blum, *Studien zur Komposition des Pentateuch* (BZAW 189; Berlin: de Gruyter, 1990), 215–18.

The essential tenets of this model are supported in a number of new studies.[8] Among them we find those who go so far as to claim that the ancestral narratives and the exodus narrative were first set side by side in the Persian era by the last main redactor of the Pentateuch.[9] We should, therefore, reexamine the question of how and when the main traditions in Genesis and Exodus came together as part of a continuous literary unit. When looking into this matter, special attention should be paid to the seam between the last chapter in the book of Genesis and the opening one of the book of Exodus. However, prior to this we should start by scrutinizing the call narrative of Moses in Exod 3–4, a section that, in the opinion of many, functions as a connecting link between the stories of the patriarchs and the exodus.

I.

The story in Exod 3–4 that relates the call of Moses by Yнwн at the mountain of God is the first pericope in the book of Exodus evincing an explicit theological program. *Inter alia,* it outlines the events about to take place during the exodus from Egypt (mainly Exod 3:18–22) and also states their goal: the *eisodos* of the Israelites to the land of Canaan (3:8, 17). The text even foretells the "worship of God on this mountain" as a significant event in the future (3:12).

In the realm of the Documentary Hypothesis, this passage in particular served as a paradigm for separating interwoven narrative strands of J and E in a single episode.[10] However, already W. Rudolph, M. Noth, and others[11] have

8. Cf. Matthias Köckert, *Vätergott und Väterverheißungen: Eine Auseinandersetzung mit Albrecht Alt und seinen Erben* (FRLANT 142; Göttingen: Vandenhoeck & Ruprecht, 1988); David M. Carr, *Reading the Fractures of Genesis: Historical and Literary Approaches* (Louisville: Westminster John Knox, 1996); Konrad Schmid, *Erzväter und Exodus: Untersuchungen zur doppelten Begründung der Ursprünge Israels innerhalb der Geschichtsbücher des Alten Testaments* (WMANT 81; Neukirchen-Vluyn: Neukirchener, 1999); Jan Christian Gertz, *Tradition und Redaktion in der Exoduserzählung: Untersuchungen zur Endredaktion des Pentateuch* (FRLANT 186; Göttingen: Vandenhoeck & Ruprecht, 2000).

9. So Schmid and Gertz (see n. 8). They believe substantial parts to be the work of this redactor, among them the book of Exodus.

10. See, for example, Werner H. Schmidt, *Exodus* (BK 1/1; Neukirchen-Vluyn: Neukirchener, 1988), and recently his pupil Axel Graupner, *Der Elohist: Gegenwart und Wirksamkeit des transzendenten Gottes in der Geschichte* (WMANT 97; Neukirchen-Vluyn: Neukirchener, 2002). However, it should be stressed that Wellhausen took care to stress the uniformity of these chapters in which there are no visible "seams" between the parallel sources. In his opinion, JE here was the author, not the editor; Julius Wellhausen, *Die Composition des Hexateuchs und der historischen Bücher des Alten Testaments* (3rd ed.; Berlin: Reimer, 1899), 70–71.

11. Wilhelm Rudolph, Der *"Elohist" von Exodus bis Joshua* (BZAW 68; Berlin: Töpelmann, 1938), 6–7; Martin Noth, *Überlieferungsgeschichte des Pentateuch* (Stuttgart: Kohlhammer, 1948), 31–32; and also Blum, *Studien zur Komposition des Pentateuch,* 20–22.

pointed to elements in this very pericope that indicate that the entire narrative of the revelation to Moses at the mountain of God was interpolated into an early pre-Priestly context. This is the evidence.

(1) A number of flaws in the literary sequence in Exod 4:18–19 are conspicuous: in verse 18 Moses takes his leave from his father-in-law: "Moses went back to his father-in-law Jether and said to him, 'Let me go back to my kinsmen in Egypt and see how they are faring.' And Jethro said to Moses, 'Go in peace.' " The exchange between Moses and Jethro in verse 18 is in tension with the command of YHWH in verse 19: "YHWH said to Moses in Midian, 'Go back to Egypt for all the men who sought to kill you are dead.' " More than that, the command in verse 19 does not show any acquaintance with Moses' mission at the mountain of God.

(2) Exodus 4:19 follows smoothly on the first sentence of 2:23, creating a flawless literary sequence: "A long time after that the king of Egypt died" (Exod 2:23aα). "And YHWH said to Moses in Midian, 'Go back to Egypt for all the men who sought to kill you are dead' " (Exod 4:19).

(3) The reason for the return of Moses to Egypt in 4:19, "for all the people who sought to kill you are dead," corresponds with the phraseology and the situation described in Exod 2: "When Pharaoh learned of the matter, he sought to kill Moses" (Exod 2:19).

(4) Corresponding to the seam between Exod 4:18, 19 there is also the trace of a diachronic seam between Exod 2 and 3: Moses' father-in-law is called "Reuel" in Exod 2:18, yet in the first and the concluding verses of 3:1–4:18 he is called "Jethro"/"Jether." These difficulties are explained quite easily by hypothesizing that the passage in Exod 3:1–4:18 is a late interpolation into an existing literary context.[12]

(5) This supposition is corroborated by textual evidence. In Exod 4:19 the LXX reads:

μετὰ δὲ τὰς ἡμέρας τὰς πολλὰς ἐκείνας ἐτελεύτησεν ὁ βασιλεὺς Αἰγύπτου
εἶπεν δὲ κύριος πρὸς Μωυσῆν ἐν Μαδιαμ βάδιζε ἄπελθε εἰς Αἴγυπτον τεθνήκασιν γὰρ πάντες οἱ ζητοῦντές σου τὴν ψυχήν

During those many days the king of Egypt died.
And the Lord said to Moses in Midian, "Go back to Egypt, for all the men who were seeking your life are dead."

---

12. Except for the Priestly verses Exod 2:23aβ–25.

The underlined "plus" at the opening of the verse in the Septuagint repeats *verbatim* the phrasing used in Exod 2:23aα, skipping over the exact same passage 3:1–4:18, which according to the literary-critical analysis proved an addition. Thus, what we have here is a classical example of *Wiederaufnahme*, which in our case cannot be considered an original literary device, seeing that against the inner dynamics of the story it takes us back to the situation before the revelation at Mount Horeb. Instead, we are dealing with an editorial device by which a composer/redactor tried to embed the story of the burning bush in a given literary context. At some later point the *Wiederaufnahme* was expunged from part of the traditions due to its clumsiness.[13]

The evidence for Exod 3:1–4:18 as an interpolation stands in the way of those who want to see J and E as continuous, parallel "sources" throughout Exod 2–4,[14] yet at the same time it opens the way to a variety of different conjectures. Thus we recently witness a tendency to argue that Exod 3:1–4:18 is based on the Priestly literature and that its aim is to bridge between Priestly and non-Priestly material. For Exod 3 there is no real evidence to bear out such an assertion.[15] However, the situation is different in Exod 4. It has long been claimed that the nomination of Aaron as Moses' spokesman in our story is fashioned on the Priestly model in Exod 6–7.[16] And, indeed, the figure of Aaron is not well rooted in the non-Priestly context: in 3:18 Moses is commanded to

---

13. The other way around, it would be difficult to explain why any copyist should add such a problematic repetition.

14. Anyone who will, for example, try to attribute the interpolation to the history of J before its being united with E would have to explain how the redactor (R[JE]), who made a greater effort to blend E into J harmoniously, making substantial changes in the text of J, left such obvious traces witnessing to Exod 3–4 being secondary, including the *Wiederaufnahme* of Exod 4:19 (LXX).

15. Detailed arguments are offered by Gertz and Schmid. One of the arguments is that Exod 3:6–7:9. depend on Exod 2:23. For full discussion of the adduced evidence, see Blum, "Die literarische Verbindung," 124–33.

16. Heinrich Valentin, *Aaron: Eine Studie zur vorpriesterlichen Aaron-Überlieferung* (OBO 18; Fribourg: Universitätsverlag; Göttingen: Vandenhoeck & Ruprecht, 1978), 82–116; Hans-Christoph Schmitt, "Redaktion des Pentateuch im Geiste der Prophetie: Beobachtung zur Bedeutung der 'Glaubens'-Thematik innerhalb der Theologie des Pentateuch," *VT* 32 (1982): 170–89, here 184; idem, "Tradition der Prophetenbücher in den Schichten der Plagenerzählung Ex 7,1–11,10," in *Prophet und Prophetenbuch: Festschrift O. Kaiser* (ed. V. Fritz et al.; BZAW 185; Berlin: de Gruyter, 1989), 196–216, here 213; Van Seters, *Life of Moses*, 53 n. 55; recently Gertz, *Tradition und Redaktion*, 315–16. In Exod 6–7 Moses is God to Pharaoh and Aaron is Moses' prophet (7:1–2); in Exod 4 Moses is God to Aaron and Aaron is spokesman to Moses with the Israelites (4:16–17). Our story foreshadows what is to come and already here attributes to Aaron the function that he is to have later in P; the reason for Moses' refusal and Aaron's appointment are also taken from Exod 7: Moses' lack of rhetorical skills. The appellation of Aaron, peculiar to Exod 4:14 ("Aaron the Levite"), could be explained in this context as a notion mediating between the representative of Second Temple priesthood and the Levites.

go to Pharaoh with the elders of Israel, but according to 5:2 Aaron accompanies him instead of the elders; yet Pharaoh's reaction in 5:4 is more appropriate to the elders: "Why do you distract the people from their tasks? Get to your labors!" It may well be that the figure of Aaron was integrated into Exod 4–5 at a later stage by a post-Priestly hand.

This supposition is supported by additional considerations: the first and the third signs given to Moses (4:3–9) to convince the Israelites seem to be molded on the plagues according to their Priestly version: the rod turning into a serpent (תנין/נחש) (7:8–13) and the Nile's water turning into blood (7:19–20).

Last but not least, in the Priestly version, the Israelites' lack of faith is indicated by the people's *actual* reaction to Moses' mission (6:9), whereas in Exod 4 the lack of faith is presented as an anticipated *potential* problem that is averted by "signs and portents." Furthermore, the issue of the *potential* reaction of the Israelites leads to a second round of questions and answers after Moses' appointment had already reached its appropriate conclusion at the end of Exod 3. The main aim of this second round—in addition to bringing Aaron into the picture[17]—is to forestall the lack of faith of the people as expressed in Exod 6. Thus we read in 4:30: "And he performed the signs in the sight of the people, and the people believed."[18] It cannot be a mere coincidence that in the stories of the patriarchs we find an exact parallel to this phenomenon: the story relating Abraham's faith and complete trust in Yнwн as told in Gen 15 (post-Priestly material[19]) anticipates and aims at redressing the story relating Abraham's laughter in Gen 17 (P).

Let us sum up the profile of Exod 3–4 as it has emerged thus far: the data culled from both textual and literary criticism show that the programmatic pericope Exod 3:1–4:18 has been embedded in a pre-Priestly story in which Exod 4:19 was the direct continuation of 2:23aα. At the same time, there are signs that the second part of the revelation at Mount Horeb in Exod 4:1–17 and further

---

17. Among other things, the redactor was partial to making Aaron participate in the first encounter at the mountain of the Lord (Exod 4:27).

18. What is told in Exod 4:27–31 cannot be severed from the stratum of Exod 4:1–17. Furthermore, there is a close proximity between Exod 4:27–28 and 18:1–12, which may serve as an important additional support for the surmised profile of this diachronic stratum: from various indicators we can deduce that the episode with Israel at the mountain of God in Exod 18 was inserted only after the priestly editors had finished the beginning of the Sinai pericope in Exod 19. For a more detailed discussion, see Erhard Blum, "Gibt es die Endgestalt des Pentateuch?" in *Congress Volume: Leuven, 1989* (ed. J. A. Emerton; VTSup 43; Leiden: Brill, 1991), 54–56.

19. At least in its present form; see, e.g., Alexander Rofé, *Introduction to the Composition of the Pentateuch* (Hebrew) (Jerusalem: Academon, 1994), 78; Blum, "Die literarische Verbindung," 142–45.

elements that are connected with this narrative[20] were added by a post-Priestly redactor.

What is the significance of these diachronic assessments regarding the literary connection between the books of Genesis and Exodus? I would maintain that it is only in the stratum of Exod 4:1–17 that we discern some links with our tradition in the book of Genesis.[21] To my mind this is not the case in the call narrative in Exod 3, and this in spite of the common opinion according to which Exod 3 forms the narrative bridge between the ancestors and the exodus. A close reading of the passage, however, reveals that it makes no reference to the patriarchs except in the self-presentation of the Deity revealing himself to Moses. Even if we assume that the mention of the names "Abraham, Isaac, and Jacob" in Exod 3:6, (15,) 16 is original (although it seems very likely that the text initially only referred to "the God of your father/fathers"[22]), this would not witness to any *literary* connection, since it presupposes only the knowledge of the patriarchs' names.

Moreover, if the call narrative of Moses were primarily part of a literary context that included the ancestral tradition, we would expect to find the topics central to this tradition. In any case, these very topics would be most relevant in the first divine speech in which the Deity expresses the intention to free the Israelites from their bondage in Egypt and to lead them into the land of Canaan. Indeed, this is what we find in Priestly passages such as Exod 6:3–8:

> (3) I appeared to Abraham, Isaac, and Jacob as El Shaddai, but I did not make myself known to them by my name Yhwh. (4) *I also established my covenant with them, to give them the land of Canaan, the land in which they lived as sojourners....* (5) I have now heard the moaning of the Israelites because the Egyptians are holding them in bondage, and *I have remembered my covenant.* (6) Say, therefore, to the Israelite people: "I am Yhwh. I will free you from your labors of the Egyptians.... (8) *I will bring you into the land that I swore to give to Abraham, Isaac and Jacob.*"

In Exod 3:16–17, however, Moses is commanded to tell the elders of Israel the following:

---

20. I assign to this redactional stratum at least the following texts: Exod 4:1–17, *27–31; 7:15b, 17b, 20aβb; 12:12–27; 14:31; 18:1–12. In most of these passages there are clear but divergent signs to their being secondary from a diachronic point of view (Blum, "Die literarische Verbindung," 134–35).

21. Mainly through the topic of faith/disbelief dealt with above.

22. Attention should be paid to the *Wiederaufnahme* in v. 15 and to the formulation in the singular of "the God of your father" in verse 6. For a detailed discussion, see Blum, "Die literarische Verbindung," 139–40.

(16) ... I have taken note of you and of what is being done to you in Egypt,
(17) and I have declared: I will take you out of the misery of Egypt to the land
of the Canaanites, the Hittites, the Amorites, the Perizzites, the Hivites, and
the Jebusites, to a land flowing with milk and honey.

We find no mention here of God's covenant with the patriarchs nor of the
promise of the land. Could it be that an author who has just dealt with these
very matters would not reiterate them when describing the first revelation of
the Deity, thereby sanctioning Moses' mission as well as creating a firm literary
sequence? Such an omission seems most unlikely after witnessing to the narrator's theological and literary skill in the story of the burning bush.

We should therefore deduce that the entire interpolated story in Exod 3
with its abundant divine rhetoric is either not familiar with the narrative cycle
of the ancestors or ignores it. Moreover, we must establish that the pre-Priestly
literary narrative about the exodus from Egypt formed an autonomous tradition that did not presuppose the literary context of the patriarchal narratives as
its introduction.

2.

Thus the question is to be asked: What was the literary context within
whose framework the narratives of the patriarchs and the narratives about Moses
were put side by side? In order to provide an answer we should first examine the
passages connecting the books of Genesis and Exodus.

Genesis 50:21 concludes the narrative about Joseph and his brothers. The
Documentary Hypothesis attributed the last verses of Gen 50 (24–26) to E,
mainly due to its use of the title *'elohim*. Yet in this case again that hypothesis
faces a problem: Gen 50:24 shows a striking similarity to Exod 3:16–17, verses
that hitherto were attributed to J:

Gen 50:24:	פקד יפקד אתכם	ואלהים
Exod 3:16:	נראה אלי ... לאמר פקד פקדתי אתכם	יהוה ...
Gen 50:24:	... והעלה אתכם מן־הארץ הזאת אל־הארץ	
Exod 3:17:	... אעלה אתכם מעני מצרים אל־ארץ	

Two possible explanations can be given to the literary parallel: either one
author is responsible for both Gen 50:24 and Exod 3:16–17, or the passages are
dependent on each other. Various reasons, into which we will go at a later stage,
suggest that Gen 50:24 is based on YHWH's words in Exod 3 and serves as a pre-
paratory comment; indeed, in Gen 50:24 we have the promise to the patriarchs
so conspicuously absent from Exod 3.

Crucial to our discussion are verses 25–26, which conclude the book of Genesis. On the one hand, they are a continuation of verse 24, with which they form a closed, identifiable, literary unit. On the other hand, they belong to an intricate contextual fabric, the strands of which are traceable throughout Gen 33 up to Josh 24:

(1) Joseph's bones: in Gen 50:25–26 Joseph asks to have his bones carried up from Egypt to the promised land; in Exod 13:19 Moses takes Joseph's bones with him; in Josh 24:32 we read that the Israelites bury Joseph's bones, which they had brought up from Egypt, in a piece of land Jacob had bought for a hundred *kesitah* from the children of Hamor, Shechem's father; this takes us back to Gen 33:19, which tells about the purchase of that parcel of land. In addition, Joseph is associated with Shechem already in Gen 48:21–22 in Israel's blessing. The blessing of Israel in Gen 48:21–22 is parallel in form and in subject matter to the speech of Joseph in Gen 50:24. Both speeches focus on the imminent death of the hero. The speech of Joseph leads into his request in verses 25–26 concerning the burial of his bones:

| Gen 50:24 –26 | Gen 48:21–22 |

(2) There is a typological connection between the ritual acts of Jacob/Israel and his household in Shechem under the terebinth (Gen 35:1–7) and the deeds of the Israelites at that same place (Josh 24). The elements common to the two include the preservation in the way and over against the cities/peoples around, the removal of the foreign gods, the place Shechem, the terebinth, and the altar/ sanctuary. Some of the parallels occur in the very same language in the two

texts. The parallels create a typological correspondence: "like fathers like sons" (אבות סימן לבנים). These observations are, of course, well known, yet it is important to stress that what we have here are not only intertextual phenomena, nor a one-sided dependence of one literary unit on another. Rather they are elements of a common redactional stratum. The evidence is as follows.

(a) Jacob's buying of the land from the children of Hamor, Shechem's father, is the act that opens his sojourn in Shechem (ending in Gen 35!) and is referred to at the conclusion of Josh 24. Thus this reference forms a kind of *inclusio*.

(b) The mention of Joseph's bones in several instances in the Pentateuch (Gen 50:25–26; Exod 13:19) are meaningless without the deed of burial in Josh 24; by the same token, the prolepsis in Gen 35:1–7 has no significance without its parallel in Josh 24.

(c) Meanwhile, Josh 24 is based on the prolepsis in Gen 35 at least in regard to one matter: the motif of the gods that the forefathers had worshiped when living beyond the Euphrates (Josh 24:2, 14; Gen 35). This is a tradition unique to Josh 24, never mentioned in the narratives about Abraham. What is the origin of this tradition? The answer lies in the narrative context of the redactional fabric we have described. The whole idea is anchored in a late innerbiblical midrash on the ancient narrative-cycle about Jacob: those "foreign gods" in the possession of Jacob's household, which he buried "under the terebinth at Shechem," were none other than "the gods of Laban" (mentioned in Gen 31:30, 32), that is, the teraphim that Rachel carried away from her father's house. These teraphim had not been objectionable to Jacob nor to the ancient narrators. The author-exegete of Gen 35:1–7 and of Josh 24 was the one to identify them as the foreign gods that had been worshiped by Terah the father of Nahor father of Bethuel father of Laban beyond the Euphrates.[23]

Joshua 24, however, is not only a key component in the compositional-editorial fabric that goes back to the narratives of the patriarchs. The chapter in its own right is a summary of the story told in the book of Genesis up to the

---

23. The link in Gen 31:19, 21 of "and Rachel stole her father's household idols" with "and he arose and crossed the river" may well have contributed to the coming into being of the summarizing comment: "in olden times, your forefathers—Terah, father of Abraham and father of Nahor—lived across the river and worshiped other gods" of Josh 24:2, though it could be that the sentence "and he crossed the river" (Gen 31:21) was added in order to accommodate such a commentary. In any case, the "river," the Euphrates, does not fit the original geographical space of the Jacob story. The details that Jacob, with his children and the livestock in his possession, reaches the Gilead within nine days (Gen 31:22–23) and that the hill country of Gilead was considered the borderline between the household of Jacob and that of Laban witness to the fact that Jacob sojourned with Laban in "the land of the *bne qedem*" (= Hauran?), not in Aram-Naharaim, and that Laban actually does represent the Arameans of Damascus.

book of Joshua, or, to quote G. von Rad, "Ein Hexateuch in kleinster Form."
In many ways Josh 24 can be considered as a "younger brother" of the book of
Deuteronomy.[24]

Like the book of Deuteronomy, so also Josh 24 is a leave-taking speech
uttered by a national leader; Joshua, as had Moses in the book of Deuteronomy,
sums up all God's mighty deeds with his people Israel up to his own days. Joshua,
too, "gave statutes and rules for them" (24:25), although there is no explication
of these rules. Joshua, like Moses, demanded that the people make a decision,
and he also made a covenant with them. In sum, M. Anbar is right in stating
that Joshua is depicted here according to the figure of Moses in the book of Deuteronomy. Last but not least, there is an additional motif that fits this depiction:
Joshua's recording of a divine *torah* in writing (cf. Deut 31:9, 24). The remarkable statement אלהים תורת בספר האלה הדברים את יהושע ויכתב (Josh
24:26) is commented on with utmost reticence by many exegetes. An outstand-
ing commentator such as M. Noth, for example, ignores it completely; other
commentators postulate that a law codex has been lost or that there may, at a
certain point, have existed a "law of Joshua," never mentioned anywhere except
in our chapter. A. Rofé maintains that the very fact that in Josh 24 no mention is made of "the Torah of Moses" points to an essential difference between
this chapter and the Deuteronomistic tradition.[25] In his opinion, the author of
Josh 24 was not yet familiar with the term "'the Torah of Moses." Should we
thus suppose that Joshua did not act as a "second Moses" but Moses as a "first
Joshua"?

The decisive question here is the following: What is meant by the expression
האלה הדברים in Josh 24:26a? In my opinion, it cannot be read as a reference
back to the words ומשפט חוק in the previous verse.[26] The expression הדברים
with a demonstrative (or a semantic equivalent) may refer either to previously
spoken words, or to occurrences explicitly described, as for example in Exod
34:27; Jer 36:17–18; Exod 17:14, or as a self-reference to the text itself, as for
instance in Jer 45:1; 51:60–61. If the meaning were that Joshua wrote down the
ומשפט חוק we would expect a phrasing similar to that in 1 Sam 10:25a.

Therefore, we should conclude that Josh 24:26a refers either to Joshua's
recording in writing the events of the meeting in Shechem or to the chapter

---

24. Here I go back to ideas Moshe Anbar expressed in *Josué et l'alliance de Sichem (Josué
24:1–28)* (BETL 25; Frankfurt: Lang, 1992), 7–22.

25. Alexander Rofé, "Ephraimite versus Deuteronomistic History," in *Storia e tradizioni di
Israel: Festschrift J. A. Soggin* (ed. D. Garrone and F. Israel; Brescia: Paideia, 1991), 233–34; idem,
Introduction to the Historical Literature in the Hebrew Bible (Hebrew) (Jerusalem: Carmel, 2001),
47.

26. See, e.g., Shmuel Achituv, *Joshua: Introduction and Commentary* (Miqra leYisrael; Tel Aviv:
Am Oved, 1995), 371.

itself. Thus, if the phrase means either of these two, it obviously does not refer to the Torah of Moses. At the same time, it cannot be separated entirely from the Torah of Moses. For, on the one hand, the concept of a "Torah-book" did not exist before Deuteronomy (i.e., before the "Torah of Moses"); on the other hand, the stratum to which Josh 24 belongs is based on an extensive composition comprising not only pre-Priestly material in the books of Genesis, Exodus, and Joshua (cf. the "contextual fabric" described above) but probably also its expansion by the Priestly material.[27]

In sum, the ספר התורה of Josh 24 is not called ספר תורת משה, seeing that it also contains the narrative of the conquest of the land in Joshua's days; neither is it called ספר תורת יהושע, as it also holds the "Torah of Moses" from the book of Genesis onward. Actually, it is a sort of "version of the Torah of Moses expanded by Joshua," and therefore its title is ספר תורת אלהים, "the book of the Torah of God" (an expression used once more in Neh 8:8). That is the self-nomenclature of the opus starting in the first chapter of Genesis up to the end of the book of Joshua. Joshua 24 stands as its solemn finale. If this is the case, the "book of the Torah of God" is a redactional "Hexateuch," which forms an expansion or alternative to the book of Moses. In the end, however, the canonical authority of the Torah of Moses took pride of place.

With this interpretation my position differs from that of my teacher Alexander Rofé, who does not see Josh 24 as the conclusion of a unit but instead as an introduction to a pre-Deuteronomistic composition: "the Ephraimite composition."[28] This is not the place to discuss the hypothesis of the Ephraimite composition; I shall mention only two weighty assertions that he adduces regarding Josh 24.

His first argument is a text-critical one. According to the Septuagint, the end of Josh 24 evinces several pluses over the MT.[29] One of them is a concluding remark pertaining to Israel's worship of idols as a punishment for which the Lord delivered them into the hands of Eglon, king of Moab:

24:33[2] οἱ δὲ υἱοὶ Ισραηλ ἀπήλθοσαν ἕκαστος εἰς τὸν τόπον αὐτῶν καὶ εἰς τὴν ἑαυτῶν πόλιν καὶ ἐσέβοντο οἱ υἱοὶ Ισραηλ τὴν Ἀστάρτην καὶ Ασταρωθ καὶ τοὺς θεοὺς τῶν ἐθνῶν τῶν κύκλῳ αὐτῶν καὶ παρέδωκεν αὐτοὺς κύριος εἰς χεῖρας Εγλωμ τῷ βασιλεῖ Μωαβ καὶ ἐκυρίευσεν αὐτῶν ἔτη δέκα ὀκτώ

---

27. See below; in Josh 24 itself there are not many hints to Priestly material, yet it seems that verse 6, at least, is familiar with the Priestly version of Exod 13–14.

28. Cf. Rofé, "Ephraimite versus Deuteronomistic History"; idem, *Introduction to the Historical Literature.*

29. See the detailed discussion in A. Rofé, "The End of the Book of Joshua according to the Septuagint," *Shnaton* 2 (1977), 217–27.

And the Israelites went back each to their place and their city; and they worshiped the Ashtoreth and Ashtarot and the gods of the nations surrounding them; and the Lord delivered them into the hands of Eglon, king of Moab, and he ruled over them for eighteen years.

In Rofé's opinion the Septuagint here preserves an original literary sequence, which did not yet know the sections making up Judg 1:1–3:13. This, no doubt, is a daring assumption indeed. Its main difficulty lies in the fact that the introduction to the book of Judges comprises various elements that still betray the fingerprints of several scribes including Deuteronomistic redactors, who are *inter alia* responsible for the shaping of Josh 23.[30]

This means that we must posit that the LXX witnesses to the given Deuteronomistic book of Joshua and at the same time preserves an ancient pre-Deuteronomistic connecting passage (Josh 24:33 LXX + Judg 3:15) diverging substantially from the Deuteronomistic sequence. Therefore, I prefer to see the Septuagint version of the end of the book of Joshua as a short anticipation of events to come, which were written on some separate scroll of Joshua.[31]

The second argument is indispensable to those who claim Josh 24 to be pre-Deuteronomistic in any case. What we are alluding to is, of course, the location of the congregation—the temple of YHWH in Shechem.[32] Would it be feasible for such a detail to show in a late narrative, which is already familiar with "the law of Moses"? In my opinion, there are indeed a number of reasons for Shechem in particular to be mentioned in our context; I will mention only the most relevant ones.[33]

---

30. Cf., for example, Judg 2:20 with Josh 23:16 and Judg 2:21 with Josh 23:13.

31. A different issue is the question whether the story about Othniel the Kenizzite, brother of Caleb, was already part of the *Vorlage* of that copyist.

32. Achituv, *Joshua*, 366, stresses the place of the sanctuary at Shechem, which, in his opinion, goes against both trends, the Deuteronomistic and the Priestly. One should remember, however, that there are also late traditions that tell about various places of cult, at least concerning the era preceding the temple in Jerusalem; in Priestly writings obtaining in the book of Joshua, the place of the tabernacle is in Shiloh; according to the late appendix in Judg 19–20, the people assemble in Mizpah and later on in Bethel "before the Lord/God." The pseudepigraphic book of *Jubilees* sees no difficulty in having Abraham offer sacrifices in Shechem, near Bethel, or in Hebron (*Jub.* 13–14), whereas in Gen 12–13 these places—apparently not without reason—only serve as places for revelation and prayer. As to Josh 24, it should be noted that any offering of sacrifices is absent from the described ceremony (and so from Gen 35:1–7).

33. See also Erhard Blum, "Der kompositionelle Knoten am Übergang von Josua zu Richter: Ein Entflechtungsvorschlag," in *Deuteronomy and Deuteronomic Literature: Festschrift C. H. W. Brekelmans* (ed. M. Vervenne and J. Lust; BETL 133; Leuven: Leuven University Press; Peeters, 1997), 181–212, 204–5, and literature cited there.

(1) The narrator-exegete of Gen 35 could not have had a more opportune anchorage for his prolepsis than in between two ancient etiologies about a *masseba* and/or an altar in Shechem and Bethel (Gen 33:20 and Gen 35:6–7):[34] "the terebinth that was near Shechem" of Gen 35:4 refers to a consecrated space, and the root טמן, which may be surprising when used in connection with strange gods, actually makes sense in the context of putting away cult objects at such a place.[35]

(2) The author who wanted to ascribe to Joshua an augmented version of the "Torah of Moses" could not have found a better place than Shechem, since "the only places of worship which are explicitly mentioned in the book of Deuteronomy are in the vicinity of Shechem."[36] There—near Shechem—the words of the Torah were to be inscribed upon large stones and read out loud (Deut 27; Josh 8:30–35), and that is where "the terebinths of Moreh" are (Gen 12:6; Deut 11:30).

(3) At the same time, there are still questions that require an explanation: What is it that makes our author emphasize the "foreign gods that your forefathers served beyond the Euphrates" (Josh 24:14–15)? And why does he put into Joshua's mouth the demand to choose between those gods and YHWH? And what makes him in the very same breath predict that the people will fail?

> You will not be able to serve YHWH, for he is a holy God. He is a jealous God; he will not forgive your transgressions and your sins. If you forsake YHWH and serve foreign gods, he will turn and deal harshly with you and make an end of you, after having been gracious to you. (Josh 24:19–20)

This prediction can give a first hint: Can there be any doubt that this speech is formulated *ex eventu* after Israel's and Judah's destruction? And what are the "gods beyond the Euphrates" in this context if not a code for the gods worshiped in the north, the idols that, according to the tendentious tradition of 2 Kgs 17:24–41, the forefathers brought from Aram Naharaim, from beyond the Euphrates?[37] Yet, opposing the separatist-Judean outlook of 2 Kgs 17,

---

34. Regarding these etiologies, see Blum, *Die Komposition der Vätergeschichte*, 61–65, 204–9.

35. Jacob's action follows the custom of burying idols or cult utensils in a holy place; see Othmar Keel, "Das Vergraben der 'fremden Götter' in Genesis xxxv 4b," *VT* 23 (1973): 305–36. The tension between the use of טמן and "put away the foreign gods" may be rooted also in the midrashic character of the passage, for it points to the problem that the "foreign gods" are actually the family gods of Rachel and Leah.

36. Alexander Rofé, *Introduction to Deuteronomy: Part I and Further Chapters* (Hebrew) (Jerusalem: Aqademôn, 1988), 19.

37. It may well be that verse 14 throws light on an additional dimension pertaining to the forefathers and their gods; in this verse the Mesopotamian gods are linked with the gods of Egypt.

our author presents a pan-Israelite outlook; he does not make any distinction between Israel and the people of Samaria. The placement of the assembly in Shechem, the major interest the story evinces in Joseph, and the explicit reference to Jacob—all these, as it were, proffer a single common heritage for the citizens of Samaria and Judea. At the same time our story endeavors to make its readers, among them the tribes dwelling in the north, choose between the gods of "beyond the Euphrates," the gods of the Amorites, and YHWH.[38]

Here too the exegetical conclusion is strengthened by text-critical evidence, although not from Josh 24 but from a passage closer to it than any other in the Former Prophets: Judg 6:7–10.[39]

Scholars have long since recognized, on grounds of literary-critical analysis of the context, that Judg 6:7–10 forms a late interpolation into the Deuteronomistic context.[40] Typologically these verses may be compared with the warnings of the prophets in the Chronicles. And, indeed, the verses are absent from a fragment of a Judges manuscript found in Qumran—4QJudg[a]. To my mind there is no probability for a technical error or an intentional omission in this case. If so, we should assume that the short version of 4QJudg[a] represents a textual tradition into which the prophetic warning had not been inserted. This find is, in an

---

In a postexilic context this could hardly fail to be seen as an allusion to the two main centers of the Jewish Diaspora. If so, the demand to remove the foreign gods was (also) addressed to the returnees from the exile. Keeping in mind the pan-Israelite view of the author, this should not be seen as an alternative to the supposed appeal to the northern Israelites.

38. For a more detailed discussion of the matter, see Blum, *Die Komposition der Vätergeschichte*, 45–61; more recently Blum, "Der kompositionelle Knoten," 194–204.

39. Compare Judg 6:8b with Josh 24:17a; Judg 6:9b with Josh 24:18a; Judg 6:10a with Josh 24:15a, and Judg 6:10b with Josh 24:24b.

40. See especially Alexander Rofé, *The Book of Bileam (Numbers 22:2– 24:25)* (Hebrew) (JBS 1; Jerusalem: Simor, 1979), 56; he sees this addition as what he calls a "related expansion." I will sum up here the main arguments in favor of seeing the passage as secondary. (1) Vv. 7–10 are coupled to v. 6 by means of the repetition "and the Israelites cried out to the Lord." (2) Vv. 8–10 give an answer (in advance) to the question to be asked by Gideon in v. 13: "and why has all this befallen us." The anticipated answer explains the aim of the passage on the one hand, whereas on the other it causes a disruption in the continuity of the story. (3) The prophet's words are only very loosely connected with the situation: the scenic background of the speech is never given (such as the place, time, the participating characters, the reason); moreover, the prophet's appearance is cut off without coming to a conclusion. (4) The passage does not continue the plot but forms a programmatic-theological explanation of the events against the backdrop of the *Heilsgeschichte*. (5) In the passage we encounter expressions and conceptions such as גרשׁ, "the gods of the Amorites," "in whose land you dwell," all typical of Josh 24 but differing from DtrG. (6) The appearance of the prophet is reminiscent of the warning or reprimanding prophets in the book of Chronicles (as in, e.g., 2 Chr 11:2–4; 15:1–7; 16:7–10). (4) The close literary relation between v. 11 and vv. 1–6, which fits a prevalent Deuteronomistic pattern, renders the conclusion plausible that Judg 6:7–10 is a post-Deuteronomistic interpolation.

indirect way, of significance also for Josh 24, seeing that the unique proximity between these texts points to a common author or at least to the same circle of tradents.[41] At the same time, we cannot draw from 4QJudg[a] any conclusions regarding the textual history of Josh 24.

Let us now go back to the literary connection between the books of Genesis and Exodus, keeping in mind the transition between Joshua and Judges. Following the analysis I have presented so far, the verses concluding the book of Genesis are the product of the same postexilic redactional stratum to which Josh 24 belongs. Yet there is an additional link between the two transitory passages: a considerable similarity exists between Exod 1 and Judg 2:

<table>
<tr><td align="center">Exod 1:6, 8</td><td align="center">Judg 2:8, 10</td></tr>
<tr><td align="right">וימת יוסף וכל־אחרו</td><td align="right">וימת יהושע בן־נון ...</td></tr>
<tr><td align="right">וכל הדור ההוא:</td><td align="right">וגם כל־הדור ההוא נאספו אל־אבותיו</td></tr>
<tr><td align="right">ויקם מלך־חדש על־מצרים</td><td align="right">ויקם דור אחר אחריהם</td></tr>
<tr><td align="right">אשר לא־ידע את־יוסף:</td><td align="right">אשר לא־ידעו את־יהוה ...</td></tr>
</table>

Such verbatim agreement cannot be accidental. Furthermore, in the present case there is little doubt about who borrowed from whom: Exod 1 imitates Judg 2 by changing the perfect word coupling of the parallel "all that generation" and "another generation" of Judg 2:10 into the asymmetric contrast consisting of the phrases "all that generation" and "a new king" of Exod 1.

There is a general consensus that Judg 2:6–10 forms the transition from the Deuteronomistic book of Joshua to the Deuteronomistic introduction to the period of the judges. If, indeed, Exod 1:6, 8 are based on the pattern of Judg 2, the question begs to be asked: What is the correlation between these texts and the stratum of Josh 24, to which we assigned the concluding verses of the last chapter of the book of Genesis, which is the transition to the opening of Exodus.

Here we should mention that the verses that serve as a summary for the book of Joshua (24:28–30) follow the pattern of Judg 2:6–10.

<table>
<tr><td align="center">Judg 2:6–10</td><td align="center">Josh 24:28–31</td></tr>
<tr><td align="right">6 וישלח יהושע את־העם</td><td align="right">28 וישלח יהושע את־העם איש לנחלתו</td></tr>
<tr><td align="right">וילכו בני־ישראל איש לנחלתו</td><td align="right">29 ויהי אחרי הדברים האלה</td></tr>
</table>

---

41. This hypothesis does not contradict our supposition that the same redactor(s)/tradent(s) tried to create a kind of "Hexateuch" that was to end with Josh 24, for the "books" of Former Prophets were (in such *Gestalt* or another) at their disposal, and they could make additions in these writings (beyond their own "Torah-composition").

וימת יהושע בן־נון עבד יהוה בן ...
30 ויקברו אתו בגבול נחלתו ...
31 ויעבד ישראל את־יהוה כל ימי
יהושע וכל ימי הזקנים אשר האריכו
ימים אחרי יהושע
ואשר ידעו את כל־מעשה יהוה
אשר עשה לישראל:

7 ויעבדו העם את־יהוה כל ימי יהושע
וכל ימי הזקנים אשר האריכו ימים
אחרי יהושע
אשר ראו את כל־מעשה יהוה הגדול
אשר עשה לישראל:
8 וימת יהושע בן־נון עבד יהוה בן ...
9 ויקברו אותו בגבול נחלתו ...
10 וגם כל־הדור ההוא נאספו אל־
אבותיו ויקם דור אחר אחריהם
אשר לא־ידעו את־יהוה וגם את־
המעשה אשר עשה לישראל:

The passage Judg 2:6–8, marking the transition from Joshua to Judges, has been transformed by the redaction of Josh 24:28–31 to form the conclusion of the days of Joshua as well of an entire opus,[42] that is, of the late "Hexateuch" composition. Since we have found the redactional stratum of Josh 24 in the last verses of the book of Genesis as well (50:24–26), we find a parallel diachronic profile in both transition sections.[43] This renders it probable that Exod 1:6, 8—which imitate Judg 2:8, 10—were formulated by the same tradent(s) (of Josh 24).

Are we, finally, detecting traces of the editors/authors who were responsible for the primary transition between Genesis and Exodus? The answer must be negative, seeing that it is not feasible to connect directly between Exod 1:6 and Gen 50:24–26, nor is a direct linkage of Gen 50:25 and Exod 1:6 convincing from a literary point of view.[44] We must, therefore, deduce that we cannot read these redactional elements without the intervening Priestly passages, including the list in Exod 1:1–5.

---

42. A full comparison shows that neither were Judg 2:6–10 phrased as *Wiederaufnahme* nor were Josh 24:28–31 formulated as a prolepsis but as a concluding remark; see Blum, "Der kompositionelle Knoten," 184, 206.

43. It is worth noting the possibility that the lifespans of Joseph and Joshua—both lived 110 years—may have been adjusted to agree with each other as well.

44. In *Studien zur Komposition des Pentateuch* I advanced the assumption that in Gen 50:24 + Exod 1:6, 8 is to be found a pre-Priestly transition from the ancestral narratives to the exodus narrative. Yet, J. C. Gertz, *Tradition und Redaktion*, 360, has rightly argued against this, that the literary sequence resulting from the linkage of Exod 1:6 and Gen 50:24 would have something of a tragic-comic effect.

This find is not really surprising. It actually corroborates our previous conjecture that the redactional/compositional stratum of Josh 24 is already based on the Pentateuch, including the bulk of the Priestly material.

And indeed, following this assumption two details in Exod 1:5 and 6 may be explained easily. First, the sentence "and Joseph was in Egypt"—which already in the LXX has been moved after verse 4—was from the start meant as a transition between verses 5a and 6. Second, the words "and all his brothers" of verse 6 go back to the previous list of Joseph's brothers (Exod 1:1–5). Furthermore, the Priestly materials in Gen 50:22–23 and Exod 1:1a–5, 7 form a perfect transition from the family sagas in the book of Genesis to the narrative of the great and populous nation in the book of Exodus:

> Gen 50:22–23: So Joseph and his father's family remained in Egypt. Joseph lived one hundred and ten years. Joseph lived to see children of the third generation of Ephraim; the children of Machir son of Manasseh were likewise born on Joseph's knees.

> Exod 1:1–7: And these are the names of the sons of Israel who came to Egypt with Jacob, each coming with his family: Reuben, Simeon, Levi, and Judah; Issachar, Zebulun, and Benjamin; Dan and Naphtali, Gad and Asher. The total number of persons that were of Jacob's issue came to seventy ... And the Israelites were fertile and prolific; they multiplied and increased very greatly, so that the land was filled with them'.

Let us bring our discussion to an end with two far-reaching conclusions following from our analysis. (1) The stratum of Josh 24, which aimed at forming some sort of a "Hexateuch" (or more precisely the "book of the Torah of God" mentioned in 24:26), was composed after the completion of that huge pentateuchal work, a work that comprised the pre-Priestly traditions as well as the main of the Priestly material. (2) It seems that the Priestly editor(s)/author(s) was (were) the first to bring together into one continuous literary opus the three major traditions of the Pentateuch: the primeval history, the narratives of the patriarchs, and the exodus narrative.

On the basis of these conclusions there is, of course, no longer room for J and E of the traditional Documentary Hypothesis. Moreover, to some extent, some newer assumptions regarding the composition of the Torah that were suggested *inter alia* in previous publications of mine should be reexamined as well.[45]

---

45. This is not the place to dwell upon it, but there can be no doubt that the findings and deliberations of Alexander Rofé (see, e.g., "An Enquiry into the Betrothal of Rebekah," in *Die Hebräische Bibel und ihre zweifache Nachgeschichte: Festschrift R. Rendtorff* [ed. E. Blum et al.; Neukirchen-Vluyn: Neukirchener, 1990], 27–39) will be milestones in any such reexamination. For the time being, see Blum, "Die literarische Verbindung," 140–45, 151–56.

THE COMMISSION OF MOSES AND THE BOOK OF GENESIS

Thomas B. Dozeman

1. THE BOOKS OF GENESIS AND EXODUS AND THE COMPOSITION OF THE PENTATEUCH

The literary relationship between Exodus and Genesis has not played a significant role in modern research on the composition of the Pentateuch. Interpreters have focused instead on the relationship of Exodus to Deuteronomy or to the Deuteronomistic History, giving rise to the terms *Tetrateuch, Hextateuch,* and *Enneateuch* in contemporary theories of composition. Many have noted the problems of narrative unity and style between Genesis and Exodus and the abrupt transition in subject matter from family stories to a national epic.[1] But the tendency is to read the stories of the ancestors and the exodus as a single narrative by the same author(s) from the early development of the literature.[2] And this judgment has held firm even in the wake of tradition-historical studies to the contrary, such as Kurt Galling's conclusion that the story of the ancestors and the exodus are separate traditions of election[3] or the more recent argument of Albert de Pury that the separation of the election traditions is still evident in the book of Hosea, where the prophet uses the exodus tradition to evaluate critically the Jacob tradition of origin.[4]

---

1. See already Julius Wellhausen, *Die Composition des Hexateuchs und der Historischen Bücher des Alten Testament* (3rd ed.; Berlin: Reimer, 1899), 61.

2. See the overview by Konrad Schmid, *Erzväter und Exodus: Untersuchungen zur doppelten Begründung der Ursprünge Israels innerhalb des Geschichtsbücher des Alten Testament* (WMANT 81; Neukirchen-Vluyn: Neukirchener, 1999), 5–18.

3. Kurt Galling, *Die Erwählungstraditionen Israels* (BZAW 48; Giessen: Töpelmann, 1928).

4. Albert de Pury, "Le cycle de Jacob comme légende autonome des origins d'Israël," in *Congress Volume: Leuven, 1989* (ed. J. A. Emerton; VTSup 43; Leiden: Brill, 1991), 78–96. See the caution by Erhard Blum, "Die literarische Verbindung von Erzvätern und Exodus: Ein Gespräch mit neueren Endredaktionshypothesen," in *Abschied vom Jahwisten: Die Komposition des Hexateuch in der jüngsten Diskussion* (ed. J. C. Gertz et al.; BZAW 315; Berlin: de Gruyter, 2002), 122.

The insights from tradition history are beginning to influence theories of composition, prompting interpreters to reexamine the literary relationship between Genesis and Exodus. John Van Seters, followed by Rolf Rendtorff, established the framework for interpretation in separate studies on the related themes, God of the fathers and the promise to the ancestors. In the early 1970s Van Seters recognized that the ancestors in Ezekiel, Jeremiah, Deuteronomy, and the Deuteronomistic History are, for the most part, the generation of the exodus, not the patriarchs from the book of Genesis, while the earliest reference to the patriarch Abraham in the prophetic corpus is in the exilic writings of Ezekiel and Second Isaiah.[5] Van Seters concluded that the merging of the generation of the exodus and the patriarchal ancestors was a literary innovation by the Yahwist historian in the wake of confessional reformulation in the exilic period.[6] The commission of Moses in Exod 3:1–4:18 was a central text in this new historiography of origins.

Rendtorff came to a similar conclusion as Van Seters at the close of the 1970s, working in the opposite direction, from Genesis to Exodus.[7] Rendtorff noted that the theme, promise of land to the ancestors, was central to the formation of the book of Genesis but nearly absent in the book of Exodus, where it is clustered at the outset, mainly in the commission of Moses: three times in the Priestly history (Exod 2:24; 6:3, 8); four times in the non-P version (Exod 3:6, 15, 16; 4:5); with only two additional references later in the book (Exod 33:1; 32:13). He, too, concluded that the identification of the divine promise to the patriarchal ancestors, Abraham, Isaac, and Jacob, with the exodus generation was a late development. For Rendtorff, the literary process was the work of a Deuteronomistic editor who sought to relate the previously separate literary traditions ("complexes") of the patriarchs in Genesis to the story of the exodus.[8]

Subsequent interpreters have built on the research of Van Seters and Rendtorff, raising new questions about the literary formation of Genesis and Exodus and the authorship of the commission of Moses in Exod 3:1–4:18. Erhard Blum supported the thesis of Rendtorff, arguing that the call of Moses in Exod 3:1–4:18 is a key text in the *D-Komposition* (*KD*), a postexilic literary composition linking the patriarchal stories with the salvation from Egypt.[9]

---

5. John Van Seters, "Confessional Reformulation in the Exilic Period," *VT* 22 (1972): 448–59.

6. Ibid., 459.

7. Rolf Rendtorff, *Das überlieferungsgeschichtliche Problem des Pentateuch* (BZAW 147; Berlin: de Gruyter, 1977); English translation: *The Problem of the Process of Transmission in the Pentateuch* (trans. J. J. Scullion; JSOTSup 89; Sheffield: Sheffield Academic Press, 1990).

8. Rendtorff, *Problem*, 88.

9. Erhard Blum, *Studien zur Komposition des Pentateuch* (BZAW 189; Berlin: de Gruyter, 1990), 9–37, esp. 22–28.

The Priestly version of the commission of Moses (Exod 6:2–7:7) represents the later *P-Komposition* (*KP*), according to Blum, thus affirming the pre-Priestly authorship Exod 3:1–4:18.[10] But when Thomas Römer extended the work of Van Seters on the ancestors in Deuteronomy and related literature, he located the literary combination of Genesis with Exodus in the Priestly author's version of the commission of Moses (Exod 6:2–7:7), leading to the further conclusion that the present form of Exod 3:1–4:18 is a post-Priestly composition.[11]

The post-Priestly authorship of all or part of Exod 3:1–4:18 has been further developed in a number of recent studies, including those of Eckart Otto, Konrad Schmid, and Jan Christian Gertz.[12] Schmid and Gertz advocate a new hypothesis of pentateuchal composition in which the Priestly author is the first historian to combine the origin stories of the patriarchal ancestors and the exodus. The literary combination is achieved in the divine notice of the Israelite oppression (Exod 2:23aβ–25) and in the commission of Moses (6:2–7:7).[13] Exodus 3:1–4:18 is a reinterpretation, either in part (Gertz)[14] or in whole (Schmid),[15] of the Priestly version of the commission of Moses by the final redactor of the Pentateuch. The hypothesis has prompted Blum to identify two authors in Exod 3:1–4:18, the pre-Priestly author of the *KD* (Exod 3) and a post-Priestly author (Exod 4:1–17). Blum also restricts the literary boundaries of the pre-Priestly *KD* to Exodus–2 Kings, thus separating Genesis from Exodus until the composition of *KP*.[16]

My aim is to evaluate this emerging trend of research, in which the composition of Exod 3:1–4:18 is attributed to a post-Priestly redactor of the final form of the Pentaeuch, who is reinterpreting the Priestly version of Moses' commission in Exod 6:2–7:7. I will begin by comparing the present form of the two commissions of Moses, before evaluating the composition of Exod 3:1–4:18 and its function in the literary context of the Pentateuch.

---

10. Blum, *Studien zur Komposition des Pentateuch,* 232–42.

11. Thomas Römer, *Israels Väter: Untersuchungen zur Väterthematik im Deuteronomium und in der deuteronomistischen Tradition* (OBO 99; Fribourg: Universitätsverlag; Göttingen: Vandenhoeck & Ruprecht, 1990), 344–52, 552–54.

12. Eckart Otto, "Die nachpriesterschrifliche Pentateuchredaktion im Buch Exodus," in *Studies in the Book of Exodus: Redaction—Reception—Interpretation* (ed. M. Vervenne; BETL 126; Leuven: Leuven University Press; Peeters, 1996), 61–111; Schmid, *Erzväter und Exodus;* and Jan Christian Gertz, *Tradition und Redaktion in der Exoduserzählung: Untersuchungen zur Endredaktion des Pentateuch* (FRLANT 186; Göttingen: Vandenhoeck & Ruprecht, 2000).

13. Gertz, *Tradition und Redaktion,* 237–54.

14. Ibid., 255–328.

15. Schmid, *Erzväter und Exodus,* 190–92.

16. Blum, "Die literarische Verbindung," 119–56.

2. The Two Commissions of Moses

Konrad Schmid concluded that Exod 3:1–4:18 reinterprets Exod 6:2–7:7. This conclusion is based in a large part on the comparison of shared motifs and an evaluation of the literary design of the text.[17] The motifs of "hearing" (שמע) and "faith" (אמן) are especially important for determining the direction of literary dependence. Schmid argues that there is no reason for the Israelites not "to heed" the message of Moses in Exod 3:1–4:18.[18] The Priestly version in Exod 6:2–9 provides a better context for interpreting the motif, since it presents a clear linear development: God speaks to Moses (6:2–8), Moses conveys the message (6:9a), and the Israelites do not listen to his message (6:9b). The central role of "listening/hearing" in Exod 3:1–4:18 is more understandable as a reinterpretation of the Priestly version. The objections of Moses in conjunction with the "faith" of the Israelites thematize the motif of "not listening." The distinct geographical settings of the two commissions reinforce the literary dependence of Exod 3:1–4:18 on 6:2–7:7.[19] The setting of Egypt in the Priestly version presents no problem when read as the first account of the commission of Moses. It corresponds to Ezek 20:5–26. But if the Priestly version were later than Exod 3:1–4:18, the author would have corrected the setting of the divine mountain, Horeb, to Sinai, the mountain of revelation in the Priestly history.[20]

The comparison of shared motifs is important for identifying the innerbiblical relationship between texts. Yet it is difficult to judge the direction of literary dependence through a narrow comparison of motifs alone, especially when there is shared subject matter, as with the two commissions of Moses. Michael Fishbane notes that the direction of innerbiblical interpretation requires an analysis of both motifs and structure.[21] The latter text, he notes, often reorganizes its parent text in order to rethematize the topic. I will compare the present structure of the two commissions of Moses, utilizing past form-critical research on the genre of the prophetic commission and the innerbiblical methodology described by Fishbane. I will begin with the wilderness commission in Exod 3:1–4:18, before evaluating the literary design of the Priestly commission in Exod 6:2–7:7.

---

17. Schmid, *Erzväter und Exodus*, 199.

18. Schmid notes that Exod 3:18 even states the opposite, namely, that the elders would listen to Moses (ibid., 199).

19. Ibid., 200–2.

20. Ibid., 202–9.

21. Michael Fishbane, *Biblical Interpretation in Ancient Israel* (Oxford: Clarendon, 1985), 285.

2.1. THE COMMISSION OF MOSES IN EXODUS 3:1–4:18

The commission of Moses in the wilderness separates into two parts, 3:1–15 and 3:16–4:18.[22] Each section is organized around the motif of divine commission. In the first section (3:1–15) the Deity commands Moses in Exod 3:10: "And now, go, and I will send you to Pharaoh. Bring out my people, the Israelites, from Egypt." There are two additional commissions in the second section (3:16–4:18). The first, in Exod 3:16, marks the transition between the two sections: "Go and gather the elders, and you will say to them." The second commission is in Exod 4:12: "Now go, and I will be with you as you speak and will instruct you what to say."[23] The two sections, Exod 3:1–15 and 3:16–4:18, are interwoven by the repeated resistance of Moses to the divine commission (Exod 3:11; 4:1, 10, 13),[24] suggesting that Exod 3:1–4:18 has been fashioned into a literary unit, regardless of the history of composition.[25] Both sections explore the related themes of divine identity and Mosaic authority. Exodus 3:1–15 focuses more on the identity of the Deity, and Exod 3:16–4:18 defines the authority of Moses. Exodus 3:1–15 addresses the problem of the divine identity after the break in tradition from the time of the patriarchal ancestors (Exod 1:6).[26] The

22. The identification of the literary structure of Exod 3:1–4:18 is often obscured by a preoccupation with identifying the sources. Yet v. 16 is frequently noted as a point of transition in the literary structure, signifying the separation of the E (vv. 13–15) and the J (vv. 16ff.) sources. See, for example, Werner H. Schmidt, *Exodus 1–6* (BK 2/1; Neukirchen-Vluyn: Neukirchener, 1988), 109, 120; and compare William H. C. Propp, who notes the transition in the narrative but assigns Exod 3:16ff. to the E source (*Exodus 1–18* [AB 2; New York: Doubleday, 1999], 193). For stylistic evaluation of the transition at v. 16, see Georg Fischer, *Jahwe unser Gott: Sprache, Aufbau und Erzähltechnik in der Berufung des Moses (Ex 3–4)* (Göttingen: Vandenhoeck & Ruprecht, 1989), 89–91, 154–55; and Umberto Cassuto, *Commentary on Exodus* (trans. I. Abrahams; Jerusalem: Magnes, 1967), 30–52.

23. See Brevard S. Childs, *The Book of Exodus: A Critical, Theological Commentary* (OTL; Louisville: Westminster John Knox, 1974), 70–71.

24. Benno Jacob adds an additional objection in Exod 3:13 yielding a five-part structure of objection and divine reassurance, consisting of Exod 3:7–10; 13–22; 4:1–9, 10–12, 13–17 (*The Second Book of the Bible: Exodus* [trans. W. Jacob; Hoboken, N.J.: Ktav, 1992], 48).

25. For discussion of the literary boundaries of Exod 3:1–4:18, see Martin Noth, *A History of Pentateuchal Traditions* (trans. B. W. Anderson; Chico, Ca.: Scholars Press, 1981), 203 n. 549; Frederick V. Winnett, *The Mosaic Tradition* (Near and Middle East Studies 1; Toronto: University of Toronto Press, 1949), 20–29; with additional literature in Childs, *Book of Exodus*, 51–55. For more recent discussion, see Blum, *Studien zur Komposition des Pentateuch*, 22–29; Christoph Levin, *Der Jahwist* (FRLANT 157; Göttingen: Vandenhoeck & Ruprecht, 1993), 326, 329; Schmid, *Erzväter und Exodus*, 186–89; and Gertz, *Tradition und Redaktion*, 254–56 with bibliography.

26. For the interpretation of Exod 1:6 as indicating a transition in generations and its parallel in Judg 2:10, see Theodor Christian Vriezen, "Exodusstudien: Exodus 1," *VT* 17 (1967): 334–53. For comparison of the larger context, see John Van Seters, *The Life of Moses: The Yahwist as Historian*

section also explores the ability of God to be present with the Israelite people during their slavery in Egypt.[27] Exodus 3:16–4:18 raises the related problem of the authority of Moses in proclaiming YHWH's imminent salvation, especially when the experience of the Israelites is of slavery, suggesting divine abandonment, not salvation.

Many interpreters have recognized a commissioning form in Exod 3:1–15. Werner H. Schmidt identifies the central features of the form in Exod 3:10–12 to include: the commission (v. 10), the objection (v. 11), the reassurance (v. 12a), and the sign (v. 12b).[28] This form repeats in a wide variety of literature recounting the commission of charismatic and prophetic heroes such as Gideon (Judg 6:14–17), Saul (1 Sam 9–10), and Jeremiah (Jer 1:4–10).[29] The commission could be expanded to include verse 9, since this verse provides the circumstances giving rise to Moses' task.[30] Norman Habel extended the literary pattern even further to include Exod 3:1–12,[31] but the repetition of the motif of divine presence in verses 12a, "I will be with you" (כי אהיה עמך), and 14, "I will be who I will be" (אהיה אשר אהיה), indicates that the section must be extended beyond verse 12 through the revelation of the name, YHWH, in Exod 3:15.[32]

The genre of the commission is important for the interpretation of Exod 3:1–15. Brevard Childs pointed out that the form indicates an identification

---

in Exodus-Numbers (Louisville: Westminster John Knox, 1994), 17–18. For recent debates on dating Exod 1:6, see Gertz, *Tradition und Redaktion*, 358–60; and Schmid, *Erzväter und Exodus*, 152–53.

27. Many interpreters have clarified the theme of divine presence in Exod 3:1–15. See already Hugo Gressmann, who sought to identify an early form of divine appearance in a cult legend (*Mose und seine Zeit* [FRLANT 18; Göttingen: Vandenhoeck & Ruprecht, 1913], 21–30). See more recently Levin, *Der Jahwist*, 326; and Fischer, *Jahwe unser Gott*, 99–122. For review of the scholarship, see Schmidt, *Exodus 1–6*, 110–23; and Childs, *Book of Exodus*, 52–70.

28. Schmidt, *Exodus 1–6*, 123–30, with bibliography.

29. In addition to Schmidt, see Wolfgang Richter, *Die sogenannten vorprophetischen Berufungsberichte: Eine literaturwissenschaftliche Studie zu 1 Sam 9,1–10, 16, Ex 3f und Ri 6,11b–17* (FRLANT 101; Göttingen: Vandenhoeck & Ruprecht, 1970); Hans-Christoph Schmitt, "Das sogenannte vorprophetische Berufungsschema: Zur 'geistigen Heimat' des Berufungsformulars von Ex 3, 9–12; Jdc 6,11–24 und 1 Sam 9,1–10,16," *ZAW* 104 (1992): 202–16; and Van Seters, *Life of Moses*, 41–46.

30. The repetition between vv. 7 and 9 has been argued by many interpreters to be a strong illustration of two sources (see Schmidt, *Exodus 1–6*, 109). See, however, Moshe Greenberg (*Understanding Exodus* [Melton Research Center Series 2; New York: Behrman House, 1969], 99) and Blum (*Studien zur Komposition des Pentateuch*, 11) for discussion of the literary function of the repetition based on a comparison of Exod 3:6–10; Josh 14:6–12; and 2 Sam 7:27–29.

31. Norman Habel, "The Form and Significance of the Call Narratives," *ZAW* 77 (1965): 297–323.

32. Interpreters debate the placement of the revelation of the divine name in Exod 3:13–15 within the literary context of the commission of Moses. Schmidt notes a series of motifs linking Exod 3:9–12 and 13–14 (*Exodus 1–6*, 131–32).

of Moses with the prophetic office,[33] accentuating his role as a charismatic leader, not as a priest.[34] This imagery will be carried through in the presentation of Aaron (Exod 4:13–16), who also functions in a prophetic role. But the genre of the commission does not adequately describe the opening encounter between God and Moses, since Exod 3:9–12 is framed by accounts of divine self-revelation in Exod 3:1–8 and 13–15.[35] Exodus 3:6 includes a divine self-identification to Moses: "I am the God of your father." Exodus 3:13–15 carries the theme through to the introduction of the divine name, YHWH. The mixing of genres in Exod 3:1–15 indicates that the commission of Moses (Exod 3:9–12) is at the heart of the episode, but the point of focus is the identity of the Deity, YHWH (Exod 3:1–8 and 13–15).

The wilderness commission of Moses changes in emphasis from the identity of the Deity (3:1–15) to the authority of Moses (3:16–4:18). The change is signaled in the second commission (3:16), where the point of focus is on the authenticity of Moses' experience, not the identity of God per se. Moses is to inform the elders: "YHWH, the God of your fathers *appeared to me* (נראה אלי)." And it is the need to persuade the elders of the authenticity of his experience that prompts Moses to object in Exod 4:1: "They will say, 'YHWH *did not appear to you* (לא־נראה אליך).'" The objection calls forth the divine response in Exod 4:5: "They will believe that YHWH *appeared to you* (נראה אליך)."[36]

Mosaic authority in the wilderness commission is developed in two scenes with different characters, Exod 3:16–4:9 and 4:10–18. The separate commissions of Moses, Exod 3:16 and 4:12, signal the division. Exodus 3:16–4:9 explores the authority of Moses in relation to the elders.[37] Exodus 4:10–18 shifts to the character of Aaron as Moses' assistant in a prophetic role. In each section Moses objects to the divine commission (4:1, 10–12), an expected feature of the genre of the prophetic commission, since the hero must persuade the audience of the authenticity of the divine call.

---

33. Childs, *Book of Exodus,* 55.

34. See Schmid for discussion of the idealization of Moses as a prophet and its possible relationship to Abraham in Gen 15 and to Joshua in Josh 24 (*Erzväter und Exodus,* 180, 196, 224).

35. For discussion of the genre of divine self-revelation in general, see Walther Zimmerli, "I Am Yahweh," in *I Am Yahweh* (trans. D. W. Stott; Atlanta: John Knox, 1982), 1–28. For interpretation of Exod 3:1–8, see Greenberg, *Understanding Exodus,* 130–33; and George W. Coats, *Exodus 1–18* (FOTL 2A; Grand Rapids: Eerdmans, 1999), 34–42, with bibliography.

36. Gertz also notes the shift to Mosaic authority but locates the transition at Exod 4:1 (*Tradition und Redaktion,* 261).

37. The elders are named in Exod 3:16–22 (see vv. 16 and 18) but not in Exod 4:1–9, suggesting a possible expansion of the wilderness commission. Yet, there is no change in characters to mark a clear separation. Thus I read Exod 3:16–22 and 4:1–9 as a single scene in the present structure of the wilderness commission.

The first scene (3:16–4:9) confirms the absence of Mosaic authority and the need to equip Moses with signs. Exodus 3:16 states the need for Moses to confirm the authenticity of his experience. The objection of Moses is stated in Exod 4:1: "But suppose they do not believe me or listen to my voice." The objection of Moses introduces the central theme of faith (אמן) in Moses, which means listening (שמע) to his voice (קל). The phrase "listening to the voice" is a reference to the law in the book of Deuteronomy (e.g., 5:22; 15:5; 26:17; 28:1, 45, 62; 30:20), and the same meaning is present in this text. The motif will reappear at the outset of the wilderness journey in Exod 15:26 signifying God's voice as law. But it will become increasingly intermingled with Moses' voice in the experience of theophany, when the people appoint him to mediate law for them (Exod 19:9, 19; 20:18–20).[38]

The second scene (4:10–18) introduces the theme of eloquence in the charismatic hero, when Moses doubts his ability to speak persuasively (4:10–12). The second objection allows for a divine speech of disputation, underscoring the power of God to create persuasive speech, recalling the commission of the prophet Jeremiah (Jer 1:4–10).[39] The introduction of Aaron (4:13–17) underscores the unique status of Moses. He will function as a god over against Aaron's prophetic role.[40]

2.2. The Commission of Moses in Exodus 6:2–7:7

The Priestly account of the commission of Moses (6:2–7:7) follows the structure of the wilderness version (3:1–4:18). It, too, separates between sections focused on the identity of God (6:2–9; cf. 3:1–15) and the authority of Moses (6:10–7:7; cf. 3:16–4:18). Mosaic authority in the Priestly version is also developed through the objections of Moses to the commission (6:10–12 and 28–30).[41] The similar structure is illustrated in the following diagram.

---

38. See Otto, "Die nachpriesterschriftliche Pentateuchredaktion," 61–100; and Thomas B. Dozeman, *God on the Mountain: A Study of Redaction, Theology and Canon in Exodus 19–24* (SBLMS 37; Atlanta: Scholars Press, 1988), 37–86.

39. See Schmidt, *Exodus 1–6*, 200–2. For discussion of disputation speech in Second Isaiah, see Joachim Begrich, *Studien zu Deuterojesaja* (2nd ed.; TB 20; Munich: Kaiser, 1963), 48–53. For a more general description, see Marvin A. Sweeney, *Isaiah 1–39: With an Introduction to Prophetic Literature* (FOTL 16; Grand Rapids: Eerdmans, 1996), 28, 519.

40. Propp rightly concludes that, although Moses is compared to prophets, he is in a class apart (*Exodus 1–18*, 230–31). Propp supports the conclusion by relating the commission of Moses to Num 11–12. See below for a similar comparison.

41. Most agree that the beginning of the Priestly commission is Exod 6:2. There is more debate over its ending. For discussion, see Schmidt, *Exodus 1–6*, 269–312.

The Commission of Moses in the
Wilderness: Exod 3:1–4:18

The Commission of Moses in
Egypt: Exod 6:2–7:7

The Identify of Yʜwʜ

Exod 3:1–15
  Self-Revelation: 3:1–8
  Commission: 3:9–10
  Objection: 3:11
  Reassurance: 3:12
  Self-Revelation: 3:13–15

Exod 6:2–8
  Self-Revelation: 6:2–5
  Commission: 6:6–9

The Authority of Moses

Exod 3:16–4:18
  Moses and the Elders:
    3:16–4:9
  Moses and Aaron: 4:10–17

Exod 6:10–7:7
  Moses and Phinehas: 6:10–13
    [14–27]
  Moses and Aaron: 6:28–7:7

The Priestly account identifies the Deity by mixing the genres of divine self-revelation (6:2–5; cf. 3:1–8, 13–15) with the divine commission of Moses (6:6–9; cf. 3:9–12),[42] now fashioned into the structure of command (4:6–8) and fulfillment (4:9)—a common pattern in the Priestly history.[43] The mixing of genres in both versions of Moses' commission allows for the identification of the God of the exodus, the God of the fathers, and the patriarchal ancestors, Abraham, Isaac, and Jacob (3:6 and 6:3), thus linking the books of Genesis and Exodus. The Priestly version adds the theme of covenant as the theological basis for the relationship of the patriarchal ancestors and the exodus generation.[44]

The Priestly account of Moses' commission also changes in emphasis from the identity of God (6:2–9) to the authority of Moses (6:10–7:7). The transition is signaled by Moses' statement that he is not a persuasive speaker, creating a repetition between Exod 4:10 and 6:10–13, 28–30. In the Priestly version, Moses' objection is stated twice (6:10–12 and 28–30). The repetition indicates that Mosaic authority is developed in two scenes, which follows the pattern of his wilderness commission, where his authority was defined in relation to the elders (3:16–4:9) and Aaron (4:10–18). The first objection of Moses (6:12)

---

42. For commentary (with bibliography) on the structure and form, see Johan Lust, "Exodus 6,2–8 and Ezekiel," in Vervenne, *Studies in the Book of Exodus,* 211–12.

43. See Thomas B. Dozeman, "Numbers," *NIB* 2:31–32, 47–48, 60, 82.

44. Blum highlights the problem of interpreting the commission of Moses in Exod 3 as a reinterpretation of Exod 6, when the former lacks the motif of covenant, which is so central to the Priestly version ("Die literarische Verbindung," 131).

introduces the genealogy of Phinehas as the representative of Mosaic authority (6:14–27), as compared to the elders (3:16–4:9). The second objection (6:28) allows for the repetition of Aaron as the prophet of Moses (7:1–2) to Pharaoh and the Egyptians (7:5), as compared to the Israelite people (4:10–18). The parallel structure reinforces Schmid's conclusion of literary dependence, based on his comparison of motifs.

The comparison of the structure of the two commissions suggests that the Priestly account (6:2–7:7) is dependent on the wilderness version (3:1–4:18). The genre of the commission is rooted in the prophetic office. It explores the authority of charismatic leadership, not the priest. The genre requires the audience to encounter the hero's power directly. They must be persuaded through experience. The interplay of objection and divine reassurance is equally crucial to the genre, qualifying charismatic power as originating with God and not residing in the personal strength of the hero. Exodus 3:1–4:18 fulfills these expectations. The motif of faith requires the Israelites to experience first hand Moses' signs of authority (4:1–9). And the objections of Moses underscore that his charismatic power derives from God, not from his personal strength.

The Priestly author follows the form of the prophetic commission in fashioning Exod 6:2–7:7 around the objections of Moses. But the commission lacks the essential characteristics of the genre. The authority of Moses is not rooted in the prophetic office. It is not affirmed experientially through signs. It does not require the faith of the Israelite people. And the important interplay between objection and reassurance is absent. The objection of Moses to the divine commission is prominent (6:12, 30), but it is not about charismatic authority or the fear of fulfilling a mission. The initial objection (6:12) is embedded, rather, in a statement about past actions: "The Israelites would not listen to me; how then should Pharaoh heed me?"[45] The second objection (6:30) allows for a reinterpretation of Aaron's prophetic role as Moses' messenger to the Egyptians (7:1–2) rather than to the Israelite people.

The objections of Moses in the Priestly version of his commission fulfill the form of the genre, but not the function. This is most evident by the absence of any reassurance of the divine presence: "I will be with you." The interplay between the objection and the divine reassurance in the prophetic commission, as well as the need for experiential signs to instill "faith," give way to the genealogy of Phinehas in the Priestly version of Moses' commission. The genealogy signals

---

45. In Priestly tradition Moses does not fear future inadequacy; in fact, his sin in Num 20:2–13 is that he is too self-confident and acts independently of God. See Dozeman, "Numbers," 159–61.

a noncharismatic view of Mosaic authority, transmitted as a right of birth, not as an act of faith.

The Priestly author is not the originator of the commission of Moses. The Priestly author is following the prophetic genre of Exod 3:1–4:18, even though it conflicts with the noncharismatic view of Mosaic authority. The wilderness commission of Moses, therefore, is a pre-Priestly composition. The comparison indicates that the Priestly author has used the genre in a "lexically reorganized and topically rethematized way."[46] The result is an innerbiblical interpretation in which the Priestly author designates the Aaronide priesthood as the representatives of Mosaic authority, while defining their prophetic authority in the larger setting of the nations.

3. The Composition and Literary Context of Exod 3:1–4:18

The innerbiblical relationship between the two commissions of Moses is complicated by debate over the composition of Exod 3:1–4:18. The story is filled with literary tensions, raising questions of coherence and authorship.[47] A thorough interpretation of the literary problems is not possible.[48] I will limit my study to the recent identification of the post-Priestly authorship in Exod 3:1–4:18. Even here I will narrow my interpretation to three motifs that play an important role in the identification of the post-Priestly composition: the signs given to Moses (4:1–9); the insertion of Aaron into the commission of Moses (4:10–18); and the identification of the God of the exodus with the patriarchal ancestors, Abraham, Isaac, and Jacob (3:6, 15, 16; 4:5, focusing especially on 3:1–6). The study will begin with the problems of authorship in Exod 4, and it will conclude with an interpretation of the motif of the "God of the fathers" in Exod 3:1–6, focusing in particular on the relationship of the books of Genesis and Exodus.

3.1. The Signs of Mosaic Authority

The signs of Mosaic authority develop from the divine commission to Moses in Exod 3:16: "Go and assemble the elders of Israel and say to them, '*YHWH ... has appeared to me.*'" In Exod 4:1 Moses repeats aspects of the commission as an objection, relating the motif of faith and Mosaic authority: "What if they

---

46. Fishbane, *Biblical Interpretation in Ancient Israel*, 285.

47. See the summary of literary problems by Sean McEvenue, "The Speaker(s) in Ex 1–15," in *Biblische Theologie und gesellschaftlicher Wandel: Festschrift Norbert Lohfink, S. J.* (ed. G. Braulik et al.; Freiburg: Herder, 1993), 220–36.

48. See most recently Gertz, *Tradition und Redaktion*, 254–350

do not believe me and do not listen to my voice, but say, '*YHWH did not appear to you?*' " In Exod 4:2–9 YHWH responds to the objection, giving Moses three signs (את) to confirm his authority: (1) the transforming of Moses' staff into a snake (4:2–5); (2) the changing of the healthy hand of Moses into a leprous one (4:6–7); (3) and the instructions for turning the water of the Nile into blood (4:9).[49] The absence of a specific reference to the elders, who are the intended audience for Moses' commission in Exod 3:16, raises the question of whether Exod 4:1–9 is a literary addition to the commission of Moses in Exod 3. And the literary parallels between the first and third signs and the first two plagues in the Priestly history raise a further question concerning the post-Priestly composition of Exod 4:1–9.

The literary parallels between the signs of Moses and the Priestly plagues include (1) the turning of a staff into a snake (4:2–5 = 7:8–13) (2) and the changing of the Nile River into blood (4:9 = 7:14–24; see esp. vv. 20–21a, where Aaron is the protagonist).[50] The debate over the authorship of Exod 4:1–9 centers on the direction of the literary dependence between the signs given to Moses and the Priestly plague cycle. Some interpreters detect the influence of Priestly literature in the signs, suggesting post-Priestly authorship (e.g., Schmid, Blum, Gertz, and Otto). The reasons are varied. The order of the signs given to Moses follows the order of the plagues in the present form of the text, suggesting the dependence of Exod 4:1–9 on the Priestly history. The motif of faith is a late addition to the Pentateuch, relating prophetic presentations of Abraham (Gen 15), Moses (Exod 3–4), and Joshua (Josh 24). And shared motifs suggests that Exod 4:1–9 is reinterpreting the Priestly plague cycle: the underworld snake, תנין (7:8–13) is reinterpreted as a local creature, נחש (4:2–4); the turning of water into blood fits the setting of Egypt (7:14–24) but is out of place in the wilderness (4:9); and the motif of dry ground (יבשה) is a late addition to the story of the exodus.[51]

Others argue that the Priestly author has reinterpreted Exod 4:1–9, emphasizing the role of Aaron in the plagues (e.g., Noth, Propp, Schmidt, Van Seters). They note differences between the Priestly account of the plagues and the signs to Moses. Exodus 4:1–9 focuses on the authority of Moses and the faith of the

---

49. Schmidt notes the interplay between the motifs of action (Exod 4:2–4, 6) and interpretation (Exod 4:1, 5, 8–9) in the present structure of Exod 4:1–9 (*Exodus 1–6*, 188).

50. The parallels are interwoven with specific motifs. The first sign and the first Priestly plague employ the motifs of the staff (מטה), the act of throwing it (שלח in the hiphil), and its transformation into a snake. The third sign and the second plague include the motifs of blood, water, and the Nile River. See Gertz, *Tradition und Redaktion*, 312–13.

51. For more detailed interpretation, see Schmid, *Erzväter und Exodus*, 203–5; Gertz, *Tradition und Redaktion*, 313–15; Blum, "Die literarische Verbindung," 134; and especially Otto, "Die nachpriesterschriftliche Pentateuchredaktion," 103–6.

elders, as compared to the focus on Aaron and Pharaoh in the Priestly history. Moses' staff becomes a snake (נחש), not a water serpent (תנין), as is the case in Exod 7:8–13; the leprosy of Moses' hand does not repeat in the plague cycle; and the acts of power are called signs (את) in Exod 4:1–9, as compared to wonders (מופת) in the Priestly version of the plagues (e.g., 7:3, 9).[52]

This review of interpretation indicates that the comparison of motifs has reached an impasse in resolving the direction of literary dependence between Exod 4:1–9 and the Priestly plague cycle. The different form of the signs, however, and their sequence provide additional clues for identifying the author of Exod 4:1–9. The first two signs are in a different form than the third sign. Moses acts out the first two signs, as compared to the third sign, which consists of a divine prediction. The staff of Moses is changed into a snake (4:2–5) in the first sign, and his healthy hand becomes leprous (4:6–8) in the second sign. The changing of the water of the Nile into blood (4:9) is not acted out in the third sign. It remains simply a divine prediction about a future event.

The difference in the form of the signs is carried over into their meaning. The first two signs convey a distinct message from the third. The snake/staff of the first sign likely indicates healing, a symbolic meaning of the snake in the ancient Near East.[53] The source of healing, however, is not in the snake. Moses is presented as fleeing from its danger. The power to heal is in Moses' ability to reverse the sign and change the snake back into his staff, an action he performs before the Israelite people in Num 21:4–9. The second sign conveys the same message. Mosaic authority resides in the reversal of the leprosy, underscoring once again the power of Moses to heal, which he illustrates publicly in curing Miriam in Num 12. The emphasis on a reversal in the first two signs idealizes Moses as a healer, not as a wonder-worker. But the third sign departs from the previous two. The power of Moses is not in a reversal, signifying healing, but in a destructive action when Moses will pollute the Nile River into blood (4:9). In this sign Moses is a wonder-worker who transforms nature[54] rather than a healer who reverses a dangerous circumstance.

---

52. See Martin Noth, *Exodus: A Commentary* (OTL; Philadelphia: Westminster, 1962), 45–46; Schmidt, *Exodus 1–6*, 195–96, Van Seters, *Life of Moses*, 55–58.

53. See, for example, Joris Frans Borghouts, "Witchcraft, Magic and Divination in Ancient Egypt," *CANE* 3:1775–85. For evaluation of the Israelite cult, see Norbert Lohfink, " 'I Am Yahweh, Your Physician' (Exodus 15:26): God, Society and Human Health in a Postexilic Revision of the Pentateuch (Exod. 15:25b, 26)," in *Theology of the Pentateuch: Themes of the Priestly Narrative and Deuteronomy* (trans. L. M. Maloney; Minneapolis, Fortress, 1994), 35–95, esp. 63–71.

54. Van Seters describes such action as "metamorphoses," referring to Ovid, *Metamorphoses* (*Life of Moses*, 57 n. 68).

There are three problems with interpreting the signs to Moses in Exod 4:1–9 as a post-Priestly composition that is dependent on the Priestly plague cycle. The first is the absence of the motif of leprosy in the Priestly plague cycle. Why would a post-Priestly author include the sign of leprosy, if the intention is to reinterpret the Priestly plagues in Exod 4:1–9? The second problem is that the changing of the Nile River into blood is not restricted to the Priestly version of the plague cycle. It is also the first plague in the pre-Priestly history.[55] The presence of this sign in Exod 4:1–9 does not necessarily indicate a post-Priestly author. The author may just as well be associated with the pre-Priestly version of the plague cycle. The third problem is that Aaron is a wonder-worker in the Priestly plague cycle, not a healer, as is the case in the first two signs given to Moses. Thus the characterization of Moses in Exod 4:1–9 departs from the role of Aaron in the Priestly version of the plague cycle. The three problems are an obstacle for interpreting the Priestly account of the plague cycle as the literary source for the signs to Moses.

It is possible to account for the form, the number, and the sequence of the signs to Moses in the pre-Priestly history. The signs in Exod 4:1–9 are acted out in reverse order in the pre-Priestly version of the exodus and the wilderness journey. The last sign given to Moses is the first sign to be fulfilled. The third sign, the turning of water into blood (4:9), is demonstrated in the story of the exodus (Exod 1–14), specifically in the first plague of the pre-Priestly history (Exod 7:14–24*). The second and third signs reach beyond the exodus to the wilderness journey of the Israelite people (Exod 15–18; Num 11–21). The second sign, Moses' power over leprosy (4:6–7), is demonstrated in the story of Miriam's leprosy (Num 12). And the first sign, the snake (4:2–5), is associated with Nehoshet, at the close of the wilderness journey (Num 21:4–9). The distribution indicates that the three signs to Moses in Exod 4:1–9 provide the organization to the exodus and the wilderness journey in the pre-Priestly history.

The separate form of the signs acquires clarity in the larger narrative context of the pre-Priestly history. The form of the third sign, when compared to the first two signs, led to the conclusion that it illustrated the destructive power of Moses, who works wonders against Pharaoh and the Egyptians, not his ability to heal the Israelite people. The public demonstration of the sign reinforces this interpretation. The display of the sign in the first plague of the pre-Priestly history (Exod 7:14–24*) begins a sequence of events that culminate in the

---

55. The pre-Priestly version of the transformation of water into blood in Exod 7:14–24 includes Exod 7:14–16a, 17aα, b, 18, 20aβ–21a, 22bα, 23–24. The Priestly version includes Exod 7:16b, 17aβ, 19–20aα, 21b, 22abβ. See Thomas B. Dozeman, *God at War: Power in the Exodus Tradition* (New York: Oxford University Press, 1996), 15–18, 43–46, 110–17.

destruction of Pharaoh and the Egyptian army at the Red Sea (Exod 14*). The context clarifies the reason for the absence of a reversal in the third sign. The sign indicates the power of God and the authority of Moses to save through the destruction of the enemy, not through the healing of the Israelite people. And the idealization of Moses as a wonder-worker is underscored throughout the events of the exodus. Yet the destruction of the Egyptians is not the point of focus in the pre-Priestly history. The events of the exodus return to the Israelite people, underscoring their faith in Moses and in YHWH (14:31).

The first and second signs change in form to explore the healing power of Moses in the wilderness journey of the Israelite people, as compared to the events of the exodus. The theme of healing is introduced in the opening story of the wilderness journey, when the Israelites are promised health at Marah as a reward for obedience to the law (Exod 15:25b–26).[56] The promise of health is communicated through the divine self-revelation: "I am YHWH, your healer." The healing power of Moses is demonstrated in the second half of the wilderness journey (Num 11–21), after the revelation of law (Exod 19–34), when Moses acts out the signs of healing from his commission. Moses performs the second sign by curing the leprosy of Miriam (Num 12).[57] And he demonstrates the first sign by reversing the deadly bite of the seraphim with the construction of Nehoshet, the copper snake, at the conclusion of the wilderness journey (Num 21:4–9).[58] The mediation of Moses takes place in both stories through intercessory prayer, which Erik Aurelius has argued is crucial in the characterization of Moses as a healer in Deuteronomistic tradition.[59]

The signs given to Moses in Exod 4:1–9 may be an addition to his wilderness commission, but they do not appear to be a post-Priestly composition that arises from the Priestly version of the first two plagues. The signs to Moses provide an outline of the structure of the exodus and the wilderness journey in

---

56. On the authorship and the history of composition in Exod 15:22–26, see Noth, *Exodus,* 127; Norbert Lohfink, "I Am Yahweh, Your Physician," 51–62; Blum, *Studien zur Komposition des Pentateuch,* 144–46; and Erik Aurelius, *Der Fürbitter Israels: Eine Studie zum Mosebild im Alten Testament* (ConBOT 27; Lund: Almqvist & Wiksell, 1988), 153–56, 173–74.

57. For discussion concerning the pre-Priestly authorship of Num 11–12, see Martin Noth, *Numbers: A Commentary* (OTL; Philadelphia: Westminster, 1968), 92–93; Levin, *Der Jahwist,* 375; Van Seters, *Life of Moses,* 234–39; and Blum, *Studien zur Komposition des Pentateuch,* 76–85). Compare Thomas Römer, who identifies the author of Num 11–12 as post-Priestly ("Das Buch Numeri und das Ende des Jahwisten Anfragen zur 'Quellenscheidung' im vierten Buch des Pentateuch," in Gertz et al., *Abschied vom Jahwisten,* 215–31, esp. 225–27; and "Nombres 11–12 et la question d'une redaction deutéronomique dans le Pentateuque," in *Deuteronomy and Deuteronomic Literature: Festschrift C. H. W. Brekelmans* [BETL 133; Leuven: Leuven University Press; Peeters, 1997], 481–98).

58. See Thomas B. Dozeman, "Numbers," *NIB* 2:157–68.

59. Aurelius, *Der Fürbitter Israels,* 141–53.

the pre-Priestly history. The idealization of Moses as a wonder-worker (4:9) is demonstrated in the first plague (7:14–24) of the pre-Priestly plague cycle. The demonstration of power over the Egyptians leads eventually to the "faith" of the people in Moses and in Yhwh (14:31) at the conclusion of the exodus. The idealization of Moses as a healer (4:2–8) is demonstrated in the second half of the pre-Priestly wilderness journey (Num 12 and 21:4–9).

The Priestly author reinterprets the signs of Moses to accentuate the role of Aaron in the plague cycle, and the reinterpretation is similar in both cases. Aaron performs the signs before Pharaoh, not the Israelite people, while the meaning of the signs is no longer a unique act of healing but a demonstration of power. The action of Aaron advances the central theme of the Priestly commission of Moses: to bring Pharaoh and the Egyptians to knowledge of Yhwh (7:5). The demonstrations of power by Aaron are not unique but are repeated by the Egyptian magicians.

3.2. The Role of Aaron

The debate over Priestly authorship is even more acute in Exod 4:10–18 because of the sudden appearance of Aaron in the wilderness (4:13–16, 27–31) and in the initial confrontation with Pharaoh (5:1–6:1). The Priestly author fashions the commission of Moses to accentuate the importance of Aaron (6:2–7:7), while also including him in the plague cycle. And most references to Aaron in the Pentateuch occur in the Priestly history, where his portrayal as high priest is developed in detail.[60] Thus, the question arises whether the sudden appearance of Aaron in the wilderness is evidence of post-Priestly authorship to expand the role of Aaron from priest to prophetic teacher and to include him in the initial confrontation with Pharaoh (e.g., Valentin, Blum, Schmid, Otto, and Gertz).

Heinrich Valentin identifies the description of Aaron as "brother" (אח) of Moses and as "the Levite" (הלוי) as evidence for the influence of Priestly tradition in the composition of Exod 4:10–18. The identification of Aaron as "brother" suggests upon first reading a direct link to the Priestly history, where Moses and Aaron are fashioned into a nuclear family. The interpretation of "brother" as "sibling" would point to a post-Priestly author, who is building on the familial relationship of Aaron and Moses from the Priestly history. The aim

---

60. The problem with attributing Exod 4:10–18 to a Priestly or post-Priestly author is that Aaron appears in texts that have no relationship to Priestly literature. The clearest example is the war against the Amalekites in Exod 18:8–16, where Aaron and Hur assist Moses. For discussion, see Aelred Cody, *A History of the Old Testament Priesthood* (AnBib 35; Rome: Pontifical Biblical Institute, 1969), 150 and passim.

of a post-Priestly author, according to Valentin, is to accentuate the teaching office of the Aaronide priesthood in the postexilic period (see Lev 10:10).

But the term "brother" also plays a role in the pre-Priestly history, where it has a more general meaning, signifying the entire Israelite nation, as opposed to the Egyptians. Moses identifies the Israelite people as "brothers" in Exod 2:11, and he employs the same term at the conclusion of his wilderness commission, announcing to Jethro in Exod 4:18: "I must go and return to my brothers (אחי), who are in Egypt."[61] The initial description of Aaron as "brother" in Exod 4:14, only four verses before Moses' announcement to Jethro in verse 18, is likely the same general meaning, suggesting the pre-Priestly authorship of Exod 4:10–18.

The point of emphasis in the description of Aaron is not that he is a "brother" to Moses but that he is "the Levite." The title conflicts with the view of Aaron in the Priestly history, where Levites are separated from the Aaronide priests, as subordinate assistants in the cult (Num 3–4; 8). In Exod 4:10–16 the title "the Levite" designates an office of teaching. Aaron speaks the words that YHWH teaches (ירה) Moses (Exod 4:15). Werner H. Schmidt points to parallels in Deuteronomy (33:10), in Chronicles (2 Chr 17:8), and in Nehemiah (8:7).[62] The book of Deuteronomy provides more detail on the teaching function of the Levitical priests (Deut 24:8–9), their care of Torah (Deut 31:9–13, 25), and their ability to convey the covenant curses (Deut 27:1–26). The description of Aaron as "brother" and "the Levite" favors the pre-Priestly authorship of Exod 4:10–18.

The literary context of the appearance of Aaron provides further clarity on his function in the pre-Priestly history. The interpretation of Moses' wilderness commission (Exod 3:1–4:18) indicated that the Levites, represented by Aaron, are separated from the elders. The two groups are introduced in the second half of the commission, when the theme of Mosaic authority is developed (Exod 3:16–4:18). The elders are the point of focus in Exod 3:16–4:9, where the central theme is their need to have faith in Moses' authority, requiring a direct and an experiential encounter with his power. The introduction of Aaron, the Levite, is contained in Exod 4:10–18, where the theme is no longer belief in Mosaic authority but the need to convey it to the people through teaching.

---

61. Gertz, *Tradition und Redaktion*, 257–58.

62. Schmidt, *Exodus 1–6*, 204. See also Heinrich Valentin, *Aaron: Eine Studie zur vor-priesterschriftlichen Aaron-Überlieferung* (OBO 18; Fribourg: Universitätsverlag; Göttingen: Vandenhoeck & Ruprecht, 1978), 128–29; Van Seters, *Life of Moses*, 62. See Propp (*Exodus 1–18*, 214) for an early date to the composition of this section; and Gertz (*Tradition und Redaktion*, 321–28) for arguments supporting the post-Priestly authorship.

The distinction between the elders and Aaron is developed further in the pre-Priestly history, when the theme of Mosaic authority returns in Num 11–12, after the revelation of the law and the establishment of the tent of meeting (Exod 19–34). The structure of Num 11–12 parallels the wilderness commission of Moses, with the elders the point of focus in Num 11:4–35 (= Exod 3:16–4:9) and Aaron in Num 12 (= Exod 4:10–18). In Num 11 the elders acquire an office of leadership when they receive Mosaic authority directly from God in the tent of meeting. They even acquire momentarily the charismatic power of Moses to become prophets (Num 11:25).

Numbers 12 separates Aaron (and Miriam) from Moses, underscoring the latter's unique status before God as the only person to speak directly to the Deity. The clairvoyance of Aaron in the tent of meeting is indirect at best, arising from visions and dreams (Num 12:6–8).[63] Aaron does not receive the direct infusion of Mosaic authority, as was the case with the elders. The limitation of Aaron's authority in Num 12 corresponds to his introduction in Exod 4:10–18, where the Deity first appointed Aaron to assist Moses. Aaron is singled out for his eloquence in speaking, but he functions in a subordinate role to Moses as teacher. YHWH speaks only through Moses, who functions as a god to Aaron. Aaron, in turn, will be Moses' spokesperson to the Israelites, conveying the divine instruction (ירה, v. 16), a reference to law in the pre-Priestly history (see Exod 15:25; 24:12).

3.3. YHWH OF THE EXODUS AND THE GOD OF THE PATRIARCHS

The central theme in Exod 3:1–15 is the identification of YHWH, the God of the exodus, with the God of the patriarchs, Abraham, Isaac, and Jacob. The interweaving of the themes forms a literary relationship between the books of Genesis and Exodus. Both Van Seters and Rendtorff noted tradition-historical and literary tensions surrounding the themes, the God of the fathers and the promise to the ancestors. And as noted at the outset, the problems have received more detailed investigation in recent scholarship, leading to the conclusion that the merging of the themes in Exod 3:1–15 is the work of a post-Priestly author. The author is building on the composition of the Priestly history, where the God of the ancestors is first identified with YHWH, the God of the exodus (Exod 6:2–8).

The post-Priestly authorship of Exod 3:1–6 leads to the larger hypothesis that the Priestly history is the first composition to relate the books of Genesis

---

63. Miriam may represent other competing prophetic groups in the postexilic period (see Ursula Rapp, *Mirjam: Eine feministisch-rhetorische Lektüre der Mirjamtexte in der hebräischen Bibel* [BZAW 317; Berlin: de Gruyter, 2002], 31–193).

and Exodus. A thorough interpretation of this innovative hypothesis is neither possible nor necessary to evaluate the literary relationship between Genesis and Exodus and the post-Priestly authorship of the wilderness commission of Moses.[64] The issues converge in the divine self-revelation to Moses in Exod 3:6, when YHWH is identified as both the God of Moses' father and the God of the patriarchal ancestors, Abraham, Isaac, and Jacob. My interpretation will be restricted for the most part to this text, even though a similar identification repeats throughout the wilderness commission (Exod 3:6, 15, 16; 4:2). Is there a literary relationship between the divine self-revelation to Moses in Exod 3:1–6 and the book of Genesis? And, if so, who is the author, and what criteria do interpreters use to reach their conclusion?

Jan Christian Gertz argues for a literary relationship between the divine self-revelation to Moses (Exod 3:1–12*) and the book of Genesis by the post-Priestly redactor of the final form of the Pentateuch. The identity of the author emerges in the composition of Exod 3:1–6. The pre-Priestly form of the cultic legend includes Exod 3:1–4a, 5, and 6b. It recounts an initial event in the life of Moses without connection to the book of Genesis.

The literary relationship to Genesis is forged with the addition of Exod 3:4b, 6a. The divine statement, "Moses, Moses," with the response, "Here I am," in verse 4b is an interruption of verses 4a and 5, accentuated by the change in divine names from YHWH (v. 4a) to Elohim (v. 4b). The post-Priestly identity of the author is evident with the phrase "and God called (קרא) to him from (מן) the bush," suggesting the influence of Priestly style (see Lev 1:1). The divine self-identification, "I am the God of your father, the God of Abraham, the God of Isaac, and the God of Jacob," in Exod 3: 6a is separated from verse 5 with its own introduction, "and he said," while lacking continuity in content and in language.[65] The post-Priestly identity of the author is based, for the most part, on the limitation and concentration of the references to the three patriarchs to Exod 3:1–4:18,[66] the prior presence of the three patriarchs in the Priestly tradition (Exod 2:24; 6:2, 8), [67] and the limited and late distribution of references to the three patriarchs in the Deuteronomistic History and in Chronicles.[68]

---

64. See most recently Gertz, *Tradition und Redaktion*, 254–350.

65. Gertz concedes that the syntax of vv. 5–6a could simply be a literary transition, (1) if v. 6a continued the same thought of v. 5, merely shifting point of view; or (2) if v. 6a introduced a new section. But he concludes that these criteria are not fulfilled, thus indicating the redactional character of the verses (ibid., 270 n. 167). See the comments by Blum, "Die literarische Verbindung," 137–38 n. 85.

66. Gertz, *Tradition und Redaktion*, 280.

67. For discussion of Priestly tradition, see ibid., 237–54.

68. Ibid., 280; see also Römer, *Israels Väter*, 384–86.

The post-Priestly redaction in Exod 3:4b, 6a forges a literary tie to the divine address to Jacob in Beersheba in Gen 46:1aα–5a. The literary connections include the repetition of the person's name in the divine call ("Moses, Moses" [Exod 3:4b] and "Jacob, Jacob" [Gen 46:2aβ]), the response "Here I am" (הנני, Exod 3:4b; Gen 46:2b), and the identification of the Deity as "the God of your father" (Exod 3:6a; Gen 46:3a). Other less explicit indications of literary dependence reinforce the innerbiblical connection, including the combination of the "God of the father" with the motif of the divine promise of salvation (Exod 3:6a; Gen 46:3), the reference to the exodus with the phrase "I will bring you up [from the land]" (Exod 3:8a; Gen 46:4), and the motif of divine presence (Exod 3:12a; Gen 46:4).

A comparison of motifs in Gen 46:1aα–5a to other instances of divine self-revelation in the book of Genesis suggests an overarching literary design including the address to Abram (Gen 12:1–4a), Isaac (Gen 26:2–6), and Jacob (Gen 28:13–15). Genesis 46:1aα–5a may be a later addition to this sequence by the same post-Priestly redactor of Exod 3:4b and 6a, suggesting a more diachronic profile than a simple literary development.[69] Its function is to bridge the patriarchal literature to the exodus.[70] The self-revelation of Yhwh to Moses in Exod 3:6a, as both the "God of your father" and "the God of Abraham, the God of Isaac, and the God of Jacob," is the culmination of the literary sequence, according to Gertz, allowing for the explicit identification of the God of the patriarchs with Yhwh of the exodus.

Erhard Blum notes the literary problems that result from the identification of a pre-Priestly and a post-Priestly composition of Exod 3:1–6. The most notable is the lack of narrative logic in the pre-Priestly version of the story, with the absence of any identification of the Deity to Moses. The reaction of Moses to the Deity in verse 6b makes no sense, according to Blum, with the absence of the divine address (v. 4b) or the self-introduction (v. 6a). Moses could not know that the Deity was speaking to him.[71] And, in view of this, Blum argues against the identification of a separate author for Exod 3:4b, 6a, attributing the whole of Exod 3:1–6 to the pre-Priestly KD.

Blum does agree with Gertz that the pre-Priestly version of Moses' commission in Exod 3 is limited in scope to an initial event in the life of Moses, without connection to the book of Genesis. But this point of agreement leads to the further rejection of the literary parallels between Gen 46:1aα–5a and Exod

---

69. Gertz, *Tradition und Redaktion*, 277–83.

70. Ibid., 279.

71. Blum, "Die literarische Verbindung," 137–38. See also the more detailed arguments on קרא in v. 4b as not presupposing Priestly tradition; the literary function of the change in divine names in v. 4b; and the literary relationship between vv. 5 and 6a (138 n. 85).

3:1–6 cited by Gertz. For Blum the repetition of the person's name in the divine address and the response "Here I am" (הנני) are simply idiomatic speech in biblical narrative and not a sign of a more specific innerbiblical relationship.[72] The self-identification of the Deity in both texts is also unrelated. Genesis 46:3 is tied to Gen 31:13, according to Blum, while Exod 3:6a is grounded in the specific call of Moses.[73] Thus, Exod 3:1–6 does not presupposes Gen 46:1aα–5, nor does the latter text provide a bridge to the exodus. The reference to the three patriarchs in Exod 3:6a cannot be used to indicate a literary relationship between Genesis and Exodus, according to Blum, because Exod 3:6a cannot be attached or related to a specific text in Genesis.[74] The reference to the three ancestors may simply indicate a general knowledge of the patriarchs, independent of a literary connection between Genesis and Exodus.[75]

Blum is correct, in my judgment, that the isolation of a post-Priestly redactor in Exod 3:4b, 6a is not strongly supported by the literary structure of Exod 3:1–6. Yet the literary parallels between Gen 46:1aα–5a and Exod 3:1–6, cited by Gertz, do suggest an innerbiblical relationship. These text share "multiple and sustained linkages" in motifs and in form, to use the language of Michael Fishbane, extending beyond simple idiomatic speech in biblical narrative. There appears to be a "network of connections," in the words of David Carr, including the role of setting, which suggest a profile or horizon of meaning that encompasses both texts.[76]

4. THE CONCLUSION

My comparison of the two commissions of Moses suggests that the Priestly version in Exod 6:2–7:7 is dependent on the wilderness account in Exod 3:1–4:18. In addition to evaluating the relationship between the two commissions of Moses, my brief examination of Exod 3:1–6 has also explored the relationship between the wilderness commission of Moses and the book of Genesis in

---

72. Ibid., 137–38.

73. For discussion of Gen 46:2–4, see Erhard Blum, *Die Komposition der Vätergeschichte* (WMANT 57; Neukirchen-Vluyn: Neukirchener, 1984), 246–49; and idem, "Die literarische Verbindung," 131–32 n. 61.

74. Blum, "Die literarische Verbindung," 130.

75. Blum leaves open the possibility that the specific references to the three patriarchs in Exod 3:6 might be redactional (ibid., 139).

76. David M. Carr, "Genesis in Relation to the Moses Story: Diachronic and Synchronic Perspectives," in *Studies in the Book of Genesis: Literature, Redaction and History* (ed. A. Wénin; BETL 155; Leuven: Leuven University Press; Peeters, 2001), 273–95, esp. 279. For his interpretation of Gen 46:2–4, see *Reading the Fractures of Genesis: Historical and Literary Approaches* (Louisville: Westminster John Knox, 1996), 211–13.

a pre-Priestly narrative. The literary study has led to my conclusion that the wilderness commission of Moses in Exod 3:1–4:18 is a pre-Priestly composition and that the pre-Priestly history includes a version of Genesis and Exodus.

The study also raises a series of methodological questions about the composition of the Pentateuch. The shift in methodology from source criticism to supplemental or redaction-critical theories of composition introduces a host of problems concerning the identification of literary dependence in the composition of the Pentateuch that are presently unresolved. The criteria for judging innerbiblical relationships varies widely in different authors, ranging from a more limited study of syntax and motifs to the analysis of forms and even branching out to include the broader literary design of more extended narratives. The different criteria for judging literary dependence require further evaluation. There also remains a lack of agreement with regard to the identification of the genre of pentateuchal literature. Further research is required to clarify the difference for example between a *Komposition,* an origin tradition, and ancient historiography. How might these large distinctions in genre influence the criteria for evaluating coherence in biblical narratives, as well as the innerbiblical relationship and literary dependence between texts? The literary evaluation of Priestly tradition also looms in the background of any study of non-Priestly literature, whether it is evaluated as pre- or post-Priestly. The recent emphasis on a post-Priestly redaction of the Pentateuch rests in a large part on the evaluation of Priestly literature as an independent source or history, since the Priestly author is the first to combine the stories of Genesis and Exodus into a new master narrative of origins. Yet there are strong indications that the Priestly literature is supplemental and dependent on a pre-Priestly version. The recent arguments for a post-Priestly redaction make the evaluation of Priestly tradition a pressing problem in the study of the composition of the Pentateuch.

The theological implications of the late merging of the ancestor stories and the exodus are significant. The research by Schmid, Gertz, and Römer suggests that the relationship between the books of Genesis and Exodus is far more important than has been recognized in previous hypotheses of the composition of the Pentateuch. They have underscored the discontinuity between the ancestral stories and the narrative of the exodus, as competing traditions of origin with distinct conceptions of Yahwism. Schmid summarizes the different outlook of the two traditions at the close of his article in this volume with the following points of contrast:

Separate Origin Tradition of the Ancestors	Separate Origin Tradition of Moses/Exodus
1. Central Theme: Land Possession	1. Central Theme: Land Possession
2. Promise: Present Life in Land	2. Promise-Fulfillment: Conquest of Land
3. Indigenous to Land	3. Outsiders to Land
4. Inclusive to Other Peoples in the Land	4. Exclusive to Other Peoples in Land
5. Peaceful	5. Holy War
6. Israelite Identity: Genealogy	6. Israelite Identity: The Exodus
7. Focus Is on Abraham	7. Focus Is on Moses
8. Southern Point of View	8. Northern Point of View
9. Bearers of Tradition: People of the Land	9. Bearers of Tradition: The DTR school
10. Literary Boundaries: Ancestor Cycle	10. Literary Boundaries: Exodus–2 Kings

The implications of this insight require further research for interpreting the theology of the Pentateuch. The past models for interpreting the Pentateuch have tended to harmonize the two traditions into one story of salvation history. The result has been the subordination of the ancestral stories to the ideology of holy war in the story of the exodus. The hypothesis of the late formation of two origin traditions provides a new way of reading the canonical Pentateuch as two competing ideologies of land possession, one exclusive and violent and the other inclusive and peaceful. The insight conforms well to B. S. Childs's insight into the formation of canon as often consisting of the juxtaposition of traditions, rather than their harmonization. A new reading of the Pentateuch as the juxtaposition of two competing origin traditions may provide a way to loosen the stranglehold that the ideology of holy war has had on contemporary appropriations of the Pentateuch. I have identified a pre-Priestly author to be responsible for relating the story of the ancestors to the exodus. But this minor debate over authorship does not lessen the impact of recognizing two competing origin traditions in the formation of the Pentateuch.

THE YAHWIST AND THE REDACTIONAL
LINK BETWEEN GENESIS AND EXODUS*

Christoph Levin

In our dispute about the transition between the books of Genesis and Exodus, we concur on four basic decisions.

(1) Genesis and Exodus as books were separated at a secondary stage. Since the existence of the Priestly source has recently again become generally accepted,[1] and since the threads of this source run through Genesis and Exodus at least, these books must have once formed a literary unity. Genesis and Exodus did not yet exist as separate literary entities at the stage under discussion.[2] The focus here is the connection between the primeval history (Gen 1–11), the history of the patriarchs (Gen 12–36), and the Joseph story (Gen 37–50), on the one hand, and the Moses (Exod 2–4), exodus, and wilderness narratives (Exod 12—Num 20), on the other. To maintain that the transition between the books of Genesis and Exodus is decisive for theories about the Pentateuch goes too far.

(2) The non-Priestly narratives did not originally form a coherent composition. The hypothesis that there was a unified narrative composition extending from the creation of the world through to the conquest of Canaan cannot be maintained. In his contribution, Thomas Römer reminds us that this was already recognized by earlier research. Those aspects of the patriarchal narratives that connect to the national history cannot be reconciled with the narrative

---

*Translation of the original response by Margaret Kohl. The edited article has been revised by Bernard Levinson. Many thanks to both!

1. In recent research the serious doubts of Rolf Rendtorff and Erhard Blum have been overlooked. See Rolf Rendtorff, *The Problem of the Process of Transmission in the Pentateuch* (trans. J. J. Scullion; JSOTSup 89; Sheffield: JSOT Press, 1990); Erhard Blum, *Die Komposition der Vätergeschichte* (WMANT 57; Neukirchen-Vluyn: Neukirchener, 1984); and idem, *Studien zur Komposition des Pentateuch* (BZAW 189; Berlin: de Gruyter, 1990).

2. This is especially true if the Priestly source is seen as the basic document.

about the exodus from Egypt, as Albert de Pury has demonstrated.[3] The literary genre and narrative design of the Joseph story makes its original independence clear.[4] The Balaam narratives are also an independent composition. As regards the independence of the primeval history, I agree with Frank Crüsemann and Markus Witte, with some reservations.[5]

The idea that the Yahwist was a narrator must be abandoned. But we do not need to stress this over and over again. This is not a case of "farewell to the Yahwist," as Konrad Schmid sees it.[6] He, together with others, has failed to take account of the evidence that I have presented. I have shown that the Yahwist was not a narrator but an editor—let us call him the "editor J"—who brought the non-Priestly narrative compositions into the literary cohesion we have today.[7]

(3) The third point on which we agree is the dating. The integration of the separate blocks of tradition represented by the Tetrateuch narrative as a whole was only possible at a later period. In my opinion, the Yahwist has in view the beginning of the Jewish Diaspora.[8] This can be seen from his choice of narrative sources, as well as from his worldwide perspective and his concept of the God YHWH. As Schmid has stressed, the late date has serious consequences for our

---

3. See Albert de Pury, *Promesse divine et légende cultuelle dans le cycle de Jacob: Genèse 28 et les traditions patriarcales* (ÉB; Paris: Gabalda, 1975), and his numerous other articles on this subject. See also Thomas Römer, *Israels Väter: Untersuchungen zur Väterthematik im Deuteronomium und in der deuteronomistischen Tradition* (OBO 99; Fribourg: Universitätsverlag; Göttingen: Vandenhoeck & Ruprecht, 1990); and Konrad Schmid, *Erzväter und Exodus: Untersuchungen zur doppelten Begründung der Ursprünge Israels innerhalb der Geschichtsbücher des Alten Testaments* (WMANT 81; Neukirchen-Vluyn: Neukirchener, 1999).

4. See, for example, Herbert Donner, "Die literarische Gestalt der alttestamentlichen Josephsgeschichte," in idem, *Aufsätze zum Alten Testament* (BZAW 224; Berlin: de Gruyter, 1994), 76–120.

5. Frank Crüsemann, "Die Eigenständigkeit der Urgeschichte," in *Die Botschaft und die Boten: Festschrift Hans Walter Wolff* (ed. J. Jeremias and L. Perlitt; Neukirchen-Vluyn: Neukirchener, 1981), 11–29; and Markus Witte, *Die biblische Urgeschichte: Redaktions- und theologiegeschichtliche Beobachtungen zu Genesis 1,1–11,26* (BZAW 265; Berlin: de Gruyter, 1998).

6. *Abschied vom Jahwisten. Die Komposition des Hexateuch in der jüngsten Diskussion* (ed. J. C. Gertz et al.; BZAW 315; Berlin: de Gruyter, 2002); and my review of this volume: "Abschied vom Jahwisten?" *TRu* 69 (2004): 329–44.

7. Christoph Levin, *Der Jahwist* (FRLANT 157; Göttingen: Vandenhoeck & Ruprecht, 1993). For the English-speaking readership, Ernest W. Nicholson, *The Pentateuch in the Twentieth Century: The Legacy of Julius Wellhausen* (Oxford: Clarendon, 1998), 161–65, presents a fine outline of the thesis. However, Nicholson misses the basic argument: the redaction-critical distinction between the pre-Yahwistic narrative sources, on the one hand, and editorial additions, on the other (165–67).

8. See Levin, *Der Jahwist*, 414–35 ("Die Botschaft des Jahwisten"); idem, *The Old Testament: A Brief Introduction* (trans. M. Kohl; Princeton: Princeton University Press, 2005), 61–70; and idem, "The Yahwist: The Earliest Editor in the Pentateuch" (forthcoming).

view of the religious history of Israel and Judah. About this there is no disagreement between us. If I still adhere to the hypothesis of a Yahwist, this is only a matter of literary history in particular, which is not decisive for the history of Israelite religion nor can be decided by the history of Israelite religion.

(4) The fourth point on which we agree—at least some of us—is the enduring importance of the Documentary Hypothesis. Römer reports that among limited groups of German-speaking scholars it has become the fashion to call the Documentary Hypothesis into doubt. But in his monograph about the final redaction, Jan Christian Gertz shows very clearly that two accounts are present alongside one another in Exod 1–14, which have subsequently been linked together.[9] His results, however, cannot be reconciled with Schmid's view that the call of Moses in Exod 3 is dependent on the Priestly source.[10] The arguments that Schmid and others offer contradict the nature of the material, which is essentially narrative, not redactional. Here I emphatically agree with Thomas Dozeman.[11]

Römer has stressed that the Documentary Hypothesis was developed on the basis of the book of Genesis and was only extended to the other books from that point. It is therefore particularly interesting that Gertz based his proof on the book of Exodus. Earlier research did not find the dominance of the book of Genesis problematic. It is easy to see why. The Documentary Hypothesis can be developed only on the basis of the narratives, and it applies *prima facie* only to the narrative material. By far the greatest part of the laws in the Pentateuch, beginning with Exod 12, were added later. In the first chapters of Exodus, the narrative style is quite similar to that of Genesis. If there is a caesura, we have to look for it not between Genesis and Exodus but somewhere after Exod 14.

If we really come down to it, the controversy between us has to do merely with the redactional linking of the narrative blocks. Schmid and Gertz attribute this to the P source. By doing so, they resurrect a form of the Supplementary Hypothesis that prevailed during the first half of the nineteenth century. According to this model, P is the earliest literary foundation of the Pentateuch, while the non-P material was added subsequently. In contrast, I maintain that there was a separate redaction within the non-P material.

---

9. Jan Christian Gertz, *Tradition und Redaktion in der Exoduserzählung: Untersuchungen zur Endredaktion des Pentateuch* (FRLANT 186; Göttingen: Vandenhoeck & Ruprecht, 2000).

10. See also the strong arguments of Erhard Blum: "To sum up, in Exodus 3 there is no one single detail to make sure or at least probable that the text is diachronically dependent on the Priestly Pentateuch tradition" ("Die literarische Verbindung von Erzvätern und Exodus," in Gertz et al., *Abschied vom Jahwisten*, 127 n. 5; my translation).

11. See also the appendix to this article: "The Yahwist as Editor in Exodus 3: The Evidence of Language."

Römer, Schmid, and Gertz point out that explicit links between the books of Genesis and Exodus were added only later, after the Priestly source. This argument from silence goes back to Rainer Kessler.[12] But it is untenable. It is certain that texts such as Gen 15 and 46:2–4 are later than P.[13] The same is true of most of the promises to the patriarchs, beginning with the key text of Gen 13:15–17.[14] The promises to the patriarchs presuppose the link between Genesis and Exodus. Consequently, they cannot be used as evidence to argue that the link did not previously exist. All these texts are irrelevant for our question. With regard to the relationship of Gen 46 to Exod 3, Dozeman has raised the necessary critical questions.

Gertz falls back upon the famous image with which Wellhausen described the procedure of the Pentateuch redaction: "It is as if Q [i.e., P] were the scarlet thread on which the pearls of JE are hung."[15] But Wellhausen was wrong. Everyone who considers the role of the Priestly source in the history of the patriarchs is familiar with the problem: that a continuous thread is in fact lacking. Rolf Rendtorff has emphatically pointed this out.[16] Even if we accept Schmid's suggestion that the Priestly source did not include a Joseph story, the problems about the Priestly presentation of Abraham, Isaac, and Jacob remain unsolved. Moreover, Moses is never introduced by the Priestly source. It is significant that Schmid's reconstruction breaks off at the crucial point: the transition to the story of the exodus. Gertz, despite his concentration on the transition, is forced into highly speculative assignments as regards Gen 50. In his analysis there is a significant *petitio principii*, which can be described as: "There *must* be a Priestly thread in the Pentateuch to have created the coherence of the whole." He himself admits that the only text in Gen 50 that is certainly P consists of verses 12–13 and 22b. This follows the general consensus of research, as Schmid's list

---

12. Rainer Kessler, "Die Querverweise im Pentateuch: überlieferungsgeschichtliche Untersuchung der expliziten Querverbindungen innerhalb des vorpriesterlichen Pentateuchs" (Th.D. diss., University of Heidelberg, 1972).

13. Christoph Levin, "Jahwe und Abraham im Dialog: Genesis 15," in *Gott und Mensch im Dialog: Festschrift Otto Kaiser* (ed. M. Witte; 2 vols.; BZAW 345/1; Berlin: de Gruyter, 2004), 237–57.

14. It is essential that the promise of Gen 13:15–17 is pronounced at Bethel, i.e., in the very same place where Abraham's tent previously had been (see 12:8). The return to Bethel (see 13:3) was necessary only because in 12:10–20 Abraham went to Egypt. This excursus causes Abraham to anticipate the fate of the later people of Israel. Gen 12:17, 20 verbally foreshadows the story of the plagues in Egypt—in a form composed already of P and non-P. See my "Jahwe und Abraham im Dialog," 240–41.

15. Julius Wellhausen, *Prolegomena to the History of Ancient Israel* (trans. J. S. Black and A. Menzies; Edinburgh: Black, 1885; repr., Atlanta: Scholars Press, 1994), 332 (my addition).

16. See Rendtorff, *Problem.*

shows. When Gertz assigns verse 14 to the Priestly source, because it is indispensable as a bridge, the result is a crass contradiction to verses 12–13. There are sound reasons, therefore, why I have attributed the redactional bridge formed by Gen 50:14 and 26a, as well as Exod 1:8, to the editor J.[17]

The textual gap in the Priestly source, which Gertz tries in vain to close, does not speak against the literary unity of the P document. That unity is indicated by the well-known correspondence between creation and Sinai, as well as by the covenant theology that extends from Noah to Moses, through Abraham and Jacob.[18] But P has not come down to us unscathed.[19] It therefore cannot simply be understood as the basic document. The fact that the sequence of the whole narrative as we have it today holds together is due to the existence of a second continuous source parallel to P. From Gen 12 it took over the literary lead, just as P took the lead in the primeval history.[20] Besides the document P, the document J also existed. The Tetrateuch thus does not hang on a single thread but on a cord plaited together from two strands. This cord makes it possible for the work as a whole to avoid falling apart when one of the two threads is torn, or missing, which is several times the case. If Gertz had undertaken his investigation of the final redaction on the basis of the patriarchal narratives, he would have arrived at different basic assumptions.

To come back to Römer's survey of the research history: Kuenen was right when he stated that parts of the non-Priestly text "must … be derived from a single work which we may call the *Yahwistic* document … and which we may indicate by the letter J."[21] Wellhausen, Budde, Smend, Fohrer, and others were right in differentiating literary strata within this document.[22] Gunkel was also right when he ascribed the collecting of the material to several Yahwists, who

---

17. The argument is to be found in my *Der Jahwist*, 297–321.

18. Levin, *Old Testament*, 101–9 ("The Priestly Source").

19. In most parts of the patriarchal narratives only fragments of the former P source have survived; see Gen 16:3aβγ, 16; 21:2b, 4–5; 25:19–20, 26b; 30:22a; 31:18*; 37:2aα, b; 41:46a; 46:6–7. Traces of the thread of the source can be found in Gen 11:27, 31–32; 12:4b–5; 13:6, 11b–12aα; 19:29abα; also in Gen 26:34–35; 28:1–9; also in Gen 47:28; 49:1a, 29–32, 33aα, b; 50:12–13.

20. In Gen 12–50, the fragments of the Priestly thread (see previous note) have been woven into the tapestry of the Yahwistic narratives. By contrast, in Gen 1–11 the Yahwistic text has been fitted into the closely structured Priestly framework. See Levin, *Old Testament*, 110–14 ("The Pentateuch Redaction").

21. Abraham Kuenen, *An Historico-Critical Inquiry into the Origin and Composition of the Hexateuch* (trans. P. H. Wicksteed; London: Macmillan, 1886), 140.

22. Julius Wellhausen, *Die Composition des Hexateuchs und der historischen Bücher des Alten Testaments* (4th ed.; Berlin: de Gruyter, 1963), esp. 207; Karl Budde, *Die biblische Urgeschichte* (Giessen: Ricker, 1883), esp. 244–47; Rudolf Smend, *Die Erzählung des Hexateuch auf ihre Quellen untersucht* (Berlin: Reimer, 1912), 16–30 and passim; and Georg Fohrer, *Introduction to the Old Testament* (trans. D. E. Green; Nashville: Abingdon, 1968).

follow one another in today's text.[23] Noth was right when, along the same lines, he stressed the existence of different blocks of tradition.[24] Von Rad, not least, was right in seeing the Yahwist as an author and theologian,[25] for the J source has a clearly detectible kerygma, in spite of the diversity of the narrative material.

The method by which to integrate all these insights is redaction criticism, which distinguishes within the J document between the given narrative cycles on the one hand and the editor J on the other. As everywhere else, the theology does not emerge on the level of the ancient tradition but can be traced back to the literary intention of an editor. Von Rad himself saw the Yahwist as a theologian belonging to the "late" period—influenced, however, by the biblical presentation of history, he defined this late period as the early monarchy.[26] Von Rad also neglected to distinguish clearly between tradition and redaction:[27] he overestimated the possibility of oral tradition, as did the transmission-historical research then dominant. When in 1961 his pupil Hans Walter Wolff focused on the question about the kerygma of the Yahwist, he inadvertently demonstrated that the results require a redaction-historical approach instead.[28] This solution has been pursued step by step since the 1960s, beginning with the work of Rudolf Kilian in 1966[29] and Volkmar Fritz in 1970.[30] I myself have succeeded since 1978 in extending this investigation to the whole of the Tetrateuch and have been able to describe the editorial profile of the editor J, his language, his method, his sources, his audience, and his theology.[31] So let us understand the J

---

23. See Hermann Gunkel, *Genesis* (trans. M. E. Biddle from the 3rd ed., 1910; Macon, Ga.: Mercer University Press, 1997).

24. Martin Noth, *A History of Pentateuchal Traditions* (trans. B. W. Anderson; Eaglewood Cliffs, N.J.: Prentice Hall, 1972).

25. Gerhard von Rad, "The Form-Critical Problem of the Hexateuch," in idem, *The Problem of the Hexateuch and Other Essays* (trans. E. W. Trueman Dicken; New York: McGraw, 1966), 1–78.

26. Ibid., 68.

27. This is also the problem with the "Yahwist" of John Van Seters. See, for example, his *In Search of History: Historiography in the Ancient World and the Origins of Biblical History* (New Haven: Yale University Press, 1983). Van Seters sees the Yahwist not as an editor but as a history writer using traditions. He makes no clear distiction between traditional and editorial text. Therefore, the editorial profile is rather indistinct, including a lot of material that earlier research rightly viewed as being non-Yahwistic, such as "Elohistic" and Deuteronomistic texts.

28. Hans Walter Wolff, "Das Kerygma des Jahwisten," in idem, *Gesammelte Studien zum Alten Testament* (TB 22; Munich: Kaiser, 1973), 345–73.

29. Rudolf Kilian, *Die vorpriesterlichen Abrahamsüberlieferungen literarkritisch und traditionskritisch untersucht* (BBB 24; Bonn: Hanstein, 1966).

30. Volkmar Fritz, *Israel in der Wüste: Traditionsgeschichtliche Untersuchung der Wüstenüberlieferung des Jahwisten* (Marburg: Elwert, 1970).

31. See my *Der Jahwist*, esp. 389–98 ("Die Quellen des Jahwisten"), 399–413 ("Die Sprache des Jahwisten"), and 414–35 ("Die Botschaft des Jahwisten").

document as the work of an editor. In this way justice is done to earlier research, and there is no need for clumsy expedients. Welcome back, Yahwist!

APPENDIX

THE YAHWIST AS EDITOR IN EXODUS 3: THE EVIDENCE OF LANGUAGE

The pre-Priestly continuity between the books of Genesis and Exodus is best seen from the perspective of Exod 3. The narrative of the burning bush and the divine speech that commissions Moses includes numerous cross-references to the book of Genesis, on the one hand, and to the narratives about the crossing of the Sea of Reeds and the wandering of the Israelites in the desert, on the other. One must first, of course, cut out the many late expansions of the chapter.[32] The remaining text then bears striking linguistic and stylistic similarities to the editorial expansions that the editor J has added to both the non-Priestly primeval history and the patriarchal narratives. Therefore, it is highly probable that the editor J wrote this text, too.

The narrative of the call of Moses obviously disrupts the oldest thread of the Moses-stories, which begin with Exod 2:1. With Moses' return to Egypt, the narrative of his flight to Moab comes to an end, thus forming what can be seen as a perfect literary join: "In the course of those many days the king of Egypt died. So Moses took his wife and his sons and set them on an ass, and went back to the land of Egypt" (Exod 2:23aα; 4:20).[33] This narrative sequence is now disconnected. Probably the interpolation goes back to the editor J.

As often in Genesis, the editor J used a given tradition to put his message on stage. The story of the finding of a cultic place, which forms the core of Exodus 3, originally formed a literary fragment of its own. The original shape may have been as follows:

> (1) Now Moses was keeping the flock of his father-in-law, Jethro..., and he led the flock to the west side of the wilderness, and came ... into the desert. (2) ... And he looked, and lo, a bush was burning, yet the bush was not consumed.... (4) ... God called to him out of the bush, "Moses, Moses!" And he said, "Here am I." (5) Then he said, "Do not come near; put off your shoes from your feet, for the place on which you are standing is holy ground."

---

32. See the analysis of Exod 3 in my *Der Jahwist*, 326–33. It is indispensable to make this distinction quite clear. One should not argue with the many late additions of the chapter, some of which are obviously influenced by Deuteronomistic theology and some of which may be younger than P.

33. Translation following RSV.

Because the cultic place is not given a name, the origin of this tradition remains uncertain. Maybe some part of the original text has broken off.

The literary additions that make the text as we have it start with the editor J. He shaped the chapter like one of the well-known scenes of encounter with God to be found in the patriarchal narratives (e.g., Gen 16; 18; 28; 32), thus making it one of the key scenes of his outline of history. The oldest expanded form reads as follows (the editorial text of J given in italics):

(1) Now Moses was keeping the flock of his father-in-law, Jethro, *the priest of Midian;* and he led the flock to the west side of the wilderness, and came ...[34] into the desert. (2) *And the angel of* YHWH *appeared to him in a flame of fire out of the midst of a bush;* and he looked, and lo, a bush was burning, yet the bush was not consumed. (3) *And Moses said, "I will turn aside and see this great sight, why the bush is not burning."* (4) *When* YHWH *saw that he turned aside to see,* God called to him out of the bush, "Moses, Moses!" And he said, "Here am I." (5) Then he said, "Do not come near; put off your shoes from your feet, for the place on which you are standing is holy ground." ... (7) *Then* YHWH *said, "I have seen the affliction of my people who are in Egypt, and have heard their cry* ... (8) *and I have come down to deliver them out of the hand of the Egyptians, and to bring them up out of that land to a good and broad land* ... (16) *Go and gather the elders of Israel together, and say to them,* YHWH *the God of your fathers has appeared to me,* ... *saying,* ... (17) ... *I will bring you up out of the affliction of Egypt,* ... *to a land flowing with milk and honey....* (18) ... *And you and the elders of Israel shall go to the king of Egypt and say to him,* YHWH, *the God of the Hebrews, has met with us; and now, we pray you, let us go a three days' journey into the wilderness, that we may sacrifice to* YHWH *our God.* ... (21) *And I will give this people favor in the sight of the Egyptians; and when you go, you shall not go empty,* (22) *but each woman shall ask of her neighbor, and of her who sojourns in her house, jewelry of silver and of gold, and clothing, and you shall put them on your sons and on your daughters; thus you shall despoil the Egyptians."* ... (4:18) *Moses went back to Jethro his father-in-law and said to him, "Let me go back, I pray, to my kinsmen in Egypt and see whether they are still alive." And Jethro said to Moses, "Go in peace."*

The editorial offspring of the expansion is evidenced by language. There are quite a number of striking similarities with the narratives of the books of Genesis as well as with some narrative parts of the books of Exodus and Numbers. What is important is that those parallels are also editorial. This makes it highly probable that one and the same hand has been writing. Here are the examples:

---

34. The later, non-Yahwistic expansions are marked by ellipses. See further Levin, *Der Jahwist,* 330–32.

(1) Exod 3:2: "And the angel of Yнwн appeared to him (וירא מלאך יהוה אליו)." Compare Gen 12:7: "Then Yнwн appeared to (וירא יהוה אל־) Abram, and said, 'To your descendants I will give this land'"; Gen 16:7: "The angel of Yнwн (מלאך יהוה) found her [Hagar] by a spring of water in the wilderness"; Gen 18:1: "And Yнwн appeared to him (וירא אליו יהוה) [Abraham] by the oaks of Mamre"; and Gen 26:2: "And Yнwн appeared to him (וירא אליו יהוה) [Isaac], and said, 'Sojourn in this land, and I will be with you, and will bless you.'"

(2) Exod 3:3: "And Moses said, 'I will turn aside and see this great sight, why the bush is not burning.'" This kind of monologue counts as a stylistic device of the editor J.[35] Compare Gen 18:12: "So Sarah laughed to herself, saying, 'After I have grown old, and my husband is old, shall I have pleasure?'"; Gen 21:7: "And she [Sarah] said, 'Who would have said to Abraham that Sarah would suckle children? Yet I have borne him a son in his old age'"; Gen 28:16: "Then Jacob awoke from his sleep and said, 'Surely Yнwн is in this place; and I did not know it'"; and Gen 32:21: "For he [Jacob] thought, 'I may appease him with the present that goes before me.'"

(3) Exod 3:4: "When Yнwн saw that (וירא יהוה כי) he turned aside to see." Compare Gen 6:5: "Yнwн saw that (וירא יהוה כי) the wickedness of man was great in the earth"; and Gen 29:31: "When Yнwн saw that (וירא יהוה כי) Leah was hated, he opened her womb; but Rachel was barren."

(4) Exod 3:7: "Then Yнwн said, 'I have seen the affliction (ראה ראיתי את־עני) of my people who are in Egypt, and have heard their cry (שמעתי צעקתם)'"; also v. 17: "I will bring you up out of the affliction (מעני) of Egypt, to a land flowing with milk and honey." Compare Gen 4:10: "And Yнwн said [to Cain], 'What have you done? The voice of your brother's blood is crying (צעקים) to me from the ground'"; Gen 16:11: "And the angel of Yнwн said to her [Hagar], 'Behold, you are with child, and shall bear a son; you shall call his name Ishmael; because Yнwн has given heed to your affliction (שמע יהוה אל־עניך)'"; Gen 18:20–21: "Then Yнwн said, 'Because the outcry (זעקת) against Sodom and Gomorrah is great, I will go down to see (וארדה) whether they have done altogether according to the outcry (הכצעקתה) which has come to me; and if not, I will know'"; Gen 19:13: [The angels to Lot,] "Because the outcry (צעקתם) against its people has become great before Yнwн"; Gen 29:32: "For she [Leah] said, 'Because Yнwн has looked upon my affliction (ראה יהוה בעניי); surely now my husband will love me'"; Gen 29:33: "And [Leah] said, 'Because Yнwн has heard (שמע יהוה) that I am hated, he has given me this son

---

35. Except for the editorial stratum of the Yahwist, monologues of this kind are very rare in the Old Testament. On this point, see ibid., 411.

also'"; Exod 1:11–12: "Therefore they [the Egyptians] set taskmasters over them to afflict them (ענתו) with heavy burdens. But the more they were oppressed (יענו), the more they multiplied and the more they spread abroad"; and Exod 14:10: "And the people of Israel cried out (ויצעקו) to Yʜwʜ" (cf. 15:24–25; 17:4; Num 11:2).

(5) Exod 3:8: "I have come down (וארד) to deliver them out of the hand of the Egyptians, and to bring them up out of that land to a good and broad land (ארץ טובה ורחבה)." Compare Gen 11:5: "And Yʜwʜ came down to see (וירד יהוה לראת) the city and the tower, which the sons of men had built"; Gen 18:21: "I will go down to see (ארדה־נא ואראה) whether they have done altogether according to the outcry which has come to me; and if not, I will know"; Gen 26:22: "And he moved from there and dug another well, and over that they did not quarrel; so he called its name Rehoboth (רחבות), saying, 'For now Yʜwʜ has made room (הרחיב יהוה) for us, and we shall be fruitful in the land (בארץ)' "; and Exod 34:5: "And Yʜwʜ descended (וירד יהוה) in the cloud and stood with him [Moses] there. And he proclaimed the name of Yʜwʜ."

(6) Exod 3:16: "Go and gather the elders of Israel together, and say to them, 'Yʜwʜ the God of your fathers (יהוה אלהי אבתיכם) has appeared to me (נראה אלי)'" (cf. v. 2); also v. 18: "Yʜwʜ, the God of the Hebrews (יהוה אלהי העבריים), has met with us (נקרה)." Compare Gen 24:12: "And he [Abraham's servant] said, 'O Yʜwʜ, God of my master Abraham (יהוה אלהי אדני אברהם), grant me success (הקרה־נא) today, I pray you'" (cf. vv. 27, 48); Gen 27:20: "He answered, 'Because Yʜwʜ your God (יהוה אלהיך) granted me success (הִקְרָה)'"; and Gen 28:13: "And behold, Yʜwʜ stood above it and said, 'I am Yʜwʜ, the God of Abraham your father (יהוה אלהי אברהם אביך) and the God of Isaac.' "

(7) Exod 3:21–22: "And I will give this people favor in the sight of (ונתתי חן בעיני) the Egyptians; and when you go, you shall not go empty, but each woman shall ask of her neighbor, and of her who sojourns in her house, jewelry of silver and of gold, and clothing, and you shall put them on your sons and on your daughters; thus you shall despoil the Egyptians." Compare Gen 6:8: "But Noah found favor in the eyes of (מצא חן בעיני) Yʜwʜ" (cf. Gen 19:19); Gen 18:3: [Abraham to Yʜwʜ,] "If I have found favor in your sight (מצאתי חן בעיניך), do not pass by your servant" (cf. Gen 30:27; 32:6; 33:8, 10, 15; 47:29; Exod 34:9; Num 11:11); Gen 24:35: [Abraham's servant to Betuel and Laban,] "Yʜwʜ has greatly blessed my master, and he has become great; he has given him flocks and herds, silver and gold, menservants and maidservants, camels and asses"; Gen 26:14: "He [Isaac] had possessions of flocks and herds, and a great household, so that the Philistines envied him"; Gen 30:43: "Thus the man [Jacob] grew exceedingly rich, and had large flocks, maidservants and menservants, and camels and asses"; Gen 39:4: "Joseph found favor in his [master's]

sight (וימצא יוסף חן בעיניו) and attended him"; Gen 39:21: "But Yʜᴡʜ was with Joseph and gave him favor in the sight of (ויתן חנו בעיני) the keeper of the prison"; and Exod 12:36: "And Yʜᴡʜ had given the people favor in the sight of (ויהוה נתן את־חן העם בעיני) the Egyptians, so that they let them have what they asked. Thus they despoiled the Egyptians."

(8) Exod 4:18: "Moses went back to Jethro his father-in-law and said to him, 'Let me go back, I pray, to my kinsmen (אחי) in Egypt (אשר־במצרים, cf. v. 7) and see whether they are still alive (העודם חיים)' "; see Gen 4:9: "[Cain to Yʜᴡʜ,] 'Am I my brother's keeper?' (השמר אחי אנכי)"; Gen 13:18: "Then Abraham said to Lot, 'Let there be no strife between you and me, and between your herdsmen and my herdsmen; for we are kinsmen (אנשים אהים אנחנו)' "; Gen 29:15: "Then Laban said to Jacob, 'Because you are my kinsman (אחי אתה), should you therefore serve me for nothing? Tell me, what shall your wages be?' " (cf. Gen 33:9); Gen 37:26–27: "Then Judah said to his brothers, 'What profit is it if we slay our brother (אחינו) and conceal his blood? Come, let us sell him to the Ishmaelites, and let not our hand be upon him, for he is our brother, our own flesh (אחינו בשרנו הוא).' And his brothers heeded him"; Gen 45:26: "And they [the brothers] told him [Jacob], 'Joseph is still alive (עוד יוסף חי)' "; Gen 45:28: "And Israel said, 'It is enough; Joseph my son is still alive (עוד יוסף בני חי); I will go and see him before I die' "; Gen 46:30: "Israel said to Joseph, 'Now let me die, since I have seen your face and know that you are still alive (עודך חי)' "; and Exod 2:11: "When Moses had grown up, he went out to his people (אחיו) and looked on their burdens."

Summary

These cases prove that Exod 3 forms an integral part of the outline of the history of the people of God. That outline starts with the primeval history and includes both the history of the patriarchs and the history of the exodus. It is highly probable that the common language points to common authorship: to the editor J who has chosen, connected, and commented upon the individual narratives that would eventually form the fundamental document of the Tetrateuch. Redaction criticism allows us to recognize that earlier scholarship was correct after all. The core of the non-Priestly narrative material forms an independent literary document (in the sense of the Documentary Hypothesis): the so-called "Yahwist."

THE REPORT OF THE YAHWIST'S
DEMISE HAS BEEN GREATLY EXAGGERATED!

John Van Seters

1. INTRODUCTION

As a champion of the Yahwist for many years,[1] I have been asked to respond to the essays in this volume that seek to get rid of the Yahwist as a reminder of traditional source analysis, as reflected in the Documentary Hypothesis, and to replace it with a "new" and more sophisticated methodology, that of redaction criticism. For some inexplicable reason the source P is retained, as well as the distinction between P and non-P. The P source is regarded as providing the basic form and shape of the Pentateuch, with non-P considered as filler or post-P redactional expansion. This looks like the pre-Wellhausian source analysis of Ewald in a slightly different form and displaced from his early dates into the all-inclusive "Persian period."

However, it is the non-P corpus, traditionally associated with J (and E), that is at the heart of the debate. Now we must be very clear about what is at issue in this discussion because the matter has often been obscured by details that have nothing to do with the current status of the debate and by the use of jargon, such as the "Yahwist hypothesis," which is meant to suggest, I suppose, that the Yahwist is the real culprit in the Documentary Hypothesis. This seems to be the point of the historical survey of Thomas Römer, "The Elusive Yahwist."

---

1. John Van Seters, *Abraham in History and Tradition* (New Haven: Yale University Press, 1975); idem, *Der Jahwist als Historiker* (Theologische Studien 134; Zürich: Theologischer Verlag, 1987); idem, *Prologue to History: The Yahwist as Historian in Genesis* (Louisville: Westminster John Knox; Zürich: Theologischer Verlag, 1992); idem, *The Life of Moses: The Yahwist as Historian in Exodus-Numbers* (Louisville: Westminster John Knox; Kampen: Kok-Pharos, 1994); idem, *The Pentateuch: A Social-Science Commentary* (Sheffield: Sheffield Academic Press, 1999); idem, *A Law Book for the Diaspora: Revision in the Study of the Covenant Code* (New York: Oxford University Press, 2003). It seems pointless to cite all of my articles dealing with the Yahwist, although in some of the essays in the volume little or no attention is paid to any of this corpus of work.

For the most part I have little difficulty with the facts as he has laid them out, which have also been pointed out in my own publications. Our difference has to do with the viewpoint taken toward these facts and on a few important details to which we will return below. However, the point of his survey and of the remarks by Konrad Schmid, Jan Christian Gertz, and others is to suggest that this Yahwist comes in so many different forms that it is difficult to deal with all of them and one must therefore generalize by the use of such a term as "Yahwist hypothesis."[2] All of this I consider a smoke screen. It may be observed that there are many different understandings of P, whether as source or supplement, with different limits producing as many P's as there are J's. The dating of P has been changed more radically than J, from being the earliest source to the latest. Yet these scholars seem to have no difficulty with the acceptance of P, which was as important to the Documentary Hypothesis as J. Consequently, the great diversity of opinion about J has nothing to do with the present proclamation of the Yahwist's dismissal.

In point of fact, the Yahwist, whose demise is being prematurely mourned, is a quite particular Yahwist, namely, von Rad's Yahwist as articulated in his *Das formgeschichtliche Problem des Hexateuch* (1938).[3] It was specifically this Yahwist that was attacked by Rolf Rendtorff as the fundamental problem of the Documentary Hypothesis, which he then sought to replace by a quite different literary process, following Martin Noth, and which in turn has transmuted into the current form of redaction history. All the recent discussion of the replacement of the Yahwist with editors goes back to Rolf Rendtorff's *Das überlieferungsgeschichtliche Problem des Pentateuch* (BZAW 147; Berlin: de Gruyter, 1977), of course ignoring any of the subsequent criticism that was leveled against Rendtorff's position. In his historical survey Römer fails to mention my own critique of pentateuchal studies in *Abraham in History and Tradition* (1975), which appeared *before* the works of Hans Heinrich Schmid and Rendtorff.[4] My critique of the Documentary Hypothesis was fundamentally different from that of Rendtorff. It was not directed at source criticism, which remains basic to all historical criticism. Instead, it was directed at tradition history, especially the

---

2. See also Jean Louis Ska, "The Yahwist, a Hero with a Thousand Faces," in *Abschied vom Jahwisten: Die Komposition des Hexateuch in der jüngsten Diskussion* (ed. J. C. Gertz et al.; BZAW 315; Berlin: de Gruyter, 2002), 1–23.

3. Gerhard von Rad, "Das formgeschichtliche Problem des Hexateuch," in idem, *Gesammelte Studien zum Alten Testament* (ed. R. Smend; 4th ed.; TB 8; Munich: Kaiser, 1971), 9–86. English translation: "The Form-Critical Problem of the Hexateuch," in idem, *The Problem of the Hexateuch and Other Essays* (trans. E. W. Trueman Dicken; Edinburgh: Oliver & Boyd, 1966, repr., London: SCM, 1984), 1–78.

4. For my review of Hans Heinrich Schmid and Rolf Rendtorff, see John Van Seters, "Recent Studies on Pentateuchal Criticism: A Crisis in Method," *JAOS* 99 (1980): 663–73.

block model of Martin Noth, adopted by Rendtorff, and the use of the redactor in literary criticism.

So let us focus on the *real* issue. Simply stated, von Rad's Yahwist was understood as an author and *historian* who used an old liturgical confession of God's deliverance from Egypt, as reflected in Deut 26:5–9, as the basic structure of his historical work and who then combined this with other older traditions about the giving of the law at Sinai, the stories of the patriarchs in Genesis, and the stories of the primeval history, in order to produce a remarkable history of the people from the creation of humans down to the conquest of the land of Canaan—the basic story that underlies the Hexateuch. This understanding of the Yahwist was seriously undermined by Noth, who relegated most of J's work to a preliterary stage of tradition development in the nature of numerous blocks of tradition that were already combined in some vague way before J inherited them. From this demolition of J by Noth it was but a small step for Rendtorff to dismiss the existence of J altogether.

There is, however, a major problem with all of this. It is true that questions were raised against an early date for von Rad's "little credo" of Deut 26:5–9, but this also meant that the whole basis for Noth's confessional blocks of tradition was likewise placed in doubt. Furthermore, my own work and that of Hans Heinrich Schmid (*Der sogenannte Jahwist* [Zürich: Theologischer Verlag, 1976]) made it clear that much of the material within the "so-called" J corpus must be viewed as much later in date than was previously thought. Out of this came two competing proposals. The one, my position, was to affirm von Rad's Yahwist as indeed an author and historian,[5] who was responsible for the great literary work as he claimed but who belonged to a quite different era from the one proposed by von Rad. The other, Rendtorff's view, was to affirm Noth's block theory of tradition growth, completely disregarding his grand scheme of tradition history in a preliterary "amphictyonic age," but instead assigning the process of their amalgamation and integration of diverse traditions to Deuteronomistic, Priestly,

---

5. Rolf Rendtorff, in both his *Das überlieferungsgeschichtliche Problem des Pentateuch* and in his earlier article "Der 'Jahwist' als Theologe? Zum Dilemma der Pentateuchkritik," in *Congress Volume: Edinburgh, 1974* (VTSup 28; Leiden: Brill, 1975), 158–66, ignored von Rad's claim that the Yahwist was a historian and persisted in suggesting that von Rad spoke primarily of J as a theologian. This was a serious misrepresentation of von Rad's intention in *Das formgeschichtliche Problem des Hexateuch*. See my earlier critique of this in John Van Seters, "The Yahwist as Theologian? A Response," *JSOT 3* (1977): 15–19; also idem, "The Pentateuch as Torah *and* History: In Defense of G. von Rad," in *Das Alte Testament—Ein Geschichtsbuch?* (ed. E. Blum et al.; Altes Testament und Moderne 10; Münster: LIT Verlag, 2005), 47–63. Unfortunately, Römer has continued to repeat Rendtorff's view and consequently suggests that my characterization of the Yahwist as a historian was something new, but I was merely following von Rad's clear position on this question of literary genre.

and other *redactors*.[6] The author becomes completely superfluous. Thus, the question over the existence of the Yahwist (by whatever name one wishes to call him or her) boils down to this one issue: Is the non-P corpus of the Pentateuch or Hexateuch (excluding D and Dtr) to be regarded as the work of an author and historian, or is it to be viewed as the result of a complex editorial process?

   One argument of the redaction critics is to say that the Yahwist is simply an unfortunate carryover from the defunct Documentary Hypothesis. The same, of course, could be said for P, which still remains fundamental to their analysis. However, the problem with the Documentary Hypothesis is not source analysis, dividing the text into P and non-P, which remains basic to any literary criticism of the Pentateuch. The real problem was always the redactor whose characterization and use for solving literary problems seems so completely arbitrary, and I have spoken against this quite arbitrary *deus ex machina* for thirty years.[7] It is the redactor that is the most characteristic feature of the Documentary Hypothesis! Lest it be suggested that this method of redaction criticism is something new, let me point out that it goes back to Friedrich Wolf and his *Prolegomena ad Homerum* of 1795, in which the various blocks of tradition and songs in the *Iliad* and the *Odyssey* were put together by editors in the sixth century B.C.E. and which continued to be modified by editors until their "final form" was reached by the greatest editor of all, Aristarchus, in the second century B.C.E. This approach to the transmission history of Homer was very influential in the development of the Documentary Hypothesis in biblical studies. The notion of editors and redactional criticism was always at the heart of this shared methodology, and it took classical studies 150 years to finally see the error of its ways and abandon this "redactor theory" in favor of the "author-poet." One German scholar who led the battle against it made the following characterization of redaction analysis among German classical scholarship of his day:

> Es ist ganz unvermeidlich, sich alle diese Redaktoren mit geschriebenen Texten in der Hand vorzustellen, da streichend, dort einsetzend und verschiedene Schnittstellen aneinanderpassend. Von Schreibtisch, Schere und Kleister zu sprechen, ist natürlich ein boshafter Anachronismus, aber die Richtung, in der alle Annahmen dieser Art liegen, scheint mir treffend zu bezeichnen. Buchphilologen haben diese Theorien erdacht, und Arbeit an und mit Büchern ist für sie die Voraussetzung geblieben.[8]

---

6. Rendtorff himself is uncomfortable with the term "redactor" because he admits that it is derived directly from the Documentary Hypothesis, but he and his followers use it anyway.

7. See especially my remarks in *Abraham in History and Tradition,* 129–31.

8. Albin Lesky, "Mündlichkeit und Schriftlichkeit im Homerischen Epos," reprinted in *Homer: Tradition und Neuerung* (ed. J. Latacz; Darmstadt: Wissenschaftliche Buchgesellschaft, 1979), 299. Latacz's own comment on Lesky's critique of the Wolf position was that Lesky remained for two

In biblical studies, however, such imagined redactors still persist in spite of all evidence to the contrary.[9]

So we return to the question: Is the compositional character of the non-P corpus of the Pentateuch, the body of text usually assigned to J, to be viewed as the work of editors or as the work of an ancient historian, as suggested by von Rad? It is my conviction, based upon the comparative material from classical examples of "archaic history" that the mark of such author-historians is the development, out of a body of quite diverse traditions, of a continuous and coherent account of the past with themes and interconnections to unite its various parts.[10] So far as I can see, the ancient "editor," such as Aristarchus, never engaged in such activity but instead tried to restore the classical texts to their purest form and to stigmatize as corruptions any late additions that he might find or suspect within the text. To identify the use of particular themes and other techniques of interconnections in the text as "editorial" is, to my mind, completely without justification either in antiquity or in modern times.

2. P as the Link between Genesis and Exodus

With this introduction let me take up a few selected examples from the positions set forth above as space permits.[11] Let us first look briefly at the thesis, as set forth by Konrad Schmid, that it was the Priestly writer who first made the connection between the patriarchal stories and the exodus story and that in doing so P had no knowledge of the Joseph story. To support this view, Schmid attributes a minimal number of texts to P within Gen 37–50, and those Priestly texts that do occur within the Joseph story are then merely assigned to a Priestly redactor. That, of course, is just special pleading. Let us then examine his reconstruction of this P source. It is usual for scholars to regard Gen 37:1–2 as belonging to P, since there is a clear break after verse 2. However, this would not fit Schmid's thesis, so he discards verse 2. Yet the remark about Joseph's age in verse 2a is a regular feature of P in the patriarchal stories, and it also

---

decades as a voice crying in the wilderness ("Rufer in der Wüste"); see Latacz, "Einführung," in idem, *Homer,* 12.

9. The full case for this view will be set forth in my forthcoming book, *The Edited Bible.*

10. See John Van Seters, *Prologue to History;* idem, "Is There Any Historiography in the Hebrew Bible? A Hebrew-Greek Comparison," *JNSL* 28 (2002): 1–25.

11. I will not comment on Christoph Levin's response to the papers ("The Yahwist and the Redactional Link between Genesis and Exodus"), which would require a detailed discussion about our quite different understanding of the Yahwist, except to say that his characterizing the Yahwist as an editor greatly confuses the issue of the debate. There is nothing editorial about the compositional activity that he attributes to J. I also cannot comment on those papers that I did not receive in time for this response.

occurs again in 41:46a. Of course, that too would speak against Schmid's thesis. Furthermore, he must also discard the genealogy in 46:8–27 because it makes a clear reference to Joseph's prior period in Egypt. Schmid accepts 47:27–28, which contains the remarks about the age of Jacob at his death and the length of time he spent in Egypt, but he rejects the statement in 47:9 about Jacob's age when he arrived in Egypt and the rest of the audience with Pharaoh in 47:7–11, which accounts for their settlement in Goshen, mentioned again in verse 27. Genesis 48:3–6 is regularly assigned to P because it recapitulates the language and themes of P so closely, but this again would manifest clear dependence of P on the Joseph story, so it must also be reckoned as secondary. Thus, the only way that Schmid can support his literary theory is to invoke a Priestly redactor who uses precisely the same literary techniques, language, and themes as P but who cannot be viewed as independent from the non-P context in which his words are found, in this case the Joseph story. Even Wellhausen admitted that he could not find any significant differences between P and RP.[12]

What we have left of P in Schmid's view is Gen 37:1–2aα; 46:6–7; 47:27–28; 49:1a, 29–33; 50:12–13, which he characterizes as "an acceptable and complete description of the *eisodos* within P *without an account of Joseph.*"[13] However, any unprejudiced reading of the text that remains, even with this careful surgery, reveals the most glaring gaps in narrative continuity and coherence. Following the introduction in 37:1–2aα: "Jacob lived in the land of his father's sojourning, in the land of Canaan. These are the generations of Jacob," we expect some narrative account of Jacob's sons in Canaan. But instead we are told that what follows after 37:2aα is the statement in 46:6: "And they took their livestock and their goods, which they had gained in the land of Canaan, and they came into Egypt, Jacob and all his offspring with him." There is no explanation for why Jacob and his family should leave Canaan, the promised land, and make this great migration to Egypt with all their extensive possessions. Even grammatically it is problematic to understand why verse 6 suddenly begins with a plural verb. The recapitulation of the subject in verses 6b–7a is surely intended as an introduction to the genealogy that follows in verses 8–27. Furthermore, there is no reference to Jacob's departure from Canaan, only his arrival in Egypt. If, however, we look at the preceding verse 5, "Then Jacob set out from Beersheba, and the sons of Israel carried their father, their little ones, and their wives, in the wagons that Pharaoh had sent to carry him," the continuation in verse

---

12. Julius Wellhausen, *Prolegomena to the history of Ancient Israel* (trans. J. S. Black and A. Menzies; Edinburgh: Black, 1885; repr., Atlanta: Scholars Press, 1994), 384–85. It should be noted that Rendtorff regarded P in Genesis as a supplement, not an independent source, and therefore had no trouble with the verses that Schmid excludes.

13. See above p. 46, emphasis added.

6 makes perfectly good sense as an extension of this earlier presentation. We have exactly the same phenomenon in other places in which P has added to, and embellished, the earlier J account. Note especially Gen 31:17–18, which begins in a very similar fashion, "So Jacob arose, and set his sons and his wives on camels" (v. 17), followed in verse 18 by a rather confusing mixture of J with P embellishments (see also Gen 12:4b–5a). But if Gen 47:6 depends upon verse 5, then the whole position of Schmid falls apart.[14]

Following Schmid's P corpus we next have the statement that Israel settled in Goshen (Gen 47:27–28), without any explanation of why they chose this region in particular or why it should even be noted, since in the exodus story P pays no attention whatever to this special location and even seems to contradict it. So Goshen is not a connective in P as it is in J. In this region of Goshen they apparently prospered greatly. The period of Jacob's sojourn in Egypt is given (17 years) and his total age at 147 years (cf 47:9). This in turn is followed by the account of Jacob's death, preceded by his injunction to his sons to bury him in Machpelah (49:1a, 29–33) and the subsequent carrying out of this injunction (50:12–13). At this point, however, there is another serious gap in that it places the whole family in Canaan with no suggestion that they returned to Egypt. Gertz tries to solve this problem by adding verse 14 to the P account, but this is an act of desperation. Verse 14 reads: "After he had buried his father, Joseph returned to Egypt with his brothers and all who had gone up with him to bury his father." This obviously refers to the Joseph story in 50:1–11 in which it is Joseph who is primarily responsible for the burial. Gertz disputes this latter connection, and we will need to take this question up below. His one reason for attributing it to P is that it is necessary in order to make his understanding of P work. But that is no argument at all. If all the brothers with all their families and goods returned to Canaan, since Schmid regards 50:8b as a post-P addition, then why should they have made the arduous trip back to Egypt again? This P reconstruction as an independent work makes little sense.

Schmid does not comment above on what follows in Exod 1 after Gen 50:13, but in another publication he makes it clear that Exod 1:1–5 (since it obviously presupposes the Joseph story) belongs to his Priestly redactor,[15] which for him would mean that Exod 1:7 continued from Gen 50:13. With

---

14. David M. Carr (*Reading the Fractures of Genesis: Historical and Literary Approaches* [Louisville: Westminster John Knox, 1996], 106–7) sees the problem and assigns 46:5 to P, which then means that 45:19–21 must also be P as well as the whole of Gen 31:17–18. Such a solution, however, would be disastrous to Schmid's position.

15. Konrad Schmid, *Erzväter und Exodus: Untersuchungen zur doppelten Begründung der Ursprünge Israels innerhalb der Geschichtsbücher des Alten Testaments* (WMANT 81; Neukirchen-Vluyn: Neukirchener, 1999), 30.

this sequence, however, one would get the impression that this proliferation and great prosperity took place after their return to Canaan to bury their father. Nothing suggests that they are still in Egypt. And if this is immediately followed by Exod 1:13–14, then the gaps and confusion only become worse. Why have the fortunes of the Israelites changed so drastically? Where is this taking place, and who are their oppressors? And what happened to the brothers? Even Exod 2:23aβ,b–25 does not help to answer these questions, because without verse 23aα there is still no mention of Egypt. It is simply impossible to read these bits and pieces of the P account separate from their present context. I rest my case. Schmid's conclusions do not address my presentation of the Yahwist in a single detail and need no further comment.

3. The Yahwist as the Link between the Patriarchs and Exodus Traditions

The essay by Jan Christian Gertz builds directly upon the earlier work of Konrad Schmid, with some modifications. The heart of his paper has to do with the "post-Priestly supplements" to Gen 50 and Exod 1. It is suggested by both Schmid and Gertz that 50:14 does not really belong to the Joseph story in 50:1–11 but is either a redactional addition (Schmid) or belongs to P (Gertz). The argument to support this is the assertion that the discourse between Joseph and his brothers is not appropriate after verse 14 and should come much earlier, that is, after verse 11. This is part of Schmid's larger thesis in which he sees the whole family returning permanently to Canaan, so that 50:7b and 8b, as well as verse 14, must all be redactional (and for him, post-P).[16] But does this scheme make any sense? Joseph gives no hint in his request to Pharaoh that his return to Canaan is permanent but only that it is for the purpose of burying Jacob and for this reason he receives a large military escort. This is also suggested in verses 9 and 11; the reaction of the local population only makes sense if the whole large company was viewed as predominantly Egyptian. Without verse 14 this large Egyptian contingent must also remain in Canaan. Secondly, why should the brothers be afraid of Joseph in their homeland? Joseph, without the Egyptian escort, would now simply be one of them and would no longer have any special status. Canaan is not regarded as part of the Egyptian Empire in this story. Only after they have returned to Egypt would his brothers need to be concerned about their safety. So the passage in verses 15–21 makes the best sense right where it is. Joseph's continued provision and care for his brothers and their families must reflect a location in Egypt, not in Canaan, where they would go their separate

---

16. Ibid., 59–60.

ways. I have argued elsewhere that 50:15–21 is an addition by J that is parallel to the earlier reconciliation scene in 45:1–15.[17] Its purpose here is to anticipate the sojourn in Exod 1 with the word play on the עַם־רָב "numerous people" (50:20; cf. Exod 1:8–12). However, this still means that this unit is pre-P along with the rest. The only text that belongs to P in this chapter is the burial notice in verses 12–13. It is entirely possible that 50:22–23 belongs to the original Joseph story, since it harks back to the earlier birth of the two sons in Gen 41:50–52.

At any rate, 50:24–26 is non-P and in my view belongs to J. The argument for making these verses post-P is because they have a clear connection with Exod 13:19 and Josh 24:32, which are also reckoned as post-P. But this is just circular reasoning. I have argued that they are all J, although my case for this is never discussed.[18] But why should an editor take it upon himself to construct all of these interconnections in the text as if he were the author of the text? This is extremely unlikely. The interconnections are exactly what one would expect an author, the Yahwist, to do if he were composing a comprehensive history. The prediction that we have in 50:24–26 has its parallel in the predictions to Jacob in Gen 46:3–4 and to Abraham in 15:13–16. This is a well-known historiographic technique in classical literature and one that is also employed here.

We come now to Gertz's treatment of the "post-Priestly supplements" in Exod 1. The bald statement that Exod 1:6 presupposes the enumeration of the brothers in verses 1–5 may be disregarded. Joseph and his brothers are the subjects of the prior unit in 50:24–26. The purpose of repeating the death notice of Joseph is clear from the structure of the unit. As I have shown elsewhere, the author (J) constructs this unit on the parallel transition episode in Judg 2:6–10.[19] So close are the similarities between this unit and the one in Gen 50:26; Exod 1:6, 8 that one cannot doubt a direct literary dependence of the latter on the former. It is obvious that the whole of Exod 1:1–5 is secondary to this construction. In order to use this scheme, the author felt it necessary to repeat the mention of Joseph's death so as to include "his brothers" and the whole generation as well.

What are we to make of Exod 1:7, however, which is widely attributed to P?[20] If we must exclude verse 6 as a later addition, then we end up with a statement that is nonsense. Who are the "sons of Israel" in verse 7? If this follows immediately after verse 5, then it suggests a period during the lifetime of these brothers, for there is no hint that they have died and whatever follows takes place during this time. But that is absurd, and verse 6 is certainly presupposed.

---

17. Van Seters, *Prologue to History,* 323–24.
18. Ibid.; also idem, *Life of Moses,* 18–19.
19. Van Seters, *Life of Moses,* 16–19.
20. See my treatment, ibid., 19–21, which has been ignored by Gertz.

The reason for the attribution of verse 7 to P is the obvious P terminology. Yet it is clear that verses 9–12 also presuppose some knowledge of verse 7. This leads to the view that verses 8–12 must be later than P. Yet the unit in verses 8–12 plays upon only two terms רב and עצום and their verbal equivalents. The theme is also basic to the following unit in verses 15–22, where the same language is repeated in verse 20. The verb רבה is common to both J and P, but the term עצם never occurs in any of its forms in P, although it does occur elsewhere in J and is common also in D. It seems to me obvious that J originally had a statement in verse 7: ובני ישראל רבו ויעצמו "The Israelites increased in number and grew strong."[21] This is followed by the statement that the new king, at some later date, regarded this development as a serious threat. P has merely embellished the original statement with his own jargon, which somewhat obscures the point that follows. This reconstruction of the original text may be confirmed by the fact that in the earliest version of the descent into Egypt and their sojourn there, in Deut 26:5–9, we have the famous statement in verse 5: "A wandering Aramean was my father; and he went down to Egypt and sojourned there, few in number; and there he became a great, strong and populous nation (גוי גדול עצום ורב)."[22] On the basis of this text it is not hard to reconstruct the original version of Exod 1:7, as I have done. However, nowhere in Deuteronomy is this great population expansion related to any promise to the patriarchs. This was completely unknown to D, and it is not even clear that the "father" refers to Jacob. It was left to a post-D author, the Yahwist, to combine this theme of becoming a great nation by making it a promise to the patriarchs, along with the land promise. In the patriarchal promises, the phrase גוי גדול is preferred, but in some other places J also uses עצם/עצום and רבה/רב, as he does here. P, developing his own characteristic terminology, extends the motif back to the time of creation. So it is not hard to see the line of development in the concept.

Nevertheless, Gertz tries to turn this whole argument around and make the P version primary, which cannot be made to render any kind of narrative coherence and continuity, and to make the non-P secondary, even when it is the non-P material that provides a completely consistence and coherent story,

---

21. See also Frederick V. Winnett, *The Mosaic Tradition* (Near and Middle East Studies 1; Toronto: University of Toronto Press, 1949), 16. However, Winnett's notion that in Exod 1–2 there is an old document independent of the original J that P used and appended to the story of Moses to connect it to Genesis seems farfetched and against all the evidence set forth here.

22. Gertz's statement (p. 83 above): "The connection between Gen 12:2 and Exod 1:9 is at most conceptual, since the formulation of Exod 1:9 עם רב ועצום is not the expected correspondence to the promise of a גוי גדול in Gen 12:2" is completely overturned by this earlier combination of terms in Deuteronomy and in Gen 18:18 and 26:12–16. In fact, J draws on a wide range of terminology to express the promise theme.

and the latter is attributed to the "editor"! He ignores the use of the terminology of עם רב and עצום in J as a precedent for what we have here. We have already pointed to the use of עם רב in 50:20. The theme of the numerous people as a threat to the king is picked up again in Exod 5, the occasion of the first encounter between Moses (and Aaron) and Pharaoh. After the king dismisses Moses and Aaron we have the statement (v. 5): "Pharaoh thought, 'they [the Israelites] are now more numerous (רבים) than the people of the land....' "[23] This would agree exactly with chapter 1. Both in terms of language and perspective, this unit fits very well with Exod 1:8–12, 15–22. The use of עצום is even more instructive. In the Abraham story of J in Gen 18:18 the Deity says in a divine soliloquy that Abraham is to become "a nation great and strong" (לגוי גדול ועצום). This same phrase is repeated in exactly this form in another context. In Num 14:12 Yнwн threatens to destroy the people as a whole, because of their lack of faith in him, and in their place to make of Moses "a nation greater and stronger than they" (לגוי גדול ועצום ממנו). The connection with the patriarchal promise is obvious. In the Isaac story, Gen 26:12–16, we read that Isaac prospered in the foreign territory of Gerar and became very great (גדל, verb) and that he also had a "large household of servants" (עבדה רבה) and as a consequence the king felt threatened and asked him to leave "because you are much stronger (עצם, verb) than we are." Here is an obvious parallel to the Egyptian situation within the J corpus. This, in turn, is paralleled in another text in the Balaam story. In Num 22 the Moabites are in great dread of the Israelites because they are numerous (רב, v. 3), so Balak calls upon the prophet Balaam to curse "this people because they are stronger than us" (העם הזה כי־עצום הוא ממנו). All these texts belong to J, and the language and themes expressed are completely consistent throughout. There is nothing comparable in P.

Furthermore, as stated above, it was von Rad who pointed to the Yahwist's dependence on Deut 26:5–9 for the structure of his literary work, and in spite of the redating of both the "little credo" and the Yahwist, the basic scheme of von Rad still fits the facts. It is not hard to see how an exilic J could make this statement in Deut 26:5 the basis of his connection between the patriarchs, represented by Jacob's descent into Egypt with his family, and the exodus tradition. Furthermore, the particular selection of terminology in Exod 1:7*, 8–12 is directly suggested by D's text. Since I have long argued for the heavy dependence of J upon Deuteronomy, none of this should cause any surprise. And an

---

23. This reading and interpretation of the text follows Martin Noth, *Exodus* (OTL; London: SCM, 1962), 53, who emends the defective мт text, based on the SamP reading. See also Brevard S. Childs, *The Book of Exodus* (OTL; Philadelphia: Westminster, 1974), 93, 105; Van Seters, *Life of Moses*, 74–75.

exilic date long before P is quite appropriate for all this literary development to take place.

Gertz likewise passes lightly over the use of פרץ in combination with רבה in Exod 1:12: וכאשר יענו אתו כן ירבה כן יפרץ "The more they oppressed them, the more they increased in number and the more they expanded." This certainly does not reflect the P terminology in verse 7, which uses the more usual P term שׁרץ, "to proliferate." The term פרץ, in the sense of bursting the limits of one's territory, is rather distinctive of J, and this is the sense in which it is used in Exod 1:12. It also has a very similar sense in the divine promise of numerous offspring to Jacob in the Bethel theophany in Gen 28:14: "Your off-spring shall be like the dust of the earth and you shall burst your limits (ופרצת) to the west and to the east and to the north and to the south." Again in Gen 30:30 Jacob says to Laban: "For you had little before I arrived, and it has burst forth into abundance (ויפרץ לרב) and God has blessed you wherever I went." This also relates the term to the same theme of divine promise of blessing.[24]

Second Isaiah, in the Song of the Barren Woman, Isa 54:1–5, which is clearly an image that is taken from the patriarchal stories, makes direct allusion to the theme of the promise of great population growth with the statement: "For you shall break out of your boundaries (תפרצי) right and left, your descen-dents shall disposses nations and resettle deserted cities" (v. 3). In the light of the repeated use of this term by J in connection with precisely this same theme, as noted above, it is hard to resist the conclusion that Second Isaiah is quoting J and his special language at this point. This means further that the use of this ter-minology in Exod 1:12 is probably by the same author, J, as in the Genesis texts and that *it is deliberately used to recall this theme of the promises in the patriarchal stories.* And since Second Isaiah, whom I have long argued is a contemporary of the Yahwist,[25] already knows of this usage, it must be prior to P and not depen-dent upon P, as the "new" redactional criticism suggests.

What we have seen in our analysis is that it is not P but the earlier non-P Yahwist who is the author of this historiographic interconnection between the patriarchal and exodus traditions, precisely as von Rad proposed. J does this by modeling the transition between the era of Joseph and his brothers and the later period of the oppression (Gen 50:26; Exod 1:6–8) upon the transition from the age of Joshua and his generation to the following period of apos-tasy (Judg 2:8–10). He combines with this the description of the sojourn from

---

24. See also Gen 30:43.

25. See most recently, John Van Seters, "In the Babylonian Exile with J: Between Judgment in Ezekiel and Salvation in Second Isaiah," in *The Crisis of Israelite Religion: Transformation of Religious Tradition in Exilic and Post-Exilic Times* (ed. B. Becking and M. C. A. Korpel; OTS 42; Leiden: Brill, 1999), 71–89.

Deut 26:5, which mentions the great population growth, and then uses this as the motive for the oppression by the Egyptians. At the same time, his language makes constant allusion back to the time of the patriarchs and the theme of the divine promises so that a careful reader cannot miss the interconnection between the two. The Priestly writer adds little to this continuity; in fact, his embellishments tend to obscure what is so obvious without them. This literary artistry, which von Rad rightly attributed to the Yahwist as author and historian, should not be relegated in piecemeal fashion to innumerable hypothetical editors. They never existed!

The next level of interconnection between the patriarchs and the exodus has to do with the patriarchal promises. It is often asserted that P is the one responsible for this interconnection by means of the texts in Exod 2:23aβb–25; 6:2–8, which refer back to the P texts in Gen 17; 28:1–4; 35:9–13. There can be no doubt about the importance of this interconnection for the P scheme of divine revelation, as Wellhausen clearly recognized. And yet it is remarkable that P feels no need to make any further reference to the patriarchal covenant and blessing in the subsequent narration and laws. By contrast, J (the non-P corpus) makes repeated reference to the patriarchal promises, but these are dismissed by Rendtorff and his followers as "redactional" and of little consequence for the whole. This seems to me highly prejudicial to the discussion. We will therefore look briefly at the J interconnection in Gen 46:2–4 and Exod 3:6. It may be useful to set them down, side by side:

Gen 46:2–4	Exod 3:4b, 6
God spoke to Israel in a vision by night and said, "Jacob! Jacob!" He answered, "Here I am." Then he said, "I am El, the god of your father (אנכי האל אלהי אביך), do not be afraid of going down to Egypt, for I will make you into a great nation (לגוי גדול) there. I will go down with you to Egypt and I will also bring you up again, and Joseph's hand will close your eyes."	God called to him out of the bush, and he said, "Moses! Moses!" He answered, "Here I am." … Then he said, "I am the god of your father (אנכי אלהי אביך), the god of Abraham, the god of Isaac, and the god of Jacob." And Moses hid his face because he was afraid to look at the deity.

The similarity and interconnection between these two accounts are obvious. The setting for the first revelation is the journey by Jacob and his family to Egypt and the temporary halt at Beer-sheba, where Jacob offers sacrifices to "the god of Isaac his father." This, in turn, links the text with the Isaac story in Gen 26 and the revelations there, including the one at Beer-sheba in 26:24, which is of a very similar form: "I am the god of Abraham, your father." This is then linked to the revelations to Jacob in 28:13 and 32:10 as "the god of Isaac, your father." The use of the term "god of your father" with the meaning "god of Jacob" is used by the brothers of Joseph in their appeal to Joseph for his forgiveness in 50:17 as the deity of the Israelites in Egypt. The use of the designation האל is likewise linked to the special revelation of the god of Bethel (31:13; 35:1). There can be no doubt that all these texts are part of the same non-P corpus, J. The Yahwist has embedded his theme of the patriarchal promises within the Joseph story with the specific intention of making a connection with the exodus theme. The reference to becoming a "great nation" (לגוי גדול) not only picks up on the theme of the patriarchal promises typical of J, but it also uses the same language as in Deut 26:5: ויהי־שם לגוי גדול.

Once the whole pattern of interconnections among the passages in the J corpus of Genesis becomes clear, there is no reason left to dissociate the text of Exod 3:6 from these other texts.[26] It is only J who uses the term "god of your father," and what he means by this is the god of the three patriarchs. It certainly does not mean the god of Moses' father. Furthermore, there is simply no divine revelation, no announcement of the deity in the unit 3:1–6 without this declaration. What has created some confusion is that the author of the unit in 3:1–6 has combined two different models for his revelation, the one taken from Josh 5:13–15, the other from Gen 46:2–4, and it is the interweaving of these two that has created the impression of a combination of independent sources. Nevertheless, the whole unit in Exod 3:1–6 belongs to the same hand. Once it is admitted that 3:6 is integral to the unit, there is no need to see any of the references to the god of the patriarchs in the rest of the chapter as secondary. To do so is quite arbitrary.

I do not need to examine the rest of the call narrative in Exod 3–4, since it has been treated by Thomas Dozeman, who has given considerable space to my views and who appears to be in substantial agreement with them. Yet Dozeman, who regards the story of the commission of Moses in Exod 3:1–4:18 as a pre-P composition closely connected to Genesis, is reluctant to call this work J because of its associations with the Documentary Hypothesis, although he has no such qualms about the use of P. Instead, he prefers to follow the example of Blum and use a term such as "D History" because it has a "similar outlook to the Book of Deuteronomy and the Deuteronomistic History, although each

---

26. See my earlier treatment of Exod 3:1–6 in *Life of Moses*, 36–41; also Thomas Dozeman, in "The Commission of Moses and the Book of Genesis" above, p. 124 [§3.3].

body of literature undergoes a distinct history of composition."[27] But surely this terminology becomes more confusing than helpful, because it could easily be taken as part of D or Dtr, which it is not. The very fact that it incorporates into the history of Israel the patriarchal traditions, creating a whole new understanding of Israelite-Jewish identity, demands that it be recognized as a distinct literary work. The term Yahwist and its former equivalents have a long pedigree in historical criticism as a way of recognizing a corpus of texts distinct from P, and I see no good reason for replacing it with another designation, such as KD or D History, which to my mind creates greater misunderstanding and confusion. The Yahwist, as a quite exceptional author and historian within the biblical texts, remains well and strong and will endure for some time to come.

---

27. Quoted from his discussion of the "D History" in his forthcoming commentary on Exodus, which he has shared with me. See also idem, "Geography and Ideology in the Wilderness Journey from Kadesh through the Transjordan," in Gertz et al., *Abschied vom Jahwisten*, 173–89.

WHAT IS REQUIRED TO IDENTIFY PRE-PRIESTLY NARRATIVE CONNECTIONS BETWEEN GENESIS AND EXODUS? SOME GENERAL REFLECTIONS AND SPECIFIC CASES*

David M. Carr

The essays under consideration here deal with one of the most interesting and significant problems in pentateuchal scholarship: the question of when and how the ancestral and Moses-exodus traditions were joined into a single literary whole. In the past, scholars have focused overly much on subtle distinctions between purported J and E documents interwoven with each other throughout the Pentateuch, distinctions so subtle, in fact, that many, if not most, penta-teuchal specialists no longer see them. Meanwhile, thanks in large part to work by scholars such as Rolf Rendtorff, Erhard Blum, Konrad Schmid, Thomas Römer, and more recent authors surveyed by Thomas Römer and Thomas Doz-eman in this volume, it is becoming increasingly clear that there is another more obvious and important set of divisions between sources of the Pentateuch, that is, the divisions separating the major non-Priestly sections from each other: pri-meval history, Jacob, Joseph and Moses-exodus stories.

Of course, older transmission-historical studies also talked of these divisions between blocks of the Pentateuch, but most such earlier studies (e.g., Noth) argued that the marked difference between, say, the Jacob traditions and the Moses traditions resulted from their *oral* prehistory. The contribution of more recent studies is to suggest that many dimensions of the present Pentateuch, par-ticularly the non-Priestly materials, are best explained through hypotheses about the joining of more fixed, probably written versions of these separate sections of

---

*As is true for several other essays in this volume, this one was presented in abbreviated form in the Pentateuch Section at the 2004 Society of Biblical Literature Annual Meeting. I thank the panelists and participants in that section for their comments. In addition, I am grateful to Erhard Blum for providing extensive, very helpful critical feedback on my earlier work on this essay.

the Pentateuch. Thus Jan Christian Gertz can report in his essay, and not without reason, that "it is widely acknowledged that the patriarchal narratives and exodus story were originally transmitted separately."

That said, let us be clear on what is under discussion here. Jan Christian Gertz cites me (and Christoph Levin) as "proponents of the Yahwist thesis." But I am not the proponent of any "Yahwist" that would have been recognizable as such to Wellhausen, Gunkel, Noth, or others. After all, I, like many, if not most, specialists working on pentateuchal formation now, do not recognize an "Elohist" counterpart to the older "Yahwist."[1] Whatever pre-Priestly proto-Pentateuch I would consider would be one that contains texts once assigned to J and E. Furthermore, I am inclined to date any non-P proto-Pentateuch no earlier than the late preexilic or (more likely) exilic period. My pre-Priestly "proto-Pentateuch" is close to the older J neither in contents or context. The only way I am a proponent of a "Yahwist" is if one reduces the definition of such a document as Jan Christian Gertz does to those who posit a "running strand of pre-Priestly material in the Tetrateuch." That definition, however, makes the term "Yahwist" so different from the older use of the term as to make it functionally nonusable. In fact, no one on this panel, so far as I know, advocates a Yahwist recognizably like the J of studies up through the 1970s.[2] The question under discussion here is whether there once was some kind of pre-Priestly Pentateuch. But then "farewell to the pre-Priestly Pentateuch?" does not have the ring to it that "farewell to the Yahwist?" does, so I will move on.

1. Parallels and Differences between the Papers

Looking at the group of essays, the most prominent division is that between the paper by Dozeman and those by Römer, Schmid, Gertz, and Blum. The latter four summarize central arguments against the idea of a pre-Priestly Pentateuch, while Dozeman provides arguments for that idea.

I turn first to similarities and differences between the essays by Blum, Römer, Schmid, and Gertz. These essays raise a number of observations that

---

1. Though a few scholars continue to maintain the existence of an "E" of some sort (e.g., Horst Seebass, Werner H. Schmidt, and Axel Graupner in Bonn, Germany; Richard Elliott Friedman and Robert Coote in the U.S.A.; Sean McEvenue in Canada; and Ernest Nicholson in Britain), the contents of this E (aside from a few key texts, e.g., Gen 20–22* and parts of 28:10–22) are so varied as to make use of the common term E relatively meaningless.

2. Though John Van Seters still claims the term "Yahwist" for such a non-J document (and Christoph Levin has used the term "Jahwist" for a substantially different body of material), I think it is misleading to conduct the discussion under the heading of advocates or critics of the idea of a "Yahwist."

will be familiar to those who have followed French- and German-language pentateuchal scholarship in recent years but may be unfamiliar to others. In this context, the essay by Römer, along with the first major subsection of Dozeman's essay, provides a useful overview of the diversity of past depictions of the Yahwist, along with some early precursors to the idea that the ancestral and Moses traditions only came together at a late point.

Meanwhile, the papers by Blum, Schmid, and Gertz summarize some of the textual arguments against the idea of a pre-Priestly Pentateuch. Blum's essay both summarizes and revises some earlier proposals he made regarding the extent of the pre-P Pentateuch. Whereas in his earlier *Studien zur Komposition des Pentateuch* he argued for the idea that Exod 3:1–4:18 (except for a post-P insertion regarding Aaron in 4:13–18) were an insertion by a "KD" author who worked across both Genesis and the Moses story, this essay represents his more recent views (already expressed in his 2002 *Abschied vom Jahwisten* essay) that only Exod 3 can be assigned to the KD author (4:1–18 is now all a post-P insertion) and this KD author was exclusively focused on the Moses story. His arguments for the post-Priestly character of 4:1–18 are quite similar to those advanced by Schmid, Gertz, and others, as Blum acknowledges. He diverges from them on two main points: his contention that Exod 3 is *pre*-Priestly (Gertz and Schmid take it as post-Priestly) and that it is focused exclusively on the Moses story (Gertz and Schmid take it as focused on both Genesis and the Moses story). Then he goes on to focus on the transition between Genesis and Exodus, arguing (following Gertz and diverging from his own earlier work) that Gen 50:25–26 is the only possible non-Priestly transition from Genesis to Exodus and that these verses are inextricably connected to the transition from Joshua to Judges in Josh 24 and Judg 2:6–10, a transition that in turn is *post*-Priestly. Blum's arguments throughout are focused on the internal connections and cross-references within the passages themselves.

Central to Schmid and Gertz's arguments is the (older) observation of a sharp divide in conceptuality and ideology surrounding Egypt in the Joseph and Exodus stories: in Genesis the land of Egypt is a place of relative refuge, while in Exodus it becomes a place of genocide and oppression. Indeed, they argue that the biblical tradents themselves saw this divide and felt a need to bridge it by adding the comment in Exod 1:8 that the pharaoh of Moses's time was different from that of Joseph's. Furthermore, Schmid and Gertz argue that the other texts that link the ancestors and exodus materials are very few (e.g., Gen 15:13–16; 46:1–5; Exod 1:6, 8; also Gen 33:19; 50:25–26; Exod 13:19; Josh 24:32) and that all these texts are post-Priestly. They reject other proposed links between the ancestor and Moses stories as insufficiently explicit, particularly when compared with the highly systematic Priestly coordination of those periods. Indeed, P is the orientation point for both analyses: setting the standard by which non-Priestly cross-references qualify or fall short of qualifying as sufficient to establish a connection between these portions of the Pentateuch. For example, both Gertz and Schmid argue that Priestly promises of multiplication and reports of multiplication correspond far more closely with each other than the non-Priestly promise of multiplication in Gen 12:2 corresponds with the report of multiplication (in Pharaoh's speech) in Exod 1:9. They take this lack of a Priestly-level of correspondence as evidence that Gen 12:2 and Exod 1:9 are part of quite different literary levels. In sum, for Schmid and Gertz, P is the standard against which potential non-P connections between the ancestors and Moses are measured, and both find the non-P connections either are datable to a post-Priestly layer or fail to be as explicit as P.

Yet despite the similarities between these two essays, there are some differences. Schmid's essay provides more of an overview of the chief arguments for these shared positions, and it makes more claims about the implications of this model for the history of Israelite religion. Gertz's essay explores the join between Genesis and Exodus in more detail, reconstructing the transition in P and critiquing attempts by me and others to argue that there was a pre-Priestly bridge. Notably, Gertz's P still has a concluding Joseph story, while Schmid's essay attempts, building on a proposal by de Pury, to reconstruct a version of P that lacked such a Joseph story. Schmid's "P" moved directly from the Jacob story (including his descent into Egypt) to the story of Moses. This results for Schmid in a reconstruction of the Priestly bridge between Genesis and Exodus that is significantly different from that seen in Gertz.

Meanwhile, Dozeman's paper compares the genre and motifs of the non-P and P versions of Moses's call, arguing that—contra Schmid and Gertz in particular—the non-P version of Moses' call predates the P version rather than vice versa. If Dozeman is further correct in arguing that the non-P version of Moses' call links to the ancestral tradition (cf. Blum's essay translated in this volume), then this would represent a major piece of evidence *for* the idea of a pre-Priestly Pentateuch and we would not be saying "farewell to this [so-called] Yahwist" after all. Dozeman, however, is cautious in making broader claims on the basis of his analysis of the call of Moses (along with some comments on the Red Sea narrative). Rather, he raises some thoughtful questions toward the end of his paper, particularly one regarding distinctions in genre that is akin to concerns I have about using P as the standard against which non-P is measured.

2. P AND DIFFERENT MODELS FOR THE JOINING OF TRADITIONS

Schmid and Gertz agree that the linkage between different blocks can only be established by *explicit* forward- and back-references within a given stratum of biblical tradition. For them, the starting point is that the texts are separate until "proven combined" (to echo the famous "innocent until proven guilty" dictim). Yet we do not, in fact, have separate texts but combined texts in our present Bible, and nothing else is documented in manuscripts. Indeed, even once one has distinguished P and non-P texts, there is, at minimum, some narrative continuity in non-P texts, conceptual shifts regarding Egypt (cf. Exod 1:8) notwithstanding. The ancestors succeed one another living in the land, with Jacob-Israel eventually descending into Egypt (though cf. Schmid on this latter point), and the Moses-exodus story picks up with a people of "Israel" who start on their way back to the land. We have non-P materials that move from the one epoch to the other. Therefore, one could respond, the texts of the given non-P stratum are "connected until proven separate." Neither approach per se is preferable (assuming connection or disconnection), except insofar as we happen to have the combined pentateuchal traditions in hand, rather than the separate ones.

But say we grant, as I would, that the ancestral traditions were once separate from the Moses traditions, how do we conceptualize their joining? Schmid and Gertz conceive of the movement being from (1) separate traditions to (2) P's systematic coordination of them to (3) various post-Priestly traditions that sometimes provide additional, explicit cross-references. I suggest, on the contrary, that the movement was from (1) separate non-P compositions, to (2) a limited compositional connection of them with each other, to (3) P's systematic coordination and connection of these blocks of tradition with each other. This latter sequence of gradual movement toward coordination, I maintain, makes more sense, particularly in light of what we know about textual growth. This would be an early correlate to a widespread phenomenon we see in later, documented redactions of the Pentateuch, where the tradents that produced the *Temple Scroll*, 4QRP, and the so-called "Proto-Samaritan" manuscripts coordinated the divergent parts of an existing legal corpus with each other.[3] This move toward coordination and harmonization of disparate traditions is a characteristic of a time when such materials have become part of a common Scriptural corpus, a corpus whose parts must be coordinated. We see a similar move in the harmonizations and coordinations of diverse biblical traditions by later interpreters. In this case, I am suggesting an accelerating process of such coordination and harmonization in the formation of the Pentateuch: starting with limited redactional

---

3. I discuss this phenomenon and others in semipentateuchal traditions in David M. Carr, "Method in Determination of Direction of Dependence: An Empirical Test of Criteria Applied to Exodus 34,11–26 and Its Parallels," in *Gottes Volk am Sinai: Untersuchungen zu Ex 32–34 und Dtn 9–10* (ed. M. Köckert and E. Blum; Veröffentlichungen der Wissenschaftlichen Gesellschaft für Theologie 18; Gütersloh: Gütersloher Verlagshaus, 2001), 107–40.

linkage of originally separate compositions, and accelerating with the more systematic Priestly joins.

This proposed sequence recognizes that the Priestly stratum is not typical of other layers of biblical tradition in crucial respects. This is highlighted by Schmid's work in particular. For example, in the Priestly version of Moses' call we see explicit linkage to the patriarchs and coordination of their period with the Mosaic period. So also, he suggests that in the Priestly concept of the ancestors as "sojourners" we see an attempt to bridge between the apparent promise of the land to them and their descendants and the delay of that promise that is produced when their story is prefixed to that of the exodus and wilderness. And I have already mentioned how Gertz and Schmid's essays both find that the mention of Israel's multiplication in Exod 1:9 is insufficiently similar in wording to the promise of multiplication in Gen 12:2, especially when compared with the close agreement of the Priestly report of multiplication (Exod 1:7) and various Priestly mentions of multiplication in Genesis (1:28; 9:7; 17:2). Overall, the Priestly tradents appear to have been far more concerned than others in establishing symmetry and terminological correspondence between different parts. Whether one understands the non-P materials as part of a pre-Priestly or post-Priestly Pentateuch, the Priestly tradents contrast with them in showing an unusually high level of concern for periodization of early Israelite history and coordination of parts with it.

Therefore, precisely building on these insights by Schmid and others, we should be wary of using connections in the Priestly material as our norm for evaluating connections in non-P biblical traditions. Indeed, if it were true that the joining of these traditions was gradual, then we would not be surprised to find a more systematic joining of ancestor and Moses-exodus stories in P than in a pre-Priestly Pentateuch that preceded it, especially if that pre-Priestly Pentateuch was itself the product of a late combination of ancestral and exodus traditions.

3. Potential Pre-Priestly Connections between the Ancestral and Moses Stories

Let us turn now to look at potential pre-Priestly links of the ancestral and Moses-exodus stories. For now I will avoid focusing on those texts, such as Gen 15:13–16, that many in the current debate agree are post-Priestly. Moreover, I will not review potential connections to the exodus in texts such as the Hagar-Ishmael story in Gen 16:1–14*, partly because it is not clear how these links require a literary continuation of the story into the non-Priestly Tetrateuch. Rather, following on work in my book *Reading the Fractures of Genesis* and an essay in a Leuven Conference volume, I want briefly to point to several elements, particularly concentrated in the Abraham story, that appear to be shaped to lead into the non-Priestly exodus story found in Exodus.[4] These linkages are not of the character of P's explicit coordination of different periods. Neither are they explicit cross-references of the sort seen in Gen 15 or strings of connected texts such as the notices about Joseph's bones (Gen 33:19; 50:25–26; Exod 13:19; Josh 24:32). Nevertheless, the Abraham and exodus portions of the non-Priestly Pentateuch are linked by more than mere similarities in Yahwistic vocabulary or the like. I will focus on two sets of connections here.

One example is a network of travel commands and promises spanning Genesis that link Gen 46:1–5 to the story of Moses and the Israelites in Egypt. Each of these speeches is a divine speech relating to travel into or out of the promised land. Their similarities and differences are indicated in the following table:

TABLE 1: THE NETWORK OF TRAVEL COMMANDS
(brackets indicate placement out of order)

Gen 12:1–2	Gen 26:2–3	Gen 31:3aβb	Gen 46:3b–4
			אל-תירא
לך-לך	אל-תרד	שוב אל-ארץ	מרדה
מארצך	מצרימה	אבותיך	מצרימה
וממולדתך	שכן בארץ	ולמולדתך	
ומבית אביך	אשר אמר אליך		
אל-הארץ	גור בארץ הזאת		
אשר אראך	ואהיה עמך	ואהיה עמך	[אנכי ארד עמך
			מחרימה]
ואעשך			כי-לגוי גדול
לגוי גדול			אשימך שם
ואברכך	ואברכך		
ואגדלה שמך			
והיה ברכה:			
	כי-לך ולזרעך		ואנכי אעלך
	אתן את-		גם-עלה
	כל-הארצת האל		

---

4. David M. Carr, "Genesis in Relation to the Moses Story: Diachronic and Synchronic Perspectives," in *Studies in the Book of Genesis: Literature, Redaction and History* (ed. A. Wénin; BETL 155; Leuven: Leuven University Press; Peeters, 2001), 273–95. The contributions to this volume by Schmid and Gertz both focus primarily on critiquing my treatment in this Leuven essay of Gen 12:10–20 and 16:1–14*, by-passing the arguments regarding travel commands summarized below.

Note the particular parallels in the above table between the commands to Abraham and Jacob to travel into the land (Gen 12:1–2//31:3aβb), and the commands to Isaac and Jacob about travel out of the land (Gen 26:2–3//46:3b–4). Although these commands and associated promises often have been assigned to different layers—especially Gen 46:1–5 versus the others—they represent a remarkably cohesive and balanced system leading from the patriarchs outside of Egypt to the stay in Egypt and the trip back out. I will return to the case of Gen 46:1–5 toward the end of this response.

The other set of links between the non-Priestly narratives of the patriarchs and the Moses story is a set of terminologically linked stories of destruction in Genesis that build on God's promise to Abraham in Gen 12:2–3 and correspond to two texts in Exodus: the commissioning of Moses to initiate the exodus in Exod 3:1–4:18 and the final stage of the exodus out of Egypt at the Red Sea (Exod 14:1–31).

Non-P Sections (*)	Flood (Gen 6–8*)	Sodom (Gen 18:16–19:38*)	Exodus (Exod 3–4*, 14*)
God sees/hears that suffering or evil is "great" רבה	6:5	18:20	3:7, 9
Problem is "evil" (רעה; and related roots)	6:5	13:13; 19:7, 9	
God hears "cry" (זעקה)		18:20–21; 19:13	3:9
God descends		18:21	3:8
God tells righteous	7:1–4	19:13	3:1–4:17
God provides escape instructions	7:1–4	19:11–12	3:16–4:17 (14:13–14)
Righteous are saved	7:7 (cf. 7:1)	19:15–23	14:21–27
Destruction (by water)	7:22–23aα (cf. 7:4)	19:24 ("rain" of fire)	14:21–27

One could explain away the above network of similar themes and motifs in the three stories as chance overlaps. Nevertheless, when read together, these stories of destruction and rescue show a strikingly similar theological innovation: the extension of ideas of a god's triumph over waters (or watery monsters) at creation (e.g., Job 38:8–11; Pss 89:9–10; 104:5–9; 146:5–6; cf. re-creation in Gen 6–8*) to encompass traditions surrounding the origins of Israel (e.g., Abraham and exodus). The other place where we see this sequence of motifs established is in Second Isaiah (e.g., Isa 51:9–11), and there is a good chance that the non-P pentateuchal connections under discussion here are from a similar time.

To be sure, the above-outlined networks of thematically and terminologically connected narratives are not explicit cross-references as in the P materials. Nevertheless, they are central ways in which the existing non-Priestly pentateuchal narratives connect the ancestral stories to the exodus. These networks of connections go beyond isolated parallels in terminology (e.g,. lexica of a "Yahwist") or exodus-like structure (e.g., Gen 16:1–14*). Instead, they reflect a compositional sequence that leads from Abraham to the exodus under Moses. Contra Gertz, they cannot be explained away as attempts to reclaim the exodus tradition for the patriarchs. Rather, they are proto-exodus elements whose full import is not grasped until one gets to the exodus narrative itself. Only there does the Jacob/Israel who hears about Egypt in Genesis become a people. Only there is the God with salvific power over waters conclusively revealed in a triumph that uses the waters of the Red Sea.

4. A Pre-Priestly Bridge between Genesis and Exodus

Schmid, Gertz, and Blum devote significant attention to disproving the idea of a non-Priestly bridge between Genesis and Exodus, so in fairness to them, I will also address these arguments.

Prior to detailed engagement with individual cases, the first thing to be remembered is that it is easily possible that the conflation of this portion of two proto-Pentateuchs could have preserved material from one transition and completely eliminated the transition in the other. All documented cases of conflation involve selective use of both source traditions, and it appears in Genesis as if the R[P] redactor did eliminate non-Priestly transitions between the patriarchs in favor of Priestly ones. In light of this, anyone who assumes that there *must* be both P and non-P elements in the transition between Genesis and Exodus is mistaken about the literary process of conflation. This kind of consideration becomes a factor in Gertz's argumentation when he argues that Joseph's announcement of his death in Gen 50:24 cannot be pre-Priestly because he cannot find a corresponding pre-Priestly death notice. Generally, people only die once in narratives, including in biblical narratives, so it would be the exception rather than the rule for a conflation to include both a Priestly and non-Priestly report of Joseph's death.

That said, I will argue here that there are indications of a pre-Priestly bridge between the non-Priestly Joseph story and the non-Priestly Moses-exodus story. Like Schmid and Gertz, I take the following to be P or post-P materials: Gen 50:12–13, 22–23, 26a; Exod 1:1–5a, 7; I agree that Gen 50:15–21 probably is part of the conclusion to an earlier non-P Joseph story (though cf. Schmid on the latter point). My main points of disagreement with Schmid, Gertz, and Blum are the following: whether the notice of Joseph's return to Egypt in Gen 50:14a is a fragment of P and whether all of Gen 50:24–25 and Exod 1:6, 8 must be part of the post-P redactional layer.

5. Genesis 50:14

Genesis 50:14 is important in this discussion because it is usually treated as part of the pre-Priestly conclusion to the Joseph story, a conclusion that moves Joseph and his brothers back to Egypt after burying their father in Canaan: "and Joseph returned to Egypt, he and his brothers and all who went up to bury his father, after burying his father." Though a narrative about the exodus out of Egypt is not required as a follow-up to this return to Egypt, Gen 50:14 does create room for one to happen. Yet if Gen 50:14 is identified as Priestly or later, then a form of the non-Priestly Joseph story ends with all the brothers in Canaan. They need not leave Egypt for the land because they are already there.

Yet neither Schmid nor Gertz is able to marshal persuasive arguments for identifying Gen 50:14 as a later addition. The primary datum with which they work is a putative conflict between references to Jacob's burial in Gen 50:(12–13 P)14 and the brothers' "seeing" that their father is dead in 50:15. Gertz argues that the brothers would not just be realizing that their father was dead if they recently had completed an extended trip to Canaan to bury him. Since Gen 50:15 is generally agreed to be part of the early conclusion to the Joseph story, Gen 50:14 must be later (so Schmid and Gertz). Yet there is no need to follow this argumentation. Within the narrative world of Gen 50, there is no reason why the brothers would not "see," in the wake of Jacob's burial, that their father was dead and attempt to protect themselves by making claims to Joseph about Jacob's last wishes (50:15–18). In addition, the narrator may presuppose that such an interaction would be unlikely before the time of mourning and burial was complete. In any case, although there are signs in the manuscript tradition that parts of 50:14 may be later (50:14b is missing in the Old Greek), there is no reason to suppose that the beginning of the verse comes from a layer other than that of Gen 50:15–21, which is part of the non-Priestly Joseph story.

Even if Schmid and Gertz are right in supposing that Gen 50:14 is later than the surrounding non-Priestly texts, there is no reason to conclude that it is Priestly or later. Gertz assigns 50:14 to P because he assumes that someone expanding the non-Priestly narrative would have added such a notice of return to the end of the Joseph story, not earlier in the story's conclusion. The unusual position of Gen 50:14a, Gertz maintains, is a result of it being a part of the Priestly burial report that begins in 50:12 and concludes with a notice of the return in 50:14a. According to Gertz, this Priestly section (Gen 50:12–14a) was inserted as a block into the surrounding non-Priestly material, with 50:14b added later to smooth the transition. Yet contra Gertz, we see many occasions in which redactors add notices in the middle (not end) of sections—including his own supposition of a post-Priestly addition in 50:14b. Therefore, even if 50:14a was later, it still could be a pre-Priestly expansion of the Joseph narrative. Moreover, Gertz's assignment of 50:14a to P creates its own problems. It means that P now has a strange transition from a focus on all the brothers in 50:12–13 to Joseph in 50:14a. This clash was noticed by previous source critics. Indeed, this clash is part of what prompted them to assign 50:12–13 to P and 50:14a to non-Priestly sources.

In sum, the report of Joseph and his brothers' return to Egypt in Gen 50:14a is probably part of the early Joseph story, and even if it were not, there is no sign it was once part of P or a later layer.

6. Genesis 50:24–25

Gertz and Schmid are in more company in assigning 50:24–25 to a post-P redactor. Gertz asserts: "V. Fritz has demonstrated the dependency of this verse on the burial traditions for Abraham in Gen 25:9 and Jacob in Gen 50:13 as well as the depiction of Abraham purchasing the cave of Machpelah in Gen 23." Yet Fritz himself in his commentary on Joshua actually assigns 50:24–25 and related pentateuchal notices to E, and he merely suggests that the final burial notice for Joseph in Josh 24:32 "could be traced to the interests of a post-Priestly redactor" ("könnte die Anfügung von 32 auf das Interesse des nachpriesterschriftlichen Redaktors zurückgehen").[5] Why does Fritz suggest this? Because he thinks that it is in the P tradition of Machpelah that we first see the idea of the burial of the patriarchs in land that is purchased. This reasoning by Fritz, however, is weak. If there is a direction of dependence, it could as easily move in the reverse direction: dependence of P on the non-P traditions surrounding burial at Shechem beginning in Gen 33:19 and concluding with Josh 24:32. Nevertheless, such

---

5. Volkmar Fritz, *Das Buch Josua* (HAT 1/7; Tübingen: Mohr Siebeck, 1994), 251.

a relationship of dependence is highly unclear in any case, since there are no specific connections between the tradition about Joseph's bones and the P traditions of burial at Machpelah.[6]

Gertz argues further that Gen 50:24–25, which starts with a reference to Joseph's death, must be post-Priestly because that reference to Joseph's death now stands in a chiastic relation with a Priestly death notice for Joseph in 50:26a. Gertz outlines the chiastically related elements as follows:[7]

A   אנכי מת   50:24aβ (non-P)

B   ואלהים פקד יפקד אתכם   והעלה אתכם מן־הארץ הזאת
                                                                50:24bα (non-P)

C   אל־הארץ אשר נשבע לאברהם ליצחק וליעקב
                                                                50:24bβ (non-P)

B   והעלתם את־עצמתי מזה   פקד יפקד אלהים אתכם
                                                                50:25b (non-P)

A   וימת יוסף   50:26aα (P)

As is evident from the diagram, the elements that correspond between non-P (Gen 50:24) and P (Gen 50:26) are quite slight (אנכי מת/וימת יוסף), and these texts link different sorts of materials: Joseph's prediction of his death and the narrator's report of it. In contrast, the most specific and extensive chiastic connections occur exclusively within the speech of Gen 50:24–25, binding Joseph's speech in 24 with his oath in 25.[8] So why would there now be both

---

6. The idea of claiming land through burial of ancestors in it that is found in both texts is a widespread, cross-culturally attested idea. For discussion of reflection of these practices in the later D and P traditions of ancient Israel, see Brian Schmidt, *Israel's Beneficent Dead: Ancestor Cult and Necromancy in Ancient Israelite Religion and Tradition* (FAT 11; Tübingen: Mohr Siebeck, 1994), 278–80, 291. Cross-cultural theories regarding claims to land through burial of ancestors go back to the classic nineteenth-century work, Fustel de Coulanges, *La cité antique* (Paris: Librairie Hachette, 1883) [thanks to Brian Schmidt for this reference].

7. Jan Christian Gertz, *Tradition und Redaktion in der Exoduserzählung: Untersuchungen zur Endredaktion des Pentateuch* (FRLANT 186; Göttingen: Vandenhoeck & Ruprecht, 2000), 261.

8. See Norbert Lohfink, *Die Landverheissung als Eid: Eine Studie zu Gn 15* (SBS 28; Stuttgart: Katholisches Bibelwerk, 1967), 23 n. 43. Cf. Erhard Blum, *Die Komposition der Väter-geschichte* (WMANT 57; Neukirchen-Vluyn: Neukirchener, 1984), 255, who saw a chiastic link within these speeches between Joseph's announcement of his death in 50:24ab and his reference toward the end of 50:25 to his "bones" (עצמתי).

correspondences within Joseph's two speeches and one between Joseph's prediction of his death (non-P) and the report of it (Gen 50:26a, P)? Perhaps the latter phenomenon is best explained as a result of the confluence toward the end of the Joseph story of various traditions surrounding Joseph's death: the prediction of it, preparations, and the death itself. Indeed, it is hard to know where else the R^P redactor could or would have placed a Priestly death notice for Joseph (50:26aα) other than after Joseph's chiastically bound speeches in 50:24–25 anticipating his death, especially since the verses are constructed as a chiasm. That such placement extended the Gen 50:24–25 chiasm a bit further would have been an added benefit.[9]

The discussion of Gen 50:24–25 would not be complete without addressing Erhard Blum's somewhat different arguments in recent publications, including the essay for this volume, for the post-Priestly character of 50:24–25. Earlier he had assigned these verses to a pre-Priestly Deuteronomistic compositional layer,[10] but in 1990 he argued for the post-Priestly character of 50:25,[11] and in his most recent publications he has assigned 50:24–26 as a whole to a post-Priestly hexateuchal redaction, which developed parallel transitions from the patriarchal period to the exodus generation (Gen 50:24–25; Exod 1:6, 8; the latter modeled on Judg 2:6–8) and from the time of Joshua to that of the Judges (Josh 24:29–32; a text also modeled on Judg 2:6–8).[12] Yet building on Gertz's observation about the potentially "Tragikomik" character of a transition that leads straight from Joseph's announcement of his own death to his brothers (Gen 50:24–25) to the death of both Joseph *and* his brothers (Exod 1:6),[13] Blum concludes that Gen 50:24–25; Exod 1:6, 8 presuppose the intervening Priestly material in Exod 1:1–5a, 7*. This concurs with his conclusions that Josh 24 also presupposes the entire P/non-P Pentateuch, with the wording in Josh 24:6 paralleling that of the Priestly account of the Reed Sea in Exod 12:23.[14]

---

9. Below I argue that Exod 1:6a is a probable pre-Priestly death notice for Joseph, so the 50:24–25 chiasm may have concluded with that one before the R^P redactor's intervention.

10. Blum, *Vätergeschichte*, 255–57, 392.

11. Erhard Blum, *Studien zur Komposition des Pentateuch* (BZAW 189; Berlin: de Gruyter, 1990), 363–65.

12. See, for example, his "Die literarische Verbindung von Erzvätern und Exodus: Ein Gespräch mit neueren Endredaktionshypothesen," in *Abschied vom Jahwisten: Die Komposition des Hexateuch in der jüngsten Diskussion* (ed. J. C. Gertz et al.; BZAW 315; Berlin: de Gruyter, 2002), 150–51; idem, "Der kompositionelle Knoten am Übergang von Josua zu Richter: Ein Entflechtungsvorschlag," in *Deuteronomy and Deuteronomic Literature: Festschrift C. H. W. Brekelmans* (ed. M. Vervenne and J. Lust; BETL 133; Leuven: Leuven University Press; Peeters, 1997), 202, and his essay within the current volume.

13. Gertz, *Tradition und Redaktion*, 360.

14. Blum, "Der kompositionelle Knoten," 197.

Much depends here, however, on two elements: the mention of the death of Joseph's brothers in Exod 1:6aα and the question of whether Josh 24:6 is a sufficient basis for a post-Priestly dating of the chapter as a whole. I will return to the topic of Exod 1:6aα shortly. For now, I would simply note that Josh 24:6 is a weak hook on which to hang a post-Priestly dating of Josh 24 and associated texts. As Fritz notes, Josh 24:6–7aα diverges from the rest of Joshua's speech in speaking of those in history not as "you" (plural; see 24:5, 8, 9, 10, 11, etc.) but in the third person as "your fathers," an indicator that suggests that this section may be a later expansion of Josh 24, an expansion harmonizing this part of Josh 24 with the existing P/non-P narrative of the Reed Sea.[15]

In sum, there is little to establish that Joseph's anticipation of the exodus in Gen 50:24–25 is post-Priestly. It could be a later addition to the non-Priestly transition between Genesis and Exodus, but no one has yet given decisive reasons for identifying this section as Priestly or later. It remains a possible pre-Priestly link between the ancestral and Moses stories.

7. Exodus 1:8(–9)

Exodus 1:8 is also a potential pre-Priestly bridge between Genesis and Exodus. It is particularly important, because it appears crafted to explain the massive shift in the picture of Egypt from Genesis to Exodus: "A new king arose over Egypt who did not know Joseph." Schmid and Gertz argue that the verse is post-Priestly primarily because its continuation, the pharaoh's speech in Exod 1:9 (הנה עם בני ישראל רב ועצום ממנו) presupposes the narrator's report of multiplication in Exod 1:7 and supposedly appropriates Priestly language of multiplication from that verse (ובני ישראל פרו וישרצו וירבו ויעצמו במאד מאד) while deviating considerably from the original non-Priestly promise of multiplication to Abraham in Gen 12:2 (ואעשך לגוי גדול).

Yet here again the arguments do not hold up under scrutiny. In another context I have pointed out that Pharaoh's report of multiplication in Exod 1:9 need not be preceded by a narrator's report of such multiplication in Exod 1:7. Biblical narrators often communicate information by way of character speeches, and Exod 1:9 could be an example of that.[16] Furthermore, as Blum has pointed out, the wording of Exod 1:7 is not typically Priestly, but a combination of non-Priestly wording from Exod 1:9 and Priestly wording known elsewhere.[17]

---

15. Fritz, *Das Buch Josua,* 238.
16. Carr, "Genesis and Moses," 291.
17. Blum, "Die literarische Verbindung," 148.

This can be seen through a comparison of Exod 1:7 with Priestly and non-Priestly contexts:

P

Gen 1:28	ומלאו את־הארץ	ורבו	פרו
Gen 9:7	שרצו בארץ ורבו־בה	ורבו	פרו
Gen 17:2	במאד מאד	וארבה אותך	

D/Non-P

Exod 1:9	ועצום ממנו	רב	הנה עם בני ישראל
Deut 7:1	ועצומים ממך	רבים	ונשל ... גוים
Deut 9:14			ואעשה אותך לגוי־עצום ורב ממנו
Deut 26:5			ויהי־שם לגוי גדול עצום ורב

Exod 1:7

פרו וישרצו וירבו ויעצמו במאד מאד
ותמלא הארץ אתם

As this comparison shows, the use of עצם in Exod 1:7 distinguishes it from its Priestly parallels and links it to Exod 1:9 and other non-Priestly texts. If there is any direction of influence, it would appear to be from the typical non-P description of multiplication in Exod 1:9 to the blended P/non-P-like description of multiplication in Exod 1:7, not the other way around. Exodus 1:9 is closely linked to non-Priestly parallels and distinguished from its Priestly analogues in its use of עצם and its use of רב as an adjective (rather than the verbal רב).

In sum, Exod 1:9 shows no signs of post-Priestly authorship, nor does the crucial transition under discussion in Exod 1:8. Contra Schmid and Gertz, Exod 1:9 does not presuppose or borrow from Exod 1:7. Rather the expressions in Exod 1:7 represent a melding of non-Priestly language of the sort seen in Exod 1:9 with more typically priestly language such as that seen in Gen 1:28; 9:7. In this sense, we probably do see in Exod 1:7 a sign of Priestly "redaction."

Exodus 1:6

The last potential pre-Priestly bridge from ancestors to Moses is Exod 1:6, the notice of the death of Joseph, his brothers, and their entire generation. In the past, Nöldeke's classic discussion of P along with several other studies identified all of Exod 1:6 as part of the pre-Priestly transition from Genesis to Exodus. Nevertheless, over the years, a number of scholars, such as M. Noth, have assigned the verse or part of it to P or R[P]. This approach was given an added impetus in 1997 by H.-C. Schmitt, who argued in detail that the notice of the death of Joseph and all his brothers in Exod 1:6 linked far better to the Priestly listing of Joseph and his brothers in Exod 1:1–5 than to the preceding non-P material,[18] and Jan Christian Gertz expanded on and affirmed this argumentation in his 1990 book, pointing out, as mentioned above, the incongruity of having Joseph's brothers die (Exod 1:6) immediately after promising to bring Joseph's bones up from Egypt (Gen 50:25).[19] Nevertheless, as many have observed before, there are problems with assigning Exod 1:6 to P as well.[20] Rather, it is probable that Exod 1:6, apart from the mention of Joseph's brothers (which links to Priestly elements in Exod 1:1–5), preserves an earlier notice of the death of Joseph and his generation. *Aside from the mention of Joseph's brothers,* the notice in Exod 1:6, 8 is parallel to similar material in Judg 2:8–10:

Exod 1:6, 8	Judg 2:8–10
(6) וימת יוסף	(8) וימת יהושע בן־נון עבד יהוה
[וכל־אחיו]	בן־מאה ועשר שנים
וכל הדור ההוא	(10) וגם כל־הדור ההוא נאספו אל־אבותיו
(8) ויקם למך־חדש על־מצרים	ויקם דור אחר אחריהם
אשר לא־ידע את־יוסף	אשר לא־ידעו את־יהוה
	וגם את־המעשה אשר עשה לישראל

This set of close verbal parallels—with a divergence in the mention of Joseph's brothers in Exod 1:6—provides some weight for identifying parts of Exod 1:6 as once being part of a pre-Priestly transition from ancestors to Moses, even if the death notice in 1:6 appears to have been modified through the addition of Joseph's brothers, thus linking the verse to the list of them in Exod 1:1–5.

However much writers in the Priestly style have augmented these transitions in both Genesis-Exodus and Joshua-Judges, the parallels across Joseph/Joshua's

---

18. Hans-Christoph Schmitt, "Die Josephsgeschichte und das deuteronomistische Geschichtswerk: Genesis 38 und 48–50," in Vervenne and Lust, *Deuteronomy and Deuteronomic Literature,* 393.

19. Gertz, *Tradition und Redaktion,* 360.

20. For discussion and citations of earlier literature, see Werner H. Schmidt, *Exodus* (BK 2/1; Neukirchen-Vluyn: Neukirchener, 1988), 10–11.

final speeches (Gen 50:24//Josh 24:1–24), oath ceremonies (Gen 50:25//Josh 24:25–27), deaths (Exod 1:6a*//Judg 2:8a), deaths of their generation (Exod 1:6b//Judg 2:10a), and rise of a subsequent generation who does not "know" (Exod 1:8//Judg 2:10b) suggest a pre-Priestly core.[21] Indeed, they are related to each other by way of Joseph's provisions for his burial in Gen 50:25 and the execution of it in Josh 24:32, a linkage that suggests that some of the parallels may have been created by the same pre-Priestly author—albeit a late pre-Priestly author—intervening in both loci. On this point, as well as the links between the Jacob and Joshua Shechem narratives, the essay by Blum in the present volume is very helpful, even if I do not agree with him on the post-Priestly character of these connections.

In the final analysis, however, the argumentation here does not depend on the acceptance of each part of the pre-Priestly transition outlined above. It is also possible, of course, that the R[P] redactor—or a post-Priestly "hexateuchal redactor"—completely eliminated a pre-Priestly transition from ancestors to Moses, as apparently happened in the case of some transitions between the patriarchs in Genesis. Nevertheless, I have attempted to show that the arguments for the post-Priestly authorship of sections such as Gen 50:24–25 and Exod 1:8–9 are not compelling. Instead, at least some of the non-Priestly verses linking Genesis and Exodus (Gen 50:24–25; Exod 1:6*, 8–9) were probably part of a pre-Priestly link between ancestral and Moses traditions.[22]

8. Identification of Post-Priestly Material

The above cases are examples of a broader phenomenon in pentateuchal scholarship where contemporary scholars too easily have identified swaths of non-Priestly material as post-Priestly. This is a place where I find Thomas Dozeman's contribution to this volume particularly helpful. He provides good generic grounds for refuting Schmid's, Gertz's, and others' identification of Exod 3:1–4:17 as post-Priestly. Responding to Schmid and Gertz, Erhard Blum had already provided some arguments for regarding the bulk of Exod 3 as pre-Priestly, even as he moved to assign 4:1–17 to a post-Priestly layer seen also in Exod 4:27–31 and 18.[23] Nevertheless, Dozeman provides grounds for the identification of the call narrative in Exod 3:1–4:17 as a whole as pre-Priestly.

---

21. See Blum's brief discussion of a similar alternative in note 137 of his "Die literarische Verbindung," 148–49.

22. Gen 50:14 is not included in this list because it does not necessarily link literary compositions. It would be easily possible for an independent Joseph story to end with the return of him and his brothers to Egypt, with the author assuming a knowledge on the part of his readers of the subsequent Exodus from Egypt.

23. Blum, "Die literarische Verbindung," 124–30, and the essay in the present volume.

This does not mean, of course, that Exod 3:1–4:17 is of a piece with the surrounding material. On the contrary, one of Blum's main contributions, one picked up by Schmid and Gertz in different ways, is his expansion of Noth's argumentation that Exod 3:1–4:18 represents an insertion into the surrounding context.[24] If (Noth and) Blum is right about this, we should not be surprised to find that ideas in 3:1–4:18 are not reflected in that context or are reflected only partially. Moreover, even more than its context, the insertion could reflect relatively late elements of Israelite language and ideology. Nevertheless, once one grants the special character of Exod 3:1–4:18, the arguments for the post-Priestly character of 3:1–4:9 and even 4:10–17 are not as strong as they first appear. Disjunctions between the conceptuality of 3:1–4:18 and surrounding non-P material can be explained by the fact that this insertion represents a partially executed reconceptualization of the Moses story. Yet as Dozeman has shown, this is not a post-Priestly reconceptualization. Instead, in every instance where Exod 3:1–4:18 shows affinities with P, it diverges from it. Though P picks up on and develops some ideas found in Exod 3:1–4:18 in distinctive ways (e.g., signs, Aaron), this insertion into the non-P context, as treated by Dozeman, is probably prior to P.[25]

This is significant because parts of this insertion appear to link the Moses story with the preceding ancestral stories. Building on earlier studies, Gertz outlined specific parallels between God's theophanic appearance to Jacob (Gen 46:2–4) and the same God's appearance to Moses (Exod 3:4–8). These parallels extend beyond mere formal similarities, such as God's double address to Jacob and Moses and the response "here I am" (הנני; Gen 46:2aβ//Exod 3:4b), God's self-introduction as the "god of your father" (Gen 46:3a//Exod 3:6aα), and the generic promise to "go down" to Egypt and "bring up" Israel from there.[26] What is important is that these formal parallels occur along with connections in

---

24. Blum, *Studien zur Komposition des Pentateuch*, 20–22, and see the helpful summary of his arguments in the essay for the present volume.

25. Cf. arguments for the post-P character of Exod 3:1–4:18 in Heinrich Valentin, *Aaron: Eine Studie zur vor-priesterschriftlichen Aaron-Überlieferung* (OBO 18; Fribourg: Universitätsverlag; Göttingen: Vandenhoeck & Ruprecht, 1978), 75–81, 96, 101–6; Ferdinand Ahuis, *Der klagende Gerichtsprophet: Studien zur Klage in der Überlieferung von den alttestamentlichen Gerichtspropheten* (Stuttgart: Calwer, 1982), 44–49; Peter Weimar, *Die Berufung des Mose: Literaturwissenschaftliche Analyse von Exodus 2,23–5,5* (OBO 32; Fribourg: Universitätsverlag; Göttingen: Vandenhoeck & Ruprecht, 1980), 350–57; Konrad Schmid, *Erzväter und Exodus: Untersuchungen zur doppelten Begründung der Ursprünge Israels innerhalb der Geschichtsbücher des Alten Testaments* (WMANT 81; Neukirchen-Vluyn: Neukirchener, 1999), 197–209; Blum, *Studien zur Komposition des Pentateuch*, 27–28; Gertz, *Tradition und Redaktion*, 315–18, among others discussed in this essay.

26. See Gertz, *Tradition und Redaktion*, 278–79. In attempting to refute Gertz, Blum focuses on these in "Die literarische Verbindung," 232.

content. Contra Blum and with Gertz, the theophany to Jacob in Gen 46:1–5 represents a crucial anticipation of the exodus story in the ancestral narratives. It moves in chiastic fashion, from an initial command to the elderly Jacob not to be afraid of going down into Egypt (46:3bα) to a final promise that the Joseph he has just heard about (45:26–28) will close his eyes (46:4b). In between, God makes a promise of nationhood in 46:3bβ: "I will make you into a great nation there." That this promise anticipates the distant story of the exodus and not Jacob's own story is seen from the fact that the Jacob story does not narrate his becoming a great nation (cf. 46:3bβ). Rather, the story of the exodus develops the divine promise to Jacob in Exod 1:9 with the notice that his family became "a numerous and great people" (עם ... רב ועצום). Furthermore, 46:3bβ is elaborated—as signalled by asyndesis—by God's dual promise in 46:4a to "go down with" Jacob and "bring [him] up" (hiphil עלה). Once again, the latter part of this promise relates to a more distant future; God does not bring Jacob up out of Egypt in Genesis. Instead, this language, particularly the description of *God* "bringing up" (hiphil עלה) "from Egypt" is associated with the exodus (e.g., Exod 3:17; 17:3; 32:1–8, 23; 33:1; Lev 11:45; Num 20:5; 21:5; Deut 20:1; Josh 24:17; 24:32; Judg 2:1; 6:8; Jer 2:6; 11:7; Amos 2:10; 3:1; 9:7; Mic 6:4). Such language in 46:4aβ signals to the reader that the "bringing up" of "Jacob" will go far beyond Joseph's obligation to "bring up" his bones from Egypt (cf. Gen 50:7–11, 14), and it encompasses God's "bringing up" the "great people" that Jacob is to become. In sum, the speech in Gen 46:3b–4 moves in the following way from command to two reassuring promises:

I.	Command: Do not be afraid of going down to Egypt	46:3bα
II.	Reassuring Promises to Reinforce Command	46:3bβ–4
	A. Promise 1: Distant Future into Exodus	46:3bβ–4a
	1. Initial Statement: will make "you" into "great nation" there	46:3bβ
	[Thus: "Jacob" and "the great nation" are made equivalent]	
	2. Asyndetically Connected Elaboration:	46:4a
	a. "will go down with you" [you=Jacob]	46:4aα
	b. "will certainly bring you up" [you=great nation]	46:4aβ
	B. Promise 2: Immediate Future of Command—Joseph	46:4b

In these ways, the core of the promise of Gen 46:1–4 concludes the Genesis series of travel commands and promises, sharing with all of them a focus on "going into" and "coming out of" Egypt, but now linking in more direct ways with the following story of the exodus.

    Meanwhile, the theophany to Moses in Exod 3:1–4:18 implicitly links to promises such as Gen 46:1–4 (and others) by identifying the God who appears to Moses as the God "of Abraham, Isaac, and Jacob" (Exod 3:6, 16; 4:5; see also the insertion in 3:15). Elsewhere in the Bible (e.g., Deut 1:8; 6:10; 9:5, 27; 29:12; 30:20; 34:24; 2 Kgs 13:23; Jer 33:26; Ps 105:9; 1 Chr 16:16), these three figures are joined together by one thing: the inheritance of the promise.[27] Moreover, two of the three contexts (outside Exod 3–4) where the expression "the God of Abraham, Isaac, and Jacob" is mentioned (cf. Exod 3:6, 15, 16; 4:5) are in Chronicles, a composition that clearly presupposes a completed Pentateuch (1 Chr 29:18; 2 Chr 30:6; cf. also 1 Kgs 18:36).[28] Whatever the separate history of the traditions regarding these figures and the relative dating of the various references to the patriarchs (e.g., Genesis and Deuteronomy), the indicators both inside and outside of Genesis suggest that the coordination of these three personages was built around the idea of a promise that was shared by them. As a result, the promise is implicitly in play in the call of Moses in Exod 3:1–4:18, even if it is not mentioned explicitly. To be sure, God promises in this narrative to "go down" and "bring up" Israel from Egypt, *having heard their cry* (Exod 3:7–8; see also 3:9), but this is not an alternative explanation for God's intervention. It does not stand in place of the promises given to these figures. Rather, the promise is invoked already through the mention of Abraham, Isaac, and Jacob (e.g., Exod 3:16). The references in Exod 3:7, 9 to God's perception of Israel's suffering function to explain why God is intervening on Israel's behalf at that particular point.

The only way one could take Exod 3:1–22 as not building on and explicitly linking to narratives such as Gen 46:1–5 would be to treat formal and content elements separately, as Blum does. But the fact is that these elements occur together in Exod 3:1–4:17. The combination of verbal, formal, and substantial connections between the insertion in Exod 3:1–4:18 and the preceding narratives, especially Gen 46:1–5 and 50:24, make it quite likely that these texts in Genesis and Exodus were once part of a common pre-Priestly narrative that included both ancestors and Moses.

That said, at least something should be said about Gen 46:1–5, since Gertz and some others would assign it, like many texts discussed above, to a post-Priestly layer. Gertz does this based on the argument that Gen 46:1–5 is dependent on and later than Gen 26:1–5, 24, texts that in turn are dated by him (building on Weimar and Levin) to a post-Priestly *Endredaktion*. This dating is based on a supposed mixture of Priestly and non-Priestly language in

---

27. Their biological-genealogical connection is not unique to them, since several genealogical sidelines are presupposed as well, e.g., Ishmael and Esau.

28. Note that the expression, אלהי ... אלהי ... אלהי is unique to Exod 3:6, 15, while the other occurences of this phrase all have just one אלהי (Exod 3:16; 1 Kgs 18:36; 1 Chr 29:18; 2 Chr 30:6).

Gen 26:3b–5, especially the expanded description of Abraham's obedience in 26:5b, and on affinities between Gen 26:3b–5 and another late addition to the Abraham story, Gen 22:15–18.[29] Yet on closer examination, the terminological indicators of a post-Priestly dating of Gen 26:3b–5, 24 and 46:1–5 are slight and not decisive. The mere presence of a common word or phrase between a text in Genesis and one in Chronicles or a portion of P is hardly a basis for post-Priestly dating of the Genesis text.[30] Post-Priestly dating is always possible, but it needs to be established on the basis of disciplined use of well-documented, extensive, and reliable criteria.

Unfortunately, many contemporary identifications of texts as post-Priestly do not depend on such reliable criteria. Instead, such identifications all too often are based on a combination of methodologically problematic uses of vocabulary and/or tenuous links of certain texts with a tissue of other non-P texts likewise identified on equally problematic grounds as post-Priestly. And, as we have seen, once one set of texts is so identified on weak grounds as post-Priestly, it often brings with it a train of other connected texts as post-Priestly as well. This is not the locus for discussion of the full range of texts where this has occurred, so I have focused here on texts particularly crucial to the question of a pre-Priestly literary linkage of ancestral and Moses traditions.

9. Conclusion

Let me conclude not on a note of disagreement but agreement. Schmid's contribution concludes with a discussion of how discarding the hypothesis of a pre-Priestly "Yahwist" would alter the way the history of Israelite religion is done, linking it more integrally with cultures around it. Yet, as they acknowledge, most of these insights would also be compatible with the idea of the relatively late combination of ancestral and exodus traditions in a pre-Priestly Pentateuch. Whether one agrees with Schmid, Gertz, and Römer that P was the first to join ancestors and Moses in a literary whole or agrees with me and others that a late pre-Priestly author/editor created the first proto-Pentateuch, there is

---

29. See Peter Weimar, *Untersuchungen zur Redaktionsgeschichte des Pentateuch* (BZAW 146; Berlin: de Gruyter, 1977), 82–84 (who adds some weaker arguments regarding wording in 26:3b, 4b); and Christoph Levin, *Der Jahwist* (FRLANT 157; Göttingen: Vandenhoeck & Ruprecht, 1993), 205–6 (who finds that the reference to Abraham as "servant of Yʜwʜ" and the rest of 26:24 sounds "Deutero-Isaianic"). In actuality, though cited in support by Gertz (277 n. 203), Claus Westermann only identifies one word in Gen 46:3, מַרְאֹת ("visions"), as late, hardly a basis for dating any section of text (*Genesis 37–50* [BK 1; Neukirchen-Vluyn: Neukirchener, 1992], 170–71).

30. For extensive and detailed discussion of problems with such isolated lexical arguments, see now the essays in *Biblical Hebrew: Studies in Chronology and Typology* (ed. I. Young; JSOTSup 369; New York: T&T Clark, 2003).

agreement that the joining of the ancestral and the Moses traditions came relatively late and—outside the Abraham story—is reflected primarily in insertions such as Gen 46:1–5 or Exod 3:1–4:18. Thus we agree that the interpretation of the history of the literature and the religion of ancient Israel should presuppose that the ancestral and the exodus traditions were separate most of the preexilic period, if not also through much of the exilic period as well.

Thus, although the essays in the volume debate the existence of a pre-Priestly Pentateuch, they reflect a remarkably strong emerging consensus with regard to the dating of the literature among many contemporary pentateuchal scholars of varying methodological backgrounds. We share the idea that the non-Priestly ancestral and Moses-exodus traditions were separate in the monarchical period. No one in the present volume works with the idea of an early preexilic "Yahwistic" proto-Pentateuch nor with an E source. Furthermore, most essays share the judgment that texts such as Gen 46:1–5, the non-P bridge between Genesis and Exodus (e.g., Gen 50:24–25; Exod 1:6, 8–9), and Exod 3:1–4:18 are later additions to their contexts, whether they are pre- or post-P insertions.

Scholars such as Thomas Römer, Konrad Schmid, Jan Christian Gertz, Erhard Blum, and others have been helpful in forming this new consensus, particularly in sharpening our sense of the separation of ancestral and Mosaic traditions and the lateness of their literary connection with each other. And for this major contribution, as well as their stimulating essays, we can be grateful.

BIBLIOGRAPHY

Anbar, Moshé. *Josué et l'alliance de Sichem (Josué 24:1–28)*. BET 25. Frankfurt: Lang, 1992.

Blum, Erhard. *Die Komposition der Vätergeschichte*. WMANT 57. Neukirchen-Vluyn: Neukirchener, 1984.

———. "Der kompositionelle Knoten am Übergang von Josua zu Richter: Ein Entflechtungsvorschlag." Pages 181–212, 204–5 in *Deuteronomy and Deuteronomic Literature: Festschrift C. H. W. Brekelmans*. Edited by Marc Vervenne and Johan Lust. BETL 133. Leuven: Leuven University Press; Peeters, 1997.

———. "Die literarische Verbindung von Erzvätern und Exodus: Ein Gespräch mit neueren Forschungshypothesen." Pages 119–56 in *Abschied vom Jahwisten: Die Komposition des Hexateuch in der jüngsten Diskussion*. Edited by Jan Christian Gertz, Konrad Schmid, and Markus Witte. BZAW 315. Berlin: de Gruyter, 2002.

———. *Studien zur Komposition des Pentateuch*. BZAW 189. Berlin: de Gruyter, 1990.

Campbell, Antony F., and Mark A. O'Brien. *Sources of the Pentateuch: Texts, Introductions, Annotations*. Minneapolis: Fortress, 1993.

Carr, David M. "Genesis in Relation to the Moses Story. Diachronic and Synchronic Perspectives." Pages 273–95 in *Studies in the Book of Genesis: Literature, Redaction and History*. Edited by André Wénin. BETL 155. Leuven: Leuven University Press; Peeters, 2001.

———. *Reading the Fractures of Genesis: Historical and Literary Approaches*. Louisville: Westminster John Knox, 1996.

Childs, Brevard S. *The Book of Exodus: A Critical, Theological Commentary*. OTL. Louisville: Westminster John Knox, 1974.

Crüsemann, Frank. "Die Eigenständigkeit der Urgeschichte: Ein Beitrag zur Diskussion um den 'Jahwisten.'" Pages 11–29 in *Die Botschaft und die Boten: Festschrift H. W. Wolff*. Edited by Jörg Jeremias and Lothar Perlitt. Neukirchen-Vluyn: Neukirchener, 1981.

Dietrich, Walter. *Die Josephserzählung als Novelle und Geschichtsschreibung: Zugleich ein Beitrag zur Pentateuchfrage*. BTS 14. Neukirchen-Vluyn: Neukirchener, 1989.

Dozeman, Thomas B. *God at War: Power in the Exodus Tradition.* New York: Oxford University Press, 1996.

———. *God on the Mountain: A Study of Redaction, Theology and Canon in Exodus 19–24.* SBLMS 37. Atlanta: Scholars Press, 1988.

Friedman, Richard Elliott. *The Bible with Sources Revealed.* San Francisco: HarperSanFrancisco, 2003.

Galling, Kurt. *Die Erwählungstraditionen Israels.* BZAW 48. Giessen: Töpelmann, 1928.

Gertz, Jan Christian, Konrad Schmid, and Markus Witte, eds. *Abschied vom Jahwisten: Die Komposition des Hexateuch in der jüngsten Diskussion.* BZAW 315. Berlin: de Gruyter, 2002.

Gertz, Jan Christian. "Die Stellung des kleinen geschichtlichen Credos in der Redaktionsgeschichte von Deuteronomium und Pentateuch." Pages 30–45 in *Liebe und Gebot: Studien zum Deuteronomium. Festschrift Lothar Perlitt.* Edited by Reinhard G. Kratz and Hermann Spieckermann. FRLANT 190. Göttingen: Vandenhoeck & Ruprecht, 2000.

———. *Tradition und Redaktion in der Exoduserzählung: Untersuchungen zur Endredaktion des Pentateuch.* FRLANT 186. Göttingen: Vandenhoeck & Ruprecht, 1999.

Ha, John. *Genesis 15: A Theological Compendium of Pentateuchal History.* BZAW 181. Berlin: de Gruyter, 1989.

Hendel, Ronald S. *The Epic of the Patriarch: The Jacob Cycle and the Narrative Traditions of Canaan and Israel.* HSM 42. Atlanta: Scholars Press 1987.

Houtman, Cees. *Der Pentateuch: Die Geschichte seiner Erforschung nebst einer Auswertung.* Kampen: Kok Pharos, 1994.

Koch, Klaus. "P—kein Redaktor! Erinnerung an zwei Eckdaten der Quellenscheidung." *VT* 37 (1987): 446–67.

Kaiser, Otto. *Die erzählenden Werke.* Vol. 1 of *Grundriss der Einleitung in die kanonischen und deuterokanonischen Schriften des Alten Testaments.* Gütersloh: Gütersloher Verlagshaus, 1992.

Kessler, Rainer. "Die Querverweise im Pentateuch: Überlieferungsgeschichtliche Untersuchung der expliziten Querverbindungen innerhalb des vorpriesterlichen Pentateuchs." Th.D. diss., University of Heidelberg, 1972.

Kratz, Reinhard G. *Die Komposition der erzählenden Bücher des Alten Testaments: Grundwissen der Bibelkritik.* Uni-Taschenbücher 2157. Göttingen: Vandenhoeck & Ruprecht, 2000.

Levin, Christoph. "Das israelitische Nationalepos: Der Jahwist." Pages 63–86 in *Große Texte alter Kulturen: Literarische Reise von Gizeh nach Rom.* Edited by Martin Hose. Darmstadt: Wissenschaftliche Buchgesellschaft, 2004.

———. *Der Jahwist.* FRLANT 157. Göttingen: Vandenhoeck & Ruprecht, 1993.

Moberly, Robert W. L. *The Old Testament of the Old Testament: Patriarchal Narratives and Mosaic Yahwism*. OBT. Minneapolis: Fortress, 1992.

Nicholson, Ernest. *The Pentateuch in the Twentieth Century: The Legacy of Julius Wellhausen*. Oxford: Clarendon, 1998.

Noth, Martin. *Überlieferungsgeschichte des Pentateuch*. Stuttgart: Kohlhammer, 1948. English translation: *A History of Pentateuchal Traditions*. Translated by B. W. Anderson. Eaglewood Cliffs, N.J.: Prentice Hall, 1972. Repr., Atlanta: Scholars Press, 1981.

Otto, Eckart. *Das Deuteronomium im Pentateuch und Hexateuch: Studien zur Literaturgeschichte von Pentateuch und Hexateuch im Lichte des Deuteronomiumsrahmen*. FAT 30. Tübingen: Mohr Siebeck, 2000.

———. "Die nachpriesterschrifliche Pentateuchredaktion im Buch Exodus." Pages 61–111 in *Studies in the Book of Exodus: Redaction—Reception—Interpretation*. Edited by Marc Vervenne. BETL 126. Leuven: Leuven University Press; Peeters, 1996.

Pola, Thomas. *Die ursprüngliche Priesterschrift: Beobachtungen zu Literarkritik und Traditionsgeschichte von P^g*. WMANT 70. Neukirchen-Vluyn: Neukirchener, 1995.

Pury, Albert de, and Thomas Römer eds. *Le Pentateuque en question: Les origines et la composition des cinq premiers livres de la Bible à la lumière des recherches récentes*. MdB 19. Geneva: Labor et Fides 32002.

Pury, Albert de. "Le choix de l'ancêtre." *TZ* 57 (2001): 105–14.

———. "Le cycle de Jacob comme légende autonome des origines d'Israël." Pages 78–96 in *Congress Volume: Leuven, 1989*. Edited by John A. Emerton. VTSup 43. Leiden: Brill, 1991.

———. "Hosea 12 und die Auseinandersetzung um die Identität Israels und seines Gottes." Pages 413–39 in *Ein Gott allein? JHWH-Verehrung und biblischer Monotheismus im Kontext der israelitischen und altorientalischen Religionsgeschichte*. Edited by Walter Dietrich and Martin A. Klopfenstein. OBO 139. Fribourg: Universitätsverlag; Göttingen: Vandenhoeck & Ruprecht, 1994.

———. "Der priesterschriftliche Umgang mit der Jakobsgeschichte." Pages 33–60 in *Schriftauslegung in der Schrift: Festschrift O.H. Steck*. Edited by Reinhard G. Kratz, Thomas Krüger, and Konrad Schmid. BZAW 300. Berlin: de Gruyter, 2000.

———. *Promesse divine et légende cultuelle dans le cycle de Jacob: Genèse 28 et les traditions patriarcales*. ÉB. Paris: Gabalda, 1975.

Rad, Gerhard von. "Das formgeschichtliche Problem des Hexateuch." Pages 9–86 in idem, *Gesammelte Studien zum Alten Testament*. Edited by Rudolf Smend. 4th ed. ThB 8. Munich: Kaiser, 1971. English translation: "The Form-Critical Problem of the Hexateuch." Pages 1–78 in *The Problem of the*

Hexateuch and Other Essays. Translated by E. W. Trueman Dicken. Edinburgh: Oliver & Boyd, 1966. Repr., London: SCM, 1984.

Redford, Donald B. *A Study of the Biblical Story of Joseph (Gen 37–50).* VTSup 20. Leiden: Brill, 1970.

Rendtorff, Rolf. "Der 'Jahwist' als Theologe? Zum Dilemma der Pentateuchkritik," Pages 158–66 in *Congress Volume: Edinburgh, 1974.* VTSup 28. Leiden: Brill, 1975. English translation: "The 'Yahwist' as Theologian? The Dilemma of Pentateuchal Criticism." *JSOT* 3 (1977): 2–10.

———. *Das überlieferungsgeschichtliche Problem des Pentateuch.* BZAW 147. Berlin: de Gruyter, 1977. English translation: *The Problem of the Process of Transmission in the Pentateuch.* Translated by J. J. Scullion. JSOTSup 89. Sheffield: JSOT Press, 1990.

Rofé, Alexander. *Introduction to the Composition of the Pentateuch.* Jerusalem: Academon, 1994.

Römer, Thomas. *Israels Väter: Untersuchungen zur Väterthematik im Deuteronomium und in der deuteronomistischen Tradition.* OBO 99. Fribourg: Universitätsverlag; Göttingen: Vandenhoeck & Ruprecht, 1990.

Rose, Martin. *Deuteronomist und Jahwist: Untersuchungen zu den Berührungspunkten beider Literaturwerke.* ATANT 67. Zürich: Theologischer Verlag, 1981.

Rudolph, Wilhelm. *Der "Elohist" von Exodus bis Joshua.* BZAW 68. Berlin: Töpelmann, 1938.

Schmid, Hans Heinrich. *Der sogenannte Jahwist: Beobachtungen und Fragen zur Pentateuchforschung.* Zürich: Theologischer Verlag, 1976.

Schmid, Konrad. *Erzväter und Exodus: Untersuchungen zur doppelten Begründung der Ursprünge Israels innerhalb der Geschichtsbücher des Alten Testaments.* WMANT 81. Neukirchen-Vluyn: Neukirchener, 1999.

———. "Die Josephsgeschichte im Pentateuch." Pages 83–118 in *Abschied vom Jahwisten: Die Komposition des Hexateuch in der jüngsten Diskussion.* Edited by Jan Christian Gertz, Konrad Schmid, and Markus Witte. BZAW 315. Berlin: de Gruyter, 2002.

Schmitt, Hans-Christoph. "Die Josephsgeschichte und das Deuteronomistische Geschichtswerk." Pages 295–308 in idem, *Theologie in Prophetie und Pentateuch.* BZAW 310. Berlin: de Gruyter, 2001.

———. "Redaktion des Pentateuch im Geiste der Prophetie: Beobachtung zur Bedeutung der 'Glaubens'-Thematik innerhalb der Theologie des Pentateuch." *VT* 32 (1982): 170–89 = pages 220–237 in idem, *Theologie in Prophetie und Pentateuch.* BZAW 310. Berlin: de Gruyter, 2001.

Ska, Jean-Louis. *Introduction à la lecture du Pentateuque: Clés pour l'interprétation des cinq premiers livres de la Bible.* Bruxelles: Lessius, 2000.

Sparks, Kenton L. *The Pentateuch. An Annotated Bibliography*. Grand Rapids: Baker, 2002.

Van Seters, John. *Abraham in History and Tradition*. New Haven: Yale University Press. 1975.

———. "Confessional Reformulation in the Exilic Period." *VT* 22 (1972): 448–59.

———. *Der Jahwist als Historiker*. Theologische Studien 134. Zürich: Theologischer Verlag, 1987.

———. *The Life of Moses: The Yahwist as Historian in Exodus-Numbers*. Louisville: Westminster John Knox, 1994.

———. *The Pentateuch: A Social Science Commentary*. Sheffield: Sheffield Academic Press, 1999.

———. *Prologue to History: The Yahwist as Historian in Genesis*. Zürich: Theologischer Verlag, 1992.

Wellhausen, Julius. *Die Composition des Hexateuchs und der historischen Bücher des Alten Testaments*. Berlin: de Gruyter, 1963.

———. *Grundrisse zum Alten Testament*. Edited by Rudolf Smend. Munich: Kaiser, 1965.

———. *Prolegomena zur Geschichte Israels*. 6th ed. Berlin: de Gruyter, 1927. English translation: *Prolegomena to the History of Israel*. Translated by J. S. Black and A. Menzies. Atlanta: Scholars Press, 1994.

Winnett, Frederick V. *The Mosaic Tradition*. Near and Middle East Studies 1. Toronto: University of Toronto Press, 1949.

———. "Re-examining the Foundations." *JBL* 84 (1965): 1–19.

Witte, Markus. *Die biblische Urgeschichte: Redaktions- und theologiegeschichtliche Beobachtungen zu Genesis 1,1–11,26*. BZAW 265. Berlin: de Gruyter, 1998.

Contributors

Erhard Blum, University of Tübingen, Germany

David M. Carr, Union Theological Seminary, New York

Thomas B. Dozeman, United Theological Seminary, Dayton, Ohio

Jan Christian Gertz, University of Heidelberg, Germany

Christoph Levin, University of Munich, Germany

Albert de Pury, University of Geneva, Switzerland

Thomas Römer, University of Lausanne, Switzerland

Konrad Schmid, University of Zurich, Switzerland

John Van Seters, Waterloo, Canada

Index of Biblical and Related Literature

INDEX OF AUTHORS

Printed in the United States
206446BV00003B/133-144/A

9 781589 831636